Cities and
Sports Stadiums

Cities and Sports Stadiums

A Planning Handbook

Edited by ROGER L. KEMP

McFarland & Company, Inc., Publishers
Jefferson, North Carolina, and London

LIBRARY OF CONGRESS CATALOGUING-IN-PUBLICATION DATA

Cities and sports stadiums : a planning handbook / edited by Roger L. Kemp.
p.   cm.
Includes bibliographical references and index.

ISBN 978-0-7864-3808-2
softcover : 50# alkaline paper ∞

1. Sports facilities — United States — Case studies.   2. Urban renewal —
United States — Case studies.   3. City planning — United States —
Case studies.   4. Community life — United States — Case studies.
I. Kemp, Roger L.
GV429.A2C57   2009   796.06' 80973 — dc22   2009000729

British Library cataloguing data are available

Cover images ©2009 Shutterstock

Manufactured in the United States of America

*McFarland & Company, Inc., Publishers
Box 611, Jefferson, North Carolina 28640
www.mcfarlandpub.com*

To Anika,
the best and the brightest

Acknowledgments

Grateful acknowledgment is made to the following organizations and publishers for granting permission to reprint the materials contained in this volume.

American Planning Association
Associated Construction Publications
Congressional Quarterly Inc.
Eastern Economic Association
International Association of Sports Economists
National Association of Realtors
National Housing Institute
New Urban News Publications
Penton Media, Inc.
Reed Construction Data
Sports Business News
The Cato Institute
The Next American City Inc.
The Seattle Times Company
United States Sports Academy
Urban Land Institute
World Future Society

Table of Contents

Section III. The Future

Appendices

Preface

In cities and towns throughout the country, there is significant evidence that community development and renovation is being centered around multi-use stadiums and arenas. Sporting games, entertainment events, and cultural expositions have provided a focal point and gathering place for people in cities for centuries. What used to be done at ballparks and public markets is increasingly being undertaken in multi-use stadiums and arenas. Organized sports teams — major and minor league — are a driving force behind the national movement to build and rebuild these facilities in many communities throughout America.

Many public officials at all levels of government have approved the public financing of sports facilities over the years, and many of these projects have not proven to be in the public's best interest. In fact, many elected officials have approved public financing of these new facilities without ever seeking approval of their taxpayers. With the proper safeguards, such as those presented in the Best Practices section of this volume, citizens can benefit first-hand from new public multi-purpose stadiums and arenas. The selected best practices described in detail in this volume can set elected officials, as well as the citizens they serve, on the right track — politically, financially, and economically.

The various case studies represent state-of-the-art examples of how local governments, nonprofit and profit organizations, and public officials are using new planning, development, and redevelopment practices to encourage, review, and approve profit-making multi-use stadiums and arenas that provide the best inner-city venues for games and concerts, as well as cultural and business expositions.

The case studies contained in this volume are typically applied in a piecemeal and incremental fashion in cities and towns. For the most part, citizens, nonprofit organizations, and public officials are preoccupied with existing projects within their own communities. They do not have the time to find out what neighboring cities and towns are doing in this area, let alone what other communities are doing throughout the nation. For this reason, the case studies presented represent an important codification of knowledge.

This reference work assembles, for the first time, materials based on a national literature search, and makes this important and timely information available to citizens and public officials throughout the United States. The goal of this volume is to help educate citizens, as well as their public officials, on how to use these new planning, economic development, and redevelopment principles and practices to improve the economic conditions within their own communities.

For ease of reference, this volume is divided into four sections. The first section introduces the reader to the rapidly evolving field of cities and how they negotiate, approve, finance, design, and build stadiums and arenas. The second section and, by design, the longest, includes numerous case studies, or best practices, on how cities and towns are taking the proper measures and safeguards when approving agreements with major and minor league sports team franchises. The next section focuses on trends in this new and rapidly evolving discipline. Several appendices provide a greater understanding of this new field. Based on this brief background information, and the conceptual schema developed to assemble and present this material, the four primary sections of this volume are briefly highlighted below.

Cities and Sports Facilities

The first section of this volume provides the reader with an introduction to the new and rapidly evolving field of cities, arenas, and stadiums. To provide this context, several articles are presented that examine how sports facilities have traditionally been financed, an overview of the public benefits of sports developments, and how they impact our inner cities and downtowns, as well as how sports facilities contribute to local economic prosperity. The final two chapters of this section examine such important subjects as the prudent economic precautions and public scrutiny that should precede the public financing of these facilities, as well as how these facilities contribute to the local quality of life in America's communities. This introductory material sets the stage for the presentation of numerous case studies relating to cities, and their arenas and stadiums.

The Best Practices

The cities, towns, and communities examined in this volume, including their states, are highlighted below. These cities represent great diversity based on their size, politics, form of government, geographic location, and wealth. In total, dozens of cities are examined in many states. A brief description of the best practice examined in each of these communities is set forth in alphabetical order. These case studies represent an important and significant effort to obtain a body of knowledge on the best practices available.

Cities: Anaheim, Arlington, Boise, Boston, Chicago, Corpus Christi, Denver, East Rutherford, Evansville, Fargo, Frisco, Glendale, Harrisburg, Houston, Kansas City, Landover, Los Angeles, Memphis, Miami, Montgomery, New York, Newark, Olympia, Pasadena, Richmond, Rock Hill, St. Paul, Salem, San Francisco, Seattle, Sioux Falls, Trenton, and Washington, D.C.

States: Alabama, Arizona, California, Colorado, Florida, Idaho, Illinois, Maryland, Massachusetts, Minnesota, Missouri, New Jersey, New York, North Dakota, Pennsylvania, South Carolina, South Dakota, Tennessee, Texas, Virginia, and Washington.

Selected Best Practices: Citizen review and approval processes, creation of sports districts, creation of affordable housing by sports facilities, downtown renewal practices, designing sports stadiums, influence and impact of major league sports teams, influence and impact of minor league sports teams, inner-city revitalization incentives, multi-use facilities (as opposed to single use), municipal competition for sports teams, new types of stadium and arena revenues, new uses for old stadiums, politics of sports facility financing, powerful influence of the sports teams, public financing feasibility studies, public financing versus private financing, public ownership of sports teams, public-private partnerships for sports facilities, social versus economic benefits of sports facilities, sports facilities and political debates, sports facilities as major anchor tenants, state funding of community sports facilities, stadium and arena revenues and expenses, types of facilities and their economic impact, use of citizen advisory boards, use of Community Benefit Agreements, and voting for public financing arrangements.

The Future

The third section examines the future of sports facilities in cities. The topics examined include the "real" economic impact of publicly financed sports facilities, the changing nature of America's sports facilities due to the impact of science and technology, and assessments of the public benefits of sports facilities to determine if government funding of these facilities is in the best interests of citizens. The last two topics examined in this section encompass major trends and issues impacting and shaping our nation's sports industry and, lastly, the future of league sports and their aging facilities.

Appendices

Several important resources are included:

Glossary: Commonly used terms related to planning, land use, and economic development.

Acronyms and Abbreviations: Common acronyms and abbreviations related to planning, land use, and economic development.

Periodicals Bibliography: A list of major periodicals focusing on contemporary issues in communities, as well as the disciplines of building, economic development, the environment, land and water, planning, public works, real estate, and major sports issues.

Books and Articles Bibliography: Major published works that focus on significant sports issues, sports facilities such as stadiums and arenas, economic development as it relates to sports teams, the public financing of sports facilities, as well as their development and maintenance, and related issues.

Foundation Resources: Major foundations in the United States providing resources and possible funding for neighborhood and community projects. This list was assembled by the National Association of Development Organizations in Washington, D.C.

Federal Reserve Bank Resources: The title and address, along with the website, of each district office is provided. Each district branch location has a community development office with local, regional, and national resources related to timely and important development topics, including how to analyze requests for the public funding of sports facilities.

Federal Government Resources: Information on brownfields remediation, demographics, economic and community development, the environment, historic preservation, housing, land revitalization, transportation issues, urban development, and related urban issues.

Regional Resource Directory: A listing of all of the community governments and websites included in the Best Practices section. In those communities with the council-manager form of government, it is suggested that citizens direct their questions to the city manager. In cities with the strong-mayor form of government, it is recommended that all inquiries be made directly to the mayor.

National Resource Directory: All major national professional, membership, and research organizations serving public officials, as well as concerned professionals and citizens. Many of these organizations focus on various issues relating to cities and sports facilities, and major programs relating to this topic. The websites are listed.

International Resource Directory: Major

international professional, membership, and research organizations serving public officials, as well as concerned professionals and citizens. Many of these international organizations focus on various programs relating to local authorities and sports facilities, as well as major issues relating to these subjects.

The use of sports teams — major and minor league — and the facilities they utilize to play their games have been a fact of life on the American scene for decades. Under the correct circumstances, these stadiums and arenas can be used as a positive force to revitalize our inner cities and neighborhoods. The practices creating these positive circumstances include the proper review and approval of stadium and arena requests by citizens as well as their elected political leaders.

As more public officials and citizens become educated as to the options available, and representatives of major and minor league sports teams become aware of increasing public expectations, this field will increase in importance during the coming years.

I: Cities and Sports Facilities

CHAPTER 1

Cities and the Financing of Sports Facilities

Adam M. Zaretsky

Americans love sports. Watching the home team in any of the four major sports — baseball, football, basketball and hockey — march to victory in the World Series, Super Bowl, NBA Finals or Stanley Cup Finals arguably generates more excitement and local pride in a town than any other event. Fans love when the hometown boys win. But even when they don't, fans stick by their teams. By and large, so do the cities these teams play in. In fact, cities with home teams are often willing to go to great lengths to ensure they stay home. And cities without home teams are often willing to dangle many carrots to entice teams to move. In either case, the most visible way cities do this is by building new stadiums and arenas.

Between 1987 and 1999, 55 stadiums and arenas were refurbished or built in the United States at a cost of more than $8.7 billion.[1] This figure, however, includes only the direct costs involved in the construction or refurbishment of the facilities, not the indirect costs — such as money cities might spend on improving or adding to the infrastructure needed to support the facilities. Of the $8.7 billion in di-

rect costs, about 57 percent — around $5 billion — was financed with taxpayer money. Since 1999, other stadiums have been constructed or are in the pipeline, much of the cost of which will also be supported with tax dollars. Between $14 billion and $16 billion is expected to be spent on these post-'99 stadiums and arenas, with somewhere between $9 billion and $11 billion of this amount coming from public coffers. The use of public funds to lure or keep teams begs several questions, the foremost of which is, "Are these good investments for cities?"

The short answer to this question is "No." When studying this issue, almost all economists and development specialists (at least those who work independently and not for a chamber of commerce or similar organization) conclude that the rate of return a city or metropolitan area receives for its investment is generally below that of alternative projects. In addition, evidence suggests that cities and metro areas that have invested heavily in sports stadiums and arenas have, on average, experienced slower income growth than those that have not.

Originally published as "Should Cities Pay for Sports Facilities?" *The Regional Economist*, April 2001, by The Federal Reserve Bank, St. Louis, MO.

Why, then, would cities engage in such activities? This question is actually harder to answer than the former one because, more often than not, the reasons cited are not quantifiable. In other words, the reasons are not as easily measured as, say, costs, because they include many intangible variables, such as civic pride and political self-interest. Moreover, cities generally justify these decisions — and convince taxpayers of their virtue — with analyses that many economists consider suspect because the studies generally overlook some basic economic realities.

Not Always Built with Tax Dollars...

In 1862, William Cammeyer enclosed the Union Club Grounds in Brooklyn, N.Y., and began charging admission, making it the first recorded baseball "stadium" in the United States. The facility was quite attractive to the fledgling sport of baseball because it enabled the exclusion of non-paying spectators and impressed the up-and-coming players, for whom teams were beginning to compete. By the time the National Association was formed in 1871, owners of such enclosed ballparks had a distinct advantage in the competition for teams.

In many ways, not much has changed since then. Teams today are still attracted by modern facilities, and cities go out of their way to provide them. In other ways, though, much has changed. Nowadays, facilities are not usually owned privately by individuals, but, rather, publicly by a government agency. And even though public financing of stadiums is a more common practice today, cities did pony up for a few of the older, well-known stadiums in times past.

Some prime examples of government-owned stadiums from yesteryear are the Los Angeles Coliseum and Soldier Field, both of which are still in use today. Other famous venues, such as Fenway Park, Ebbets Field, Wrigley Field, Yankee Stadium and the original Comiskey Park, were all privately financed and owned. In fact, prior to World War II, of the 28 major league sports facilities that were built — for which data are available — only five were paid for in part or whole with taxpayer dollars.[2] Since World War II, however, of the roughly 140 sports facilities that have been built or refurbished, only 14 did not use taxpayer dollars.

...But When They Are, Are They Worth It?

The dollars being invested in sports facilities are quite substantial considering the overall contribution the industry makes to the economy. In testimony before the U.S. Congress, economist Robert Baade said that Chicago's professional sports industry — which includes five teams — accounted for less than one-tenth of 1 percent of Chicago's 1995 personal income.[3] Baade further commented that even when compared with the revenue of other industries, professional sports teams contribute small amounts to the economy. He noted, for example, that "the sales revenue of Fruit of the Loom exceed[ed] that for all of Major League Baseball (MLB), while the sales revenue of Sears [was] about thirty times larger than that of all MLB revenues."

Still, cities are driven by the idea that playing host to professional sports teams builds civic pride and increases local tax receipts from the team-related sales and salaries. When it comes to salaries, however, economist Mark Rosentraub noted in a 1997 article that there is no U.S. county where professional sports accounts for more than 1 percent of the county's private-sector payroll.

Although sports facilities certainly generate tax revenues from their sales, the pertinent question is whether these revenues are above and beyond what would have occurred in the region anyway. To address this question, city proposals to use taxpayer money to finance sports facilities are routinely accompanied by "economic impact studies." These studies, which are often commissioned by franchise owners and conducted by an accounting firm or local chamber of commerce, generally use spurious economic techniques to demonstrate the number of new jobs and additional tax revenues that will be generated by the project. The assumptions that are made in these studies — such as how much of the newly generated income will stay in the region and how many "secondary" jobs will be created — often cannot be substantiated by economic theory.

Estimates of income that will be generated and, hence, spent in the region are often overstated. Most of the "big" money in sports goes to the owners and players, who may or may not spend the money in the hometown since many live in other cities. And because athletic careers are usually short-lived, much of the players' income is invested. Moreover, league rules often require ticket revenues be shared with franchise owners in other cities as a way to subsidize teams in smaller markets. In the case of the National Football League, every visiting team leaves town with 34 percent of the gate receipts from each game.

On top of all this, the value of the subsidy a team receives when a city foots the bill for a new stadium or arena often shows up as a higher team resale price, which then ends up in the owner's pocket. For example, Eli Jacobs bought the Baltimore Orioles for $70 million in 1989, just after the team had convinced the state of Maryland to build it a new $200 million ballpark from lottery revenues. The enormously popular Oriole Park at Camden Yards opened in 1992. The following year, Jacobs sold the Orioles for $173 million. The sale netted Jacobs an almost 150 percent return, with no money out-of-pocket for the new ballpark.[4]

And the Dollars Keep Turning Over

Economic impact studies also tend to focus on the increased tax revenues cities expect to receive in return for their investments. The studies, however, often gloss over, or outright ignore, that these facilities usually do not bring new revenues into a city or metropolitan area. Instead, the revenues raised are usually just substitutes for those that would have been raised by other activities. Any student of economics knows that households have budget constraints that are binding, which means that families have only so much money to spend, particularly on entertainment. If the family chooses to spend the money at the ballpark, for example, then those funds cannot be spent on other activities. Thus, no new revenues are actually being generated.

Public funds used for a stadium or arena can generate new revenues for a city only if one of the following situations occurs: 1) the funds generate new spending by people from outside the area who otherwise would not have come to town; 2) the funds cause area residents to spend money locally that would not have been spent there otherwise; or 3) the funds keep turning over locally, thereby "creating" new spending.

Very little evidence exists to suggest that sporting events are better at attracting tourism dollars to a city than other activities. More often than not, tourists who attend a baseball or hockey game, for example, are in town on business or are visiting family and would have spent the money on another activity if the sports outlet were not available.[5]

Economists Roger Noll and Andrew Zimbalist have examined the issue in depth and argued that, as a general rule, sports facilities attract neither tourists nor new industry. A good example, once again, is Oriole Park at Camden Yards. This ballpark is probably the most successful at attracting outsiders since it is only 40 miles from the nation's capital, where there is no major league baseball team. About a third of the crowd at every game comes from outside the Baltimore area. Noll and Zimbalist point out that, "Even so, the net gain to Baltimore's economy in terms of new jobs and incremental tax revenues is only about $3 million a year — not much of a return on a $200 million investment."[6]

The claim that sporting facilities cause residents to spend more money in town than they would otherwise is harder to substantiate. To prove such a claim, the agency performing the analysis would need for its report both detailed information about the spending patterns of households and the ability to ferret out the information about their spending in other regions, which, at best, is extremely difficult and may even be impossible. Without such information, the report's authors could back into this claim only with some fancy footwork and shaky assertions. That is, they would have to contend that residents are spending more in town because of higher incomes that enable households to devote more of their entertainment budgets toward local sporting events. Then, the authors would have to demonstrate that incomes are up because money was spent on the stadium. If they can't, the argument falls apart since the only conclusion is that incomes rose for unrelated reasons; throwing tax dollars at the stadium did not affect households' spending patterns.

Multipliers: A Stadium Promoter's Friend

Of the three circumstances described that purportedly generate new revenues, the third —

funds keep turning over locally, thereby "creating" new spending — is probably the most spurious from an economist's viewpoint. Such a claim relies on what are called multipliers. Multipliers are factors that are used as a way of predicting the "total" effect the creation of an additional job or the spending of an additional dollar will have on a community's economy. It works something like this: A stadium is built, which creates new jobs in the region. Because more people are working, they spend money in the area (for lunch, parking, etc.), which in turn requires local businesses to hire additional workers to support the increased demand. These extra workers further increase demand for goods and services in the area, requiring more new jobs ... and so on. That is, the dollars keep turning over locally. The story is the same for fans spending money at the arena, which provides income for arena workers, who then spend the money, generating incomes for other workers ... and so on.

On their faces, these are compelling arguments. Some researchers have even attempted to quantify these effects, developing precise multipliers that tell analysts how much the new spending or job creation should be "multiplied" by to arrive at the "total effect" the spending or job creation will have on the local economy. These multipliers are often specific enough to distinguish between various industries, occupations and locations. Thus, economic development specialists and planners will generally latch onto multipliers and confidently proclaim that the 1,000 new jobs created by this industry will actually create 4,355 new jobs and generate $5.5 million in new revenue in the community when all is said and done.[7] Makes for great headlines, but are such outcomes believable?

Probably not. As Mark Twain once said: "It's not what we don't know that hurts. It's what we know that just ain't true." For one thing, these new jobs most likely just lure workers away from other jobs in town and do not actually lead to a net change in jobs in the area. For another, many of the jobs are low-paying, part-time and needed only on game days. Moreover, authors of these economic impact studies often choose multipliers arbitrarily or with clients' wishes in mind to get the desired outcome. As economist William Hunter has pointed out, multiplier analysis can be used to justify any public works project because "even the smallest multiplier will guarantee community income growth in excess of public expenditures."[8]

Even if economic impact studies are taken at face value, however, the cost of creating these jobs is usually out of the ballpark. In Cincinnati, for example, when two new stadiums were proposed to keep the NFL Bengals and the MLB Reds in town, the economic impact study claimed that 7,645 jobs would be created or saved because of the stadium investment. Since the project was estimated at $520 million, each new or saved job was reported to cost about $68,000.

When economists John Blair and David Swindell examined the $68,000 figure a bit closer, though, they discovered it was too low because the study's estimate of 7,645 new or saved jobs was too high. Blair and Swindell then re-evaluated the report, corrected for double-counting and other problems, and concluded that only 3,530 jobs would be created or saved if the stadium proposal passed. Thus, the cost per job was actually going to run more than $147,000. In contrast, state economic development programs spend about $6,250 per job to create new jobs.[9]

Those Old Economic Saws

Another glaring omission from these economic impact studies is the value of the next-best investment alternative — what economists call the opportunity cost. "There's no such thing as a free lunch" is a favorite economist expression because it sums up exactly what opportunity cost means: When making a choice, something always has to be given up. The value of the "losing" choice must be considered when making the decision and when calculating the value, or return, of the "winning" choice. In other words, when a city chooses to use taxpayer dollars to finance a sports stadium, the city's leaders must consider not only what the alternative uses of those funds could be — such as schools, police, roads, etc. — but they must also figure what return the city would receive from these other ventures. Then, the return from the city's next-best alternative (for example, schools) must be subtracted from the total return of the "winning" choice to arrive at the "actual" return of the stadium investment. This adjusted calculation, though, is almost always missing from sports stadium impact studies. Why? Because in just about every case, the adjusted calculation would show that the next-best alternative was actually the better alternative.

Has financing sports stadiums ever been the best alternative? Research shows "No." In their book, Noll and Zimbalist — along with 15 other collaborators — examined the local economic development argument from a wide variety of angles. In every case, the conclusions were the same. "A new sports facility had an extremely small (perhaps even negative) effect on overall economic activity and employment. No recent facility appears to have earned anything approaching a reasonable rate of return on investment. No recent facility has been self-financing in terms of its impact on net tax revenues. Regardless of whether the unit of analysis is a local neighborhood, a city, or an entire metropolitan area, the economic benefits of sports facilities are de minimus."[10]

In fact, research has shown that subsidizing sports facilities usually does not affect a city's growth and, in some cases, may even hurt growth since funds are being diverted from alternatives with higher returns. In a 1994 study that examined economic growth over a 30-year period in 48 metropolitan areas, Robert Baade found that of the 32 metro areas that had a change in the number of sports teams, only two showed a significant relationship between the presence of a sports team and real per-capita personal income growth. These cities were Indianapolis, which saw a positive relationship, and Baltimore, which had a negative relationship.

Moreover, Baade found that of the 30 metro areas where the stadium or arena was built or refurbished in the previous 10 years, only three areas showed a significant relationship between the presence of a stadium and real per-capita personal income growth. And in all three cases — St. Louis, San Francisco/ Oakland and Washington, D.C. — the relationship was negative.

The "Build It and They Will Come" Syndrome

Cities go to great lengths to lure a new team to town or to keep the home team home. They feel compelled to compete with other cities that offer new or updated facilities; otherwise, the home team might make good on its threat to leave. The weight of economic evidence, however, shows that taxpayers spend a lot of money and ultimately don't get much back. And when this paltry return is compared with other potential uses of the funds, the investment, almost always, seems unwise. Still, cities eagerly propose spending the funds, and taxpayers willingly support the proposals. Why? Because home teams strike an emotional chord with the community — that intangible "civic pride" is evidently a powerful force. Thus, attacks on stadium proposals, no mat-

ter how persuasive, likely fall on deaf ears. More-convincing arguments would spell out the civic initiatives — education, housing and transportation, for example — that are passed over or forgotten in favor of a new stadium.

Notes

1. This sum is about $10.7 billion in 2000 dollars. These data are from Keating (1999).
2. See Table 1 in Keating (1999) for a complete list of these facilities.
3. See Roberts, et al. (1995).
4. See Lane (1994).
5. See Noll and Zimbalist (1997a), chapters 2 and 15.
6. See Noll and Zimbalist (1997b).
7. This example is hypothetical and solely for expository purposes.
8. See Hunter (1988).
9. See Noll and Zimbalist (1997a), chapter 9 (Blair and Swindell) for details.
10. See Noll and Zimbalist (1997b).

References

Baade, Robert A. "Professional Sports as Catalysts for Metropolitan Economic Development," *Journal of Urban Affairs* (Spring 1996), pp. 1–17.
_____. *"Stadiums, Professional Sports, and Economic Development: Assessing the Reality,"* The Heartland Institute, Heartland Policy Study No. 62 (April 4, 1994).
Baseball Almanac. *http://baseballalmanac.com/stadium. shtml*
Bast, Joseph L. *"Sports Stadium Madness: Why It Started, How To Stop It,"* The Heartland Institute, Heartland Policy Study No. 86 (February 23, 1998).
Hunter, William J. *"Economic Impact Studies: Inaccurate, Misleading, and Unnecessary,"* The Heartland Institute, Heartland Policy Study No. 21 (July 22, 1988).
Keating, Raymond J. *"Sports Pork: The Costly Relationship Between Major League Sports and Government,"* Cato Institute, Cato Policy Analysis No. 339 (April 5, 1999).
Lane, Randall. "Bread and Circuses," *Forbes* (June 6, 1994), pp. 62–65.
Merrifield, John. "A Neoclassical Anatomy of the Economic Base Multiplier," *Journal of Regional Science* (May 1987), pp. 283–94.

Mutti, John. "Regional Analysis from the Standpoint of International Trade: Is It a Useful Perspective?" *International Regional Science Review* (Winter 1981), pp. 95–120.

Noll, Roger G., and Andrew Zimbalist, eds. *Sports, Jobs and Taxes: The Economic Impact of Sports Teams and Stadiums* (Brookings Institution Press, 1997a).

_____. "Sports, Jobs, and Taxes: Are New Stadiums Worth the Cost?" *The Brookings Review* (Summer 1997b), pp. 35–39.

Roberts, Gary R., Stephen F. Ross, and Robert A. Baade. "Should Congress Stop the Bidding War for Sports Franchises?" Hearing before the Subcommittee on Antitrust, Business Rights, and Competition, Senate Committee on the Judiciary (November 29, 1995).

Rosentraub, Mark S. "Are Tax-funded Sports Arenas a Good Investment for America's Cities?" *Insight* (September 27, 1997), pp. 25–27.

Siegfried, John, and Andrew Zimbalist. "The Economics of Sports Facilities and Their Communities," *Journal of Economic Perspectives* (Summer 2000), pp. 95–114.

CHAPTER 2

Sporting Events, Public Benefits, and Urban Development

Greg Clark

The rivalry to stage the Olympic Games, EXPOs, World Cup competitions — as well as championships, cultural festivals, and global summits — is more intense than ever before. Despite widespread virtual communication, large-scale gatherings of this kind have become increasingly popular. Shortly, China will host its first Olympics and first EXPO (Beijing in 2008 and Shanghai in 2010). India will host the Commonwealth Games (Delhi 2010), Russia its first Winter Olympics (Sochi 2014), and South Africa its first Soccer World Cup (2010).

By hosting such global events, globalizing cities of fast-growing economies can accelerate their development into "gateway roles" for their nations. Such gateway roles require high-spec buildings, enhanced logistics, advanced infrastructure, and a high-quality place.

The competition to host the 2012 Summer Olympics was the most intense ever. London's eventual victory over Madrid, Paris, New York, and Moscow emphasized the notion that the Olympics are for leading global cities to host, gave the Games themselves a boost, and

ensured that Chicago, Madrid, Tokyo, and others would line up to bid for the 2016 rights to host.

Following are the four categories of events:

Categories	Events
Trade Fairs and Exhibition Events	The EXPO and others
Cultural Events	The Capital of Culture and others
Sports Events	The Olympics and others
Political Summits and Conference Events	G8, Earth Summits, and others

These four categories represent the broad range of events that cities and nations now seek to host. There is, however, great diversity within each category.

Unfortunately, too many events in the past have left the host cities worse off, with expensive facilities that have no subsequent use — and with a big bill to pay long into the future. Awarding bodies, such as International Olympic Committee (IOC), Bureau des Internationales Expositiones (BIE), Federation of International Football Associations (FIFA),

Originally published as "Landwrites: Urban Development from Global Events," *Urban Land*, Vol. 67, No. 2, February 2008, by the Urban Land Institute, Washington, D.C. Reprinted with permission of the publisher.

and others have realized this problem, and now insist upon a well-planned local legacy and program of benefits as part of their evaluation of the bids. Events of this kind are substantially justified by these requirements — and the indirect benefits they bring — not just by the purpose of the event itself.

Local benefits include improved environment, infrastructure, and amenities; increased global exposure and visitor tourism economy; and promotion of trade and investment, as well as an increase in employment and social/business development. They can also include a country or city's increased self-confidence, national pride, civic engagement, and ambition to embrace globalization and to make the necessary adjustments and interventions to succeed. Capturing local benefits from global events, however, does not happen automatically — or by accident. They must be the subject of a dedicated plan of action.

The benefits can be characterized as "primary" and "secondary" to indicate the time frame within which they occur, rather than overall significance. Primary benefits may temporarily overlap secondary benefits that are longer term in nature.

Primary benefits include:

- Alignment of the event with sector and business growth strategies in the city or nation.
- Private/public investment partnerships.
- Image and identity events attracting increased population, investment, or trade.
- Structural expansion of visitor economy and supply chain development.
- Environmental improvements, both in the built and natural environments.

Secondary benefits include:

- Post-event usages of improved land and buildings.
- Connectivity and infrastructure legacies.

- Labor market effects and social/economic inclusion.
- Wider property market benefits.
- Improved global positioning, events strategy progress, and project management capability.

The most successful host countries and cities have a long-term plan that an event helps to implement, and they dedicate management effort to secure the benefits and the legacy for some time before the event is staged — and for several years after. In short, when international events are hosted well, they become a catalyst for urban development and global reach — which occurred in Barcelona and Turin, and, perhaps shortly will occur in Beijing and Shanghai.

However, host cities and nations also need to take precise and dedicated steps to ensure that a positive local legacy is realized. Although the hosting of major international events can be seen as an end in itself, it is also an unrivaled opportunity for a nation or a city to accomplish other efforts. These events bring with them the following:

- Immovable deadlines and the disciplines that come from them.
- A global audience and professional evaluators.
- Additional investment from external sources.
- Increased numbers of visitors and intense exposure to the media, who will all pass judgment.
- Intensified local engagement with citizens, firms, and institutions.
- A chance to celebrate human skills and endeavors.
- An opportunity to extend local skills and capabilities.

Understanding the urban development benefits that come from global events is best illustrated by what selected cities have achieved in the past, and by what they plan for the future. In the past, sporting events have resulted in improvements to a city's transportation infrastructure, public facilities, urban development, as well as the local and regional economy.

Comparable evidence across the different events is limited. However, qualitative analysis reveals some important broad distinctions that can be made between the events categories presented. Specifically, the sports events category has had a positive impact on a city's urban and cultural infrastructure, existing and new businesses, as well as the community's overall image

Key points to note are the following:

• Visitor economy and city image are affected by all events to some degree, but at the other extreme, cultural and sporting infrastructure is affected only by a certain few events.
• In general, what are termed "bigger" events have greater impact than their "smaller" counterparts, but not always; some niche events (e.g., Davos or an Americas Cup) can have very specific but far-reaching impacts.
• Smaller trade events can have a more significant direct impact on business interests, whereas the impact of bigger events is more diffused, especially when the event is specialized.
• Not all events carry the same cost implications or risk factors, which would affect the relative importance of their wider impact.

Most of the benefits accrue during the preparation, hosting, and post-event phase in all categories of events, including the sports category.

Key points to note are the following:

• Managerial and events strategy development benefits are present at all times, for all events.

• Although more benefits accrue around the peak phases of hosting an event, there are plenty of benefits, before and after the Olympics, to be considered.
• The bidding phase can accrue important benefits related to transport and urban infrastructure, city image, business interests, and managerial and events strategy development, and therefore its importance should not be underestimated.
• Infrastructure is assumed to last for at least ten years after the event. This is based on appropriate levels of investment being made in the preparation stage.
• Visitors are unlikely to arrive in any numbers before the event, although in some cases new facilities attract people when they are first opened and before the event itself takes place.

These benefits can also have different impacts, varying from one localized within a neighborhood or community, to city-wide, and even to the region beyond the city. This is important in strategically assessing how, geographically, hosting an event will affect a city or even a country, and will show any differences in where costs and benefits fall.

Scales of benefits range from local areas within the city (most probably the event location itself), to a citywide scale whereby the whole city experiences some level of the benefits, and finally to a beyond-the-city scale. At this largest scale, benefits are experienced anywhere from the city's own regional hinterland up to the national scale. Differentiating more precisely at this scale is tricky due to a complex array of factors, often specific to the particular event. These scales are "cumulative" in that classifying an impact at the beyond-the-city scale means that the impact is most certainly also present at the citywide scale and so on.

Key points to note are the following:

- A single event will have different benefits that are experienced at very different geographical scales.
- The type of event does, however, affect the scale at which any particular type of benefit is experienced — the benefits for transport infrastructure, for instance, are more widely dispersed for sporting and cultural events than for trade and political events.
- Benefits that are experienced beyond the city are more likely to be "invisibles," such as image, business interest, and visitor economy.
- Sports events tend to have more widely dispersed benefits.
- Political events are, in general, events that produce the least widely dispersed benefits of the four types of events discussed.
- To achieve beyond-city benefits, the event does not necessarily have to be bigger; smaller trade and sports events, for instance, can result in benefits experienced beyond the city.
- Events with multiple sites (especially sites that straddle several regions or nations) will have very complex benefits.

Because global events provide a compelling reason to accelerate investment — and to implement city and regional strategies more fully and rapidly — they also offer the potential to help extend regional property, infrastructure, and related markets beyond what the business cycle alone will do. There may be a countercyclical dimension to this kind of activity, which will be important during a slowdown.

So, what are the urban development benefits sought by cities planning or bidding to host global events in the next eight years? For sporting events, these urban development benefits include components of the public infrastructure such as roadways and mass-transit systems, new sports facilities such as arenas and stadiums, and the economic impact created by more visitors and tourists.

How can cities optimize the positive benefits of hosting global events?

- **Pick the right event.** Because different kinds of events offer different outcomes and benefits, potential cities and nations must select the particular event that is right for them.
- **Be bold.** The greatest benefit from hosting an event comes from being imaginative and using the event to solve a problem or facilitate a leap forward to achieve something that otherwise might be difficult or impossible to achieve.
- **Get the leadership right.** Winning the right to stage the event requires great expertise in marketing and public affairs. Delivering a great event requires exceptional project leadership and substantial business acumen. A wide range of leadership skills and experience is needed.
- **Bid well and with ingenuity.** It is essential to mount a compelling and exciting bid, even if it is unsuccessful. Many benefits can come from bidding well, though losing, but nothing is gained from a bad bid.
- **Have a Plan B.** Smart cities have positive and proactive plans for both winning and losing and the ability to present both as successes.
- **Accelerate existing plans and priorities.** Events should be used to accelerate progress on core priorities, not on side shows and activities of secondary importance.
- **Integrate efforts.** The event must be well integrated with numerous other endeavors in development, planning, transport, branding, and marketing.
- **Make the legacy and benefits come first.** The post-event impact should be the

guiding driver for all decisions. The legacy comes first, not as an afterthought.

- **Manage the legacy as a separate project.** The legacy and the wider benefits should be managed as a project in itself, with its own leadership and resources. Too many cities become distracted by the event — and forget about the legacy until it is too late.

- **Make a habit of being a host.** Hosting multiple events over a period of time increases capability and adds to the cumulative benefits. Successful cities need a long-term, multiple-events strategy.

Global events today present a unique opportunity to combine national promotion with urban development and to leverage national resources to modernize cities. This opportunity can be especially important both for cities in fast-growing and emerging economies, and for established cities in developed markets that want to internationalize their appeal. Global events offer an unusual and high-profile moment for public and private collaboration on significant business and intergovernmental projects and initiatives.

CHAPTER 3

Sports Facilities and Economic Prosperity

Gretchen Barta

In a country where most kids learn the names of sports stars before the name of the president, it is no wonder that cities across the United States place so much emphasis on building stadiums to house their local teams or attract new ones. But does the opening of a sports facility really promise economic success for the surrounding area?

In the past six years, minor-league baseball has built 44 ballparks across the country, and major-league teams are leveraging their drawing power to demand bigger and better stadiums. Much of the momentum is politically driven: Local officials and business leaders want teams to locate in their cities to share in the revenue and exposure that they bring. The rush also is driven by the "pride and need of communities to put on their best face," says Richard Andersen, president of CBRE Sports in Pittsburgh. Communities want to attract corporate relocation dollars as well, and stadiums provide more entertainment options for future employees, he adds.

Several factors must be present for a sports stadium and ancillary developments to succeed. First of all, "the location must have

legs," meaning it must be able to support development now and in the future, says Gerry Dudley, chief executive officer of CBRE Sports.

In addition to location, access is critical. "The No. 1 impacting influence on whether or not people go to events is what the access is going to be like," Andersen says. But central business districts aren't necessarily the best answer. A less-central location may be successful "if access is there and it has some connectivity to a downtown area," he explains.

For ancillary developments to succeed, the right mix of properties must be in place. Retail, restaurant, and other entertainment projects easily can capitalize on the critical masses going to the stadium. Also, "Hospitality is one of the more-common uses of land around stadiums," Dudley says. Multifamily developments may work in the right location, but only after other commercial projects have taken root, he continues.

Major- and minor-league stadiums generally are expected to draw large crowds, but even smaller facilities built for a diverse range

Originally published as "Score! Cities Build Sports Stadiums for Economic Prosperity," *Commercial Investment Real Estate*, Vol. 8, No. 6, November/December 2001, by the CCIM Institute, National Association of Realtors, Chicago, IL. Reprinted with permission of the publisher.

of uses can help funnel income into their neighborhoods. The following four case studies illustrate the different economic impacts that sports venues can have on their hometowns. While in most cases stadiums equal success, they don't always promise a winning economy.

Lowe's Motor Speedway

In 1961, when Charlotte Motor Speedway was built outside of Concord, N.C., it was the only development around for miles. The surrounding area remained empty until the early 1990s, when Speedway Motorsports, the racetrack's owner, partnered with the state of North Carolina to build a five-lane access road, which jumpstarted area development.

Although it is primarily an automobile racing facility — home of three NASCAR Winston Cup events each year — the speedway also hosts car shows, concerts, political gatherings, and corporate events that keep it rented almost every day of the year, according to Bob Rourke, CCIM, director of real estate at Speedway Motorsports.

In 1999, the speedway became the first motor sports facility to sell its naming rights and became Lowe's Motor Speedway, after Lowe's Home Improvement Warehouse.

Although plans for industrial development near the speedway never came to fruition, the area received a commercial real estate boom in 1994 when the Mills Group constructed a 1.3-million-square-foot mall near the newly built access road. Land prices immediately skyrocketed, going from $5,000 to $10,000 per acre to $120,000 to $150,000 per acre, with out parcels selling as high as $700,000 per acre, Rourke says.

Since the mid–1990s, commercial real estate growth in the area has influenced the nearby cities of Charlotte and Concord. "Without the new development the county would never have been able to go on the school-building binge it is on, the home builders would not have made the northeast part of Charlotte the second-fastest residential growth area it became, and the area would not be the largest tourist location in the state," Rourke explains. He foresees the residential and retail growth continuing, with office development not far behind.

Van Andel Arena

Almost a decade ago, the southern edge of the Grand Rapids, Mich., CBD, known as Heartside, was an underutilized neighborhood scattered with vacant warehouses and office buildings, says George Bera Jr., CCIM, president of Bera Group. To spur urban redevelopment, area business leaders proposed building a stadium to attract major entertainment events as well as offer a new home for local sports franchises.

After three years of planning and construction, the 12,000-seat stadium opened in 1996 with a $75 million price tag — $56 million from a downtown development bond and $19 million from private donations, Bera says. It was named Van Andel Arena to recognize a $11.5 million gift from the Van Andel Foundation.

"The arena is a little unique in that it was designed first and foremost for music events and secondly for sporting events," Bera says. "The main uses include concerts, hockey, and arena football."

Before it was constructed, area business planners touted the arena as a "catalyst to a CBD revitalization," he says. Restaurants and bars hoping to capitalize on the expected night life quickly sprouted in the neighborhood. Approximately 20 retail establishments opened for business at the time the arena was constructed, but Bera says that around 75 percent of them have since closed.

"There seems to be a lull in revitalization as the projects that made economic sense have been developed, and developers are looking at the remaining opportunities and searching for anchor tenants," he says.

Besides retail, the new stadium spawned other commercial real estate development. Vacant warehouses were renovated into offices, loft apartments, and parking structures, and the increased commercial activity helped push up lease rates.

Bera believes that the arena has had a positive impact on the neighborhood and will continue to do so. "Currently residential is ahead of retail but residential development is nearing a critical mass where retail is sure to follow," he says. "Within 10 years it should be a pretty exciting and successful CBD."

Turner Field

Prior to the 1996 Summer Olympics, the Atlanta Braves and the Atlanta Committee for the Olympic Games combined efforts to build a new stadium that would host the Games and then be converted into a baseball stadium to replace the aging Atlanta-Fulton County Stadium just across the street. Privately financed by the Atlanta Olympic Committee, the stadium cost $207 million to build and another $28 million to turn it into a baseball stadium in 1997, according to Bill Adams, CCIM, president of W. T. Adams and Co. Originally called Olympic Stadium, the venue was renamed Turner Field after business tycoon Ted Turner.

Before the stadium was built, the local neighborhood was economically depressed. "It was hoped that the Games and the new stadium would cause a residential and retail rebirth of the area," Adams says. Several residential projects were planned and built; however, retail projects in the neighborhood had to compete with the thriving retail space inside Turner Field. Consequently, "The retail corridor near the stadium is mostly boarded up," Adams says.

Due to the expanding residential development, land prices have skyrocketed and the neighborhood is gentrifying, yet lease rates for retail space have remained unchanged because many of the storefronts stand empty, he adds. "The stadium itself had no effect on the local commercial real estate market," he says. "The catalyst for all of the residential redevelopment was a combination of the 1996 Olympic Games and the rebirth of Atlanta's close-in neighborhoods. The stadium would have had a much greater impact if it had been located closer to the CBD," since it is more than 1 mile south of the city's center.

However, all is not lost for the neighborhood. Adams believes that the residential growth eventually will spur new retail development. "The retail will be primarily for locals but will also cater to baseball fans," he says. "I think it will develop into a very healthy retail environment within the next five years."

New Orleans Arena

Built in 1999 adjacent to the Superdome, the New Orleans Arena utilizes many of the same heating, ventilation, and air conditioning facilities as the larger structure, according to Quentin Dastugue, CCIM, chief executive officer of Property One. It also shares the Superdome's parking facility, which offers easy access to the arena.

The 18,500-seat arena cost $100 million and was funded by a dedicated hotel/motel tax that was originally put in place to pay for the Superdome, Dastugue says. It hosts the New Orleans Brass hockey team and the Tulane

University basketball and hockey teams, as well as concerts, wrestling matches, and other entertainment events. Arena officials credit the stadium's size — halfway between the Superdome and the 10,000-seat New Orleans Lakefront Arena — for attracting acts such as the Backstreet Boys and Shania Twain.

However, the future of the New Orleans Arena, which has yet to find a naming sponsor, and the surrounding neighborhood is tied to the Superdome. Earlier this year, the owners of the New Orleans Saints threatened to move the National Football League team if the city didn't build it a new stadium to replace the Superdome.

In late 2001, the Saints and the state of Louisiana came to an agreement whereby the state would subsidize the team for two years while performing studies on the feasibility of building a new stadium or renovating the Superdome. In 2003, the Saints and Louisiana will decide the future of the Superdome, and only then will the ramifications of the team leaving New Orleans be known. Until then, however, the New Orleans Arena most likely will keep packing in the fans.

Fans for the Future

Obviously, location and accessibility are two main factors that will spell a stadium's success or failure. But beyond these tangibles is another, more crucial aspect: leadership. A stadium's success hinges on "who has the vision and stamina to be the catalyst for development," Dudley says. The development must be backed by a strong entity, whether it be local government, a sports team, or a private developer.

Sports stadium development, while still in its early years, has the potential to be a major force in the commercial real estate industry. "It may be a way to help smooth the peaks and valleys of more traditional property types," Dudley says. Many larger developers are viewing this type of development as a definite business project and offering it as a specialty, he continues. And the opportunities don't end with U.S. cities and teams: International markets also are embracing sports stadium development as a means of invigorating their economies.

CHAPTER 4

Economic Precautions, Public Scrutiny, and Government Financing

Charles Mahtesian

From the beginning of football training camp in July to the end of the season in January, Pittsburgh is swathed in the black and gold colors of the city's beloved Steelers. Former star running back Franco Harris smiles down benignly from billboards. On game days, the streets empty and commerce slows to a trickle. For the past 26 years, despite the region's status as one of the smallest markets in pro sports, the Steelers have sold out every single seat in Three Rivers Stadium.

Nevertheless, on the 4th of November last year, when it came time to cast an up-or-down, love 'em-or-lose 'em, 11-county referendum to save both the Steelers and the baseball Pirates by building new football and baseball stadiums financed partially with a sales tax increase, the home teams lost. Not by a whisker, either. They suffered a crushing, humbling defeat. In Pittsburgh's own Allegheny County, the vote was 58 percent to 42 percent. In the 10 surrounding counties, the margin was even wider — in one county, the measure went down by 4 to 1.

How could a place that loves its professional sports teams so much reject an effort to keep them so decisively? Easily, it turns out. Pittsburgh is just the latest city gripped by stadium backlash. It is a phenomenon that is becoming almost as commonplace as a millionaire owner extorting city officials for more concessions or a well-paid athlete running into trouble with the law. After an overexuberant run of sweetheart stadium deals and giveaways, a bitter resistance to public financing of stadiums — especially when it involves tax increases — and to sports owner demands is unmistakably taking shape.

On the same day that Pittsburgh went to the polls, Minneapolis sent a similar message by voting overwhelmingly to set a $10 million limit on any financial assistance the city might provide to build a new ballpark for the Minnesota Twins or for construction of any other pro sports facilities. In 1996, Milwaukee and Seattle voters flatly rejected the idea of stadium taxes to finance construction of new sports facilities. The same happened last year in Columbus, Ohio, and this past February in neighboring Dublin, Ohio, where residents rejected a professional soccer stadium, even though the owner planned to finance the facil-

Originally published as "The Stadium Trap," *Governing*, Vol. 11, No. 5, May 1998, by Congressional Quarterly Inc., Washington, D.C. Reprinted with permission of the publisher.

ity himself and the city would have paid only for land acquisition, road improvements and utility extensions. When taxpayer-financed stadium projects do pass muster these days, as one did in Dallas this January, it is almost always by a razor-thin majority: That measure squeaked through by just 1,700 votes.

Legislative scrutiny of public subsidies is no less withering. In the 1998 session alone, scores of stadium-related bills clogged statehouses from Pennsylvania to Minnesota to Colorado, ranging from prohibitions on the use of public resources for sports facilities without a public vote to capping taxpayer liability for stadium costs to calling for Green Bay Packers–style community ownership of sports teams.

Given this level of roiling resentment, you might think the era of public subsidies is over. But the truth is, new stadiums that are entirely privately financed remain the exception. For all the mounting evidence of a backlash, there is little to indicate that cities are any less willing to make sizable public investments to attract or retain sports franchises. Few public officials are willing to interpret a public vote against taxpayer financing of a stadium as a willingness on the part of those taxpayers to see the team leave town.

To some extent, that explains why construction has begun on new stadiums in Milwaukee and Seattle despite bitterly contested public votes not to fund them. Or how in Ohio, despite a recent poll indicating that seven out of 10 residents oppose public financing of stadiums, several controversial stadium proposals are still alive, in addition to ongoing projects in Cincinnati and Cleveland where ground has already been broken. Or how in Pittsburgh the Steelers and Pirates might just get their new stadiums after all: A new proposal for financing the facilities includes no tax hikes and would not need the approval of the voters who vented their wrath on the original plan.

Given the virtual futility of any effort to win passage of a public referendum to finance new stadiums, bypassing the voters is rapidly becoming the strategy of choice. Never was that clearer than during last year's negotiations to lure the New England Patriots to Rhode Island when, despite having advocated for referendums in the past when the state considered public debt, Governor Lincoln Almond opposed either a binding vote on stadium bonds or a nonbinding referendum in a special election. In February, pro soccer team owner Lamar Hunt offered this assessment of the political landscape. "Wherever it ends up," he said after his Dublin, Ohio, stadium proposal was trounced at the polls, "we'll make sure it's not a referendum situation."

Of course, voter resistance to taxpayer financing of pro sports facilities is not a new phenomenon. What's new is the widespread intensity of that resistance. Bolstered by an increasing body of evidence indicating that the economic benefits of new stadiums are at best modest, opponents now have the statistical ammunition to fight back against the dizzying array of rosy economic impact studies churned out by pro-stadium forces. It's no longer so easy to dismiss stadium foes as anti-tax zealots or as the usual mob of cranks and naysayers who oppose any public works project. Nor is it easy to overlook the experiences in other cities where taxpayers appeared to have been either purposely hoodwinked or inadvertently misinformed about the real numbers behind recently approved stadium projects. In Cincinnati, for example, projected costs for a new stadium are now running $200 million more than anticipated.

Elsewhere, the stadium story is even more troubling. An Oakland grand jury is investigating the $192 million deal that lured the Raiders back to the city. In St. Louis, the convention and visitors bureau brought suit against the National Football League, charging unsuccessfully that the league conspired against the city to jack up the price paid to attract the franchise. During the 1997 trial, the city's own attorney referred to the stadium package as "the worst sports deal in history." The NFL's defense argued, in effect, that St. Louis has only itself to blame for being taken to the cleaners. That's why the $300 million domed stadium is widely referred to locally not by its proper title, the Trans World Dome, but as the "Taxpayer Dome."

Of course, not all stadium deals are matters of public ridicule. But without exception, all must weather the same firestorm of hostility toward the state of professional sports in general and toward wealthy owners and players in particular. Minnesota's ongoing stadium soap opera, for example, is complicated by publicity surrounding the finances of billionaire Twins owner Carl Pohlad. Combined with the exquisitely poor timing of Timberwolves basketball player Kevin Garnett's recent rejection of a $103.5 million salary offer, it served to undermine and undercut the efforts of pro-stadium legislators in a way that opponents never could.

As a result, the legislature has been preoccupied by the issue for the past two years; a 1997 special session convened expressly to find a solution failed to settle the question. The Twins stadium issue is even sparking controversy in faraway North Carolina: Four fast-food chains in the locale where Pohlad is threatening to relocate, North Carolina's Triad region, recently renounced their support for a tax to help fund a new stadium; two of them denied that they had ever favored it. Irate customers, it seems, were browbeating local businesses.

"The structure of professional sports and franchise-shifting certainly creates public antipathy toward them," says Frank Lucchino, the controller of Pittsburgh's Allegheny County. "When you add anti-tax fever, millionaire

owners and boorish second-string athletes demanding millions, you have a volatile combination."

No one around Pittsburgh doubted that last year. Indeed, long before voters stepped into the voting booths in November, some of the staunchest supporters of the plan known as the Regional Renaissance Initiative had recognized that it was headed toward ignominious defeat.

The initiative was the brainstorm of downtown interests and the corporate community. Proponents spent millions in an effort to convince voters in Pittsburgh and its surrounding counties that the plan would keep the teams in Pittsburgh while creating thousands of new jobs. One way of muting the expected opposition was to craft the proposal to include a project that nearly everyone could agree on — expansion of the convention center. Funds also would be directed to the downtown cultural district. Various capital projects were included as sweeteners for the surrounding counties.

The half-cent sales-tax hike was designed to raise close to $700 million over seven years. Steelers ownership offered $50 million, or 27 percent of the estimated $185 million cost of a football facility. The Pirates pledged $35 million for their ballpark, a fraction of the estimated cost of between $185 million and $200 million.

The other attempt at softening the opposition took the form of scare tactics. There was no other alternative, voters were told. If the vote failed, there was no backup plan. A rejection of the measure virtually guaranteed the Pirates' exit. The Steelers were likely to follow.

Whether or not people believed that the teams would actually leave is still a matter of speculation. Everyone agrees that, in any case, initiative backers made several major miscalculations, the most serious of which was underestimating the level of voter hostility to a tax hike, especially one that stood to benefit professional sports.

At the heart of the problem, even its supporters would later admit, was the perception that the initiative, known as Plan A, was old-school economic development. It harkened back to the dynamism of post–World War II Pittsburgh, when huge public works projects were accomplished through the sheer will of a few political and corporate titans. The plan failed to take into account all the ways the city, the region and its business community had changed in the intervening years. No longer could a single politician speak for all of the officeholders. No one corporate leader could speak for the private sector. In an era when the communities surrounding Pittsburgh are more populous than the city, Plan A's advocates were handicapped by the widespread perception of who was driving it: downtown business interests. "No people who had political skills or grassroots knowledge had any involvement with that vote," says City Councilman Jim Ferlo, who opposed the plan. "The corporate elite created it."

As in most other cities, the local newspaper, a variety of prominent elected officials and the downtown business community lined up in support of passage. The opposition was composed of an underfunded assortment of anti-tax activists and others who railed against the proposed subsidies as nothing less than corporate welfare.

The huge campaign-spending disparities between the two sides highlighted the divide. Just as stadium boosters in Columbus, Ohio, outspent their foes by more than 250 to 1, Regional Renaissance Initiative backers outspent the opposition by at least 200 to 1. And just as in Columbus, it made no difference. Voters concluded that the very interests that most strongly supported the new stadiums were the ones that stood to gain the most from them. "If

you really want to keep the team, why should the little old lady down in the Mon Valley pay for it?" asks Jake Haulk, research director of the Allegheny Institute for Public Policy, a conservative think tank that spearheaded the opposition. "The only people that agree on this are the downtown people."

In the wake of Plan A's defeat, one question remained unanswered: What exactly were the voters saying? No public funds for stadiums, or no new taxes? Ultimately, city and county officials took the vote to mean that residents still wanted the new stadiums — they just didn't want to shoulder the burden themselves through increased taxes. "The debate has been framed here that no public funds should be involved. But the reality around the country is different," says Mayor Tom Murphy. "My feeling is that when people say no public money, they mean no money used from day-to-day operations."

By March, a proposal known as Plan B surfaced. During the campaign, voters had been told that no such backup plan existed. In truth, though, discussions for Plan B had begun just as Plan A was going down the tubes.

Stripped to its essentials, the $803 million Plan B calls for nearly everyone to get something and nearly everyone to give up something. Revenues from an existing countywide sales tax, state and federal aid, ticket surcharges and private investment would provide the bulk of the funding. Popular resentment over sports greed would be addressed through a proposed tax on player salaries.

The plan, of course, makes several assumptions. Harrisburg would have to kick in $300 million in state capital funds. The legislature approved stadium funding for Pittsburgh in last year's capital budget, but that was before Plan A went down in flames. State officials also must weigh another consideration: If Pittsburgh gets its money, it won't be long before Philadelphia stadium advocates are knocking on the legislature's doors.

The private financing component also needs to be worked out. As it stands, the teams have not committed any more money to the projects than they did under Plan A. It is not escaping notice that some of the Plan B revenue streams identified as "private investment"— such as the player tax — can be considered private only under the most generous of definitions.

Still, the key is that Plan B does not raise taxes. Instead, it is a reallocation of existing tax revenues. And Plan B has one big advantage over Plan A, despite the fact that it actually costs more: If finalized and agreed to by all sides, it would not have to go before the voters who crushed Plan A.

That's not to say the teams would get a free ride. Allegheny County Commissioner Bob Cranmer, one of the Plan B architects, has insisted that both teams need to increase their share of private financing, but that the Steelers, in particular, should up their contribution because — unlike the Pirates — their survival is not predicated on having a brand new stadium. Any windfall profits created by the new stadiums, Cranmer and other officials also suggested, ought to be shared with the public. Another county commissioner demanded full disclosure of both teams' financial statements, showing exactly how they expected to benefit from the new facilities.

All of those new demands shared the same underlying message. "We just can't subsidize these teams with unreasonable amounts of public dollars. Some cities have realized that," says Cranmer. "We tell the teams that we are willing to cooperate. That's a different story than them telling us what they WANT and us trying to figure out how to deliver it. Now it's them telling us what they NEED and us stating that this is what we're willing to do."

That distinction is one that other places

are beginning to make as well. Before Rhode Island Governor Lincoln Almond decided last fall that the roughly $140 million price tag for a new stadium required by the New England Patriots was simply too high to justify the expenditure, it was already obvious that state and local officials were refusing to operate from a position of weakness. During negotiations, for example, Providence Mayor Buddy Cianci insisted that the team make special payments for the police and sanitation services that would be necessary on game days.

If there is a new resolve, though, it is a tenuous one. The local pressure to subsidize stadiums remains enormous, whether it is driven by the hospitality industry and the private sector or by voters who don't want to pay for a team's stadium but nevertheless do not want to see their home teams leave town. "If the Steelers ever left town," explains Mulugetta Birru, executive director of Pittsburgh's Urban Redevelopment Authority, "elected officials would be hung."

Every public official who sits down at the negotiating table with the idea of limiting public investment also recognizes that almost from the moment they begin talks with franchise owners, they are being undermined by their counterparts in other cities. "We have two options," says Dan Onorato, a Pittsburgh city councilman and member of the Stadium Authority. "Either get involved and commit significant amounts of public money, or no public money and say goodbye to your teams. Because there are at least five cities that will do it if we don't."

Cleveland learned that the hard way in 1995. The civic trauma inflicted on the city by Maryland's theft of the beloved Browns football team was instructive, not merely because it revealed the lengths that one city and state would go to to lure a franchise — Maryland offered to build a brand-new, rent-free $200 million stadium in downtown Baltimore, along with a slew of other lucrative incentives — but also because it served notice to thrift-minded cities that their bargaining power was severely limited.

The NFL awarded an expansion franchise to Cleveland in March, nearly three years after the Browns became the Baltimore Ravens, but by then other similarly situated cities, such as Pittsburgh, had made their own assessments about the impact of a departed franchise. "We're not so far from Cleveland that we don't understand what happened," says Allegheny County Commissioner Mike Dawida, another key player in stadium negotiations. "It's stunning to think this could have happened to them."

Nothing, as Dawida and many other local officials caught between the demands of team owners and the resistance of taxpayers can attest, stands to slam the brakes on a city's revitalization momentum as abruptly as the loss of a sports franchise. And few other events highlight the decline of struggling, older urban centers so starkly as the loss of a cherished professional sports team. According to that calculus, the economic impact of a team is nearly irrelevant. Ultimately then, for a city such as Pittsburgh, the value of not losing a team will far outweigh the price it pays to keep it. "There's a big difference between never having a team and losing one," says Onorato. "So you grudgingly do this and hold your nose."

CHAPTER 5

Sports Facilities and the Quality of Life

Josh Goodman

Many traveling salesmen have met the fate David Samson encountered in Portland, Oregon, a few months ago. When the Florida businessman ventured to town to hawk his goods, he was greeted with a curt "No, thank you" and a metaphorical slam of the door. Salesmen get used to that. What makes Samson unusual, however, is that his product wasn't a line of clothing or some useless gizmo. It was a product one would expect to generate a good deal of excitement: a major league baseball team.

Samson, president of the Florida Marlins, went to Portland to discuss relocation of the two-time World Series champions. If the goal of his trip was either to pressure Florida legislators to chip in money toward a new stadium or to find a new home that would, he failed spectacularly. Tom Potter, Portland's mayor, not only reasserted his opposition to public financing of a stadium but insisted he spoke for most of his constituents. Asked whether most Portlanders "couldn't care less about a baseball team," he replied, "That's my very strong sense."

Although Potter's bluntness is unusual, his perspective is not unique. Local and state governments are putting up increasing resistance to the idea of paying for new baseball stadiums. The Minnesota Twins have spent a decade trying to win public funds for a new ballpark but have been rebuffed by the legislature every time, most recently last year. The Marlins began seeking new suitors after the Florida legislature refused to contribute state money to build the team a new home. And the District of Columbia's City Council has already demanded, and won, multiple renegotiations of the deal that brought the Washington Nationals to town last year.

Public funding for stadiums has not exactly dried up. Since 2000, the average new major league baseball stadium has been built with 54 percent public funds, compared with 55 percent for new professional football stadiums. But the trend clearly seems to be moving in the other direction. The one ballpark completed in the past two years, in St. Louis, was built almost entirely with private money.

Communities are playing hardball with the national pastime largely as a result of two developments. First, elected officials have

Originally published as "Skybox Skeptics," *Governing*, Vol. 19, No. 3, March 2006, by Congressional Quarterly Inc., Washington, D.C. Reprinted with permission of the publisher.

begun to accept academic research showing that the economic benefits of subsidizing stadiums don't justify the costs. Second, threats by team owners to leave town are losing their potency because it is widely known that there are very few attractive markets for them to move to. Against this backdrop, baseball's supporters may have to turn to a different argument: that the sport is worth subsidizing simply because it is integral to a community's quality of life.

Negative Numbers

Until recently, baseball teams didn't worry much about strategy when they sought public money for stadiums. They talked about economic development, and assumed (correctly) that few would question them. This was especially true when teams sought subsidies from new territory they were hoping to enter. To begin with, owners argued, the construction of a stadium would be a plentiful source of jobs. Then, once it became operational, hundreds of thousands of fans would pour in, patronizing restaurants, bars and retailers in the area before and after games. As a result, a new stadium could serve as the linchpin to the revival of an entire community.

Business groups and other stadium backers still make this argument, but they are facing increasing skepticism. In the past decade, economist after economist has lambasted the idea that governments are making a prudent choice when they invest in stadiums. Their central point has been that most people have relatively fixed entertainment budgets. That means a dollar spent on baseball is a dollar not spent elsewhere in the local economy. Many academics are also skeptical that stadiums can revitalize neighborhoods. When a new stadium goes up in any city, says Villanova University's Rick Eckstein, "you can see for

yourself, even if you're a lay person, that there's not much going on there except on game days."

Many elected officials who oppose subsidizing stadiums make ample use of the economic data. John Marty, a Minnesota state senator, argues that the issue should not be whether the subsidy produces some tangible benefit but whether the benefit is equal to the cost. "If I give you $150 million, it's going to stimulate the economy, I guarantee it." Marty says. "But $150 million doesn't come out of thin air."

The shift in sentiment has hit baseball harder than it has hit other sports. Despite pro football's popularity, few teams ever argued seriously that an NFL stadium could spur an economic revitalization. With only eight regular-season home games per year, there simply weren't enough game days to boost area businesses. Major League Baseball, with a home schedule in each stadium of 81 games per year, did make this argument. So baseball had more to lose if the economic reasoning came into question — and that is what is occurring now.

The result is that long-standing stadium foes — critics on the right who see public financing as an impetus for higher taxes and critics on the left who view it as welfare for billionaires — have more influence than they did in the past. The recent spats in Florida, Minnesota and D.C. have shown that political opposition, in conjunction with budgetary pressures, can turn the tide against public financing. "Local governments have enormous needs and those needs are increasing each year and they're becoming more complicated and more expensive," says Ian Yorty, Miami-Dade County's tax collector and negotiator of the Marlins stadium deal that the legislature failed to ratify last year. "If you don't have a direct mandate from the voters, it's hard to find enough money to throw at a sports stadium."

No Place to Go

Baseball owners have one other serious credibility problem, especially when it comes to cities with existing franchises: They frequently talk about moving out of town, but they almost never do. The Montreal Expos, who became the Washington Nationals last year, are the only team to change cities in the past three decades. In the Expos' case, it took years of miserable attendance before the team finally left.

Football teams switch cities far more frequently, and the reason isn't difficult to understand. Filling a stadium eight times a year is a test even small cities can meet if given the chance. Green Bay, Wisconsin, with a population of 101,000, sells out Lambeau Field for every Packers game. It could never support a baseball team, nor would any baseball owner ever consider locating there. That is true of other cities several times the size of Green Bay. In fact, some observers doubt whether any locale that doesn't already have a major league baseball team — Portland, San Antonio, Las Vegas and Norfolk, Virginia, are mentioned most frequently as possible destinations — could support a franchise. "Market size is important to baseball in a way that it isn't to any other sport," says Neil deMause, an author who is critical of public financing of stadiums. "The NFL can put teams anywhere they want."

The lack of attractive destinations hasn't stopped owners from threatening relocation, but it has made the threats much less effective in recent years. The Twins have been rumored to be heading out of town for much of John Marty's 20-year tenure in the Minnesota Senate, and at one point Major League Baseball publicly contemplated folding the franchise. "They kept hyping it so much," says Marty. "They were going to contract the team, they were going to move the team, they were going to sell the team, but after three or four times people realize it's bogus."

Supporters of public funding for a new Twins stadium continue to warn that the team might actually leave in the absence of a new ballpark, noting that the Expos, did, in the end, move to Washington. But the widespread perception that Twins threats have been idle has encouraged lawmakers to take a stance against public funding. Last year, the legislature failed to give approval to a plan for a new stadium, even though the public costs would have been borne exclusively by Hennepin County, which approved the funding package. A court ruled last month that the Twins are not bound to stay in their current stadium, the Metrodome, beyond this season, a decision that may put pressure on lawmakers to make a final decision.

In Florida, the threat of a Marlins departure also backfired. After team officials met with Las Vegas representatives to discuss a possible move there, Florida Senate President Tom Lee, rather than seeking additional state money to keep the team in town, accused the Marlins of "blackmail," declaring that "I don't negotiate with terrorists." Later in the year, the team reached a deal with Miami-Dade County officials that was predicated on the legislature kicking in $60 million in state money. Legislators balked at that sum and the measure stalled.

More Like a Museum

If baseball teams can no longer make a persuasive claim that they are engines of economic development, or pressure communities by threatening to leave town, what might they use as a strategy for obtaining public money?

Mike Opat, a commissioner in Hennepin County, Minnesota, thinks he has the answer.

Opat, a sponsor of the Twins funding proposal that the legislature rejected, makes an analogy between stadiums and cultural amenities such as museums and theaters: No one argues for a new museum on the grounds that it will create jobs or revitalize a neighborhood. But people enjoy museums, vibrant communities have them, and citizens come to expect them.

Opat acknowledges that, from an economist's perspective, publicly financed stadiums aren't always worth the price, but wishes there was more focus on the qualitative benefits of a new ballpark. "I can't put a dollar value on the number of seniors or young people who follow the team," he says. "There are just a host of intangibles."

The question going forward is whether this "quality of life" argument will be enough to sustain support for public financing — whether the situations in Florida and Minnesota are aberrations or a sign of more resistance to come. Baseball is only a quality of life issue as long as people care about the games. In this regard, there are some disturbing omens. World Series audience ratings have dropped dramatically over the past two decades, which seems to suggest that Potter's assessment of fan interest is true in many places beyond Portland. But, if baseball has been anything over the course of its history, it has been resilient. That trait may be more necessary than ever in an era in which public financing will not be easily won.

II: The Best Practices

CHAPTER 6

Anaheim and the Influence of the Angels

Brian Judd

It was the summer of 2002; the Anaheim Angels had just wrapped up the American League championship series against the Minnesota Twins and the city of Anaheim was preparing for the Angels' first World Series appearance in the 31-year history of the franchise. The city was bursting with pride. Residents and employees donned their Angels gear, banners began to appear on car windows, and city hall was draped with a multistory red banner sporting the familiar big "A." As visions of infield celebrations materialized, municipal officials began to wonder: "If we win, where will we hold the parade?"

It may have seemed odd that no one had thought of this before, considering the team had been in Anaheim since 1966. Maybe it was because playoff opportunities had been rare in the past or, at best, short lived. Or perhaps no one had dared raise the question before for fear of jinxing the team. At any rate, scouting a suitable parade route would seem a relatively simple task. The city had a resort centered around its convention center as well as Disneyland, Disney's California Adventure, and Downtown Disney; plus two major sports fa-

cilities; and its own downtown. However, after a closer look at each of those locations, it was apparent that those sites were not the type of urban places typical of ticker-tape parades.

Though the eventual World Series Championship parade ended up as two parades — the first on Main Street in Disneyworld, the second in the parking lot around Angels Stadium of Anaheim — the city of Anaheim began its plans to create new, recognizable places that not only would provide the proper home for future world championship parades, but also would attempt to come up with new, livable places yet unseen in Orange County. The city had already begun efforts to jump-start the revitalization of its downtown, which to date had functioned primarily as a civic center — home to city hall, a few office buildings, and some limited retail development — by introducing high-density residential and mixed-use development in a pedestrian-friendly environment. It also had begun to fashion a combination of economic development and redevelopment strategies to help breathe new life into the many aging commercial corridors that framed so many of

Originally published as "The Awakening of Anaheim," *Urban Land*, Vol. 63, No. 8, August 2004, by the Urban Land Institute, Washington, D.C. Reprinted with permission of the publisher.

Anaheim's single-family neighborhoods. In addition, many of the award-winning design strategies for the Anaheim Resort had come to fruition: comprehensive landscaping and signage programs had been implemented and older areas within the resort had been transformed with new uses, cohesive signage, and marked facade improvements.

With the Anaheim Resort, the convention center, and two sports franchises, Anaheim had become a popular destination, drawing over 20 million visitors annually. Anaheim, the tenth-largest city in California, also is home to over 11,000 businesses and more than 340,000 residents living in numerous diverse neighborhoods ranging from historic enclaves going back 75 years or more to post–World War II–style subdivisions, to multifamily neighborhoods of varying quality, and to master-planned suburban hillside neighborhoods. By 2025, Anaheim's population is expected to grow beyond 380,000 and the 50-square-mile city will become one of the most densely populated cities in the United States.

In 2001, when the city launched one of its largest planning efforts in its long history — a three-year effort to update its general plan and zoning code — all of these initiatives needed to be woven together. Anaheim's general plan, initially adopted in 1963, had various elements that had been amended over the years. While some policies still provided useful guidance, others needed to be strengthened to deal more effectively with contemporary issues. As a result, the city initiated a major effort to establish a new vision and prepare a new general plan to make that vision a reality. At the outset of the general plan update, many of the city's key assets were in good shape. The Anaheim Resort had recently undergone a major facelift, including the third expansion of the convention center, making it the largest on the West Coast; implementation of an award-

winning landscape and signage plan throughout the Anaheim Resort; and the opening of Downtown Disney and Disney's California Adventure. Angels Stadium of Anaheim, located nearby, had already undergone a major overhaul in 1998.

Even with all these changes, Anaheim lacked a "big city" feel — the residential communities surrounding the new facilities lacked urban densities; pedestrian amenities were limited; retail, entertainment, office, and residential uses were, for the most part, separated; and most areas, with the exception of the Anaheim Resort, lacked any cohesive design quality.

Although the Anaheim general plan dealt with a multitude of planning issues, as required by state law, the plan's major initiatives were linked by the idea of creating better places in which residents, workers, business owners, and visitors could live, work, and enjoy their lives. Revitalizing the downtown, breathing life into the many strip commercial corridors, and creating a new urban center in Orange County around Angels Stadium were some of the more notable place-making strategies incorporated into the long-range development plan. But to get there, the city first needed a vision plan.

The first step was to develop an extensive outreach program that sought insights on the values and desires of the community. Perhaps the most important part of the outreach program — the Anaheim visioning process — included a series of community events; community group presentations; meetings with the chamber of commerce; a widely distributed community survey; one-on-one meetings with the city's elected and appointed officials; and active participation of the general plan advisory committee (GPAC). The goal for each forum was to identify what people liked and disliked about their city and to capture their vision for the future. The visioning process resulted in a statement of the desired, positive future of the city, which described what Anaheim would look and feel like and how it would function as a community once the vision plan became a reality. Endorsed by the city council, this vision plan set the foundation for preparing the general plan and, over time, served as a benchmark for the implementation of the plan.

Like most other popular places in the United States and abroad, Anaheim is supported by residents who want to be part of a community that has a unique identity and a "sense of place," enhances social interaction, and fosters civic pride — one that would reflect the growing popularity of revitalized downtowns, new mixed-use urban villages, and walkable neighborhoods. The Anaheim vision and general plan laid the land use and policy foundation to provide for the creation and enhancement of many such special places.

Early on in the planning process, a market analysis was conducted by Robert Charles Lesser and Company, based in Los Angeles, to determine the long-term potential for office, retail, and industrial land uses. One of the findings of the study suggested that the area around Angels Stadium, known as the "Platinum Triangle," provided potential for creating a new urban center in Orange County. Besides Angels Stadium and the nearby Anaheim Pond, home of the Anaheim Mighty Ducks hockey franchise, the area offered extensive multimodal transportation access with its location at the confluence of two freeways and with one of the few Metrolink stations in the county. The city is currently looking into the potential for a future intermodal transit center that would serve as a hub for commuter, light, and high-speed rail. In addition, Katella Avenue, which extends east/west through the area and connects to the Anaheim Resort, is a designated bus rapid transit (BRT) route. The Orange County Transit Authority's BRT pro-

gram combines communications technology, traffic signal priority, specifically designed vehicles, rapid fare collection, and rail-style stations to create a system that offers the flexibility of buses with features more typical of rail transit. Furthermore, the area benefits from its proximity to the Anaheim Resort, the office hub around the University of California Irvine Medical Center, and the adjacent Santa Ana River, one of Orange County's largest open space and trail linkages connecting Anaheim to both the local mountains and the Pacific Ocean.

Currently, the 800-acre Platinum Triangle comprises a large amount of underused land, primarily low-rise office and industrial uses, and a surface parking lot around the stadium. Past efforts to revitalize the area focused on office development and entertainment uses, but lacked any real integration or mix of land uses, or any urban housing. According to Bob Gardner, managing director at Robert Charles Lesser and Company, "The combination of exciting locational benefits and amenities creates a natural nexus in northern Orange County where many people will choose to work, live, and play. Over time, we would expect to see the emergence of higher-density land uses [office space and housing] building on the Platinum Triangle's obvious competitive advantages."

Planned for the Platinum Triangle are a mix of uses and upscale, high-density urban housing (up to 9,175 dwelling units) integrated into a network of pedestrian walkways, streetscape improvements, and recreational spaces. In addition, the Platinum Triangle has the potential for 5 million square feet of office space, 2 million square feet of retail space, plus entertainment, hotel, and recreational uses.

Anaheim's downtown, located within the Anaheim Colony Historic District, has witnessed many changes over time. Beginning as a small, thriving commercial area in the early

1900s, it has expanded to accommodate a growing population. Through the redevelopment process that began in the 1970s, many of the historic commercial and residential buildings were replaced with newer structures. As a result, the area is mixed, both in terms of architectural styles and age of prominent buildings. Municipal officials and area residents have expressed interest in creating a more pedestrian-friendly downtown that reflects elements of Anaheim's historic past. Design guidance to ensure that new development is compatible with the area's vision to become the "cultural, artistic, historic, and civic center of the city" is now established in the new plan.

In several areas of Anaheim, particularly in the western half of the city, aging strip malls and stand-alone retail uses line arterial corridors and form the edges of many neighborhoods. Market studies confirmed that the city had an overabundance of commercially designated land in these areas. One of the reports estimated that the west Anaheim area alone had an estimated oversupply of 1.5 million to 3 million square feet, or 172 to 275 acres of land designated for retail uses. This oversupply has resulted in anemic sales, high vacancies, and marginal tenants, and has detracted from the image and visual character of the surrounding residential areas. The general plan strives to revitalize neighborhood edges by converting many of these mid-block areas to a new kind of corridor residential land use, which provides a new opportunity to reinvigorate these edges and simultaneously address a significant portion of Anaheim's housing needs. Concurrently, specific goals and policies of the plan focus commercial uses at key intersections to take advantage of the exposure and accessibility offered by such locations.

Since they are located along busy arterials, mid-block developments will be set back far enough for safety and livability purposes, but close enough to visually improve the corridor. The design goal is to encourage mid-block development that incorporates richly detailed architecture and contributes to an attractive pedestrian-friendly street environment. Design guidelines will help in the creation of residential developments with a neighborhood scale and appearance, orientation toward the street, recessed or alley-loaded parking, and landscaped parkways. Provision of open space within each development is planned to contribute to an attractive streetscape. The policies of the general plan allow for design flexibility while outlining design features that create a visually consistent environment.

Now, with plans for a rejuvenated downtown and an urban community surrounding the Angels Stadium, future championship celebrations will present a new, welcomed dilemma the next time the Angels or Mighty Ducks win a World Series or Stanley Cup.

CHAPTER 7

Arlington and Other Cities Weigh the Value of Stadiums for Public Financing

Alan Ehrenhalt

Economists have a reputation for being cool and dispassionate, but a few phrases or concepts have the capacity to turn even the meekest of them into hectoring ideologues, exasperated with the inability of others to exercise simple common sense.

Try it some time. Tell an economist there may be some hidden virtues in rent control. Or that an expensive urban light-rail system might turn out a good investment. Odds are you will soon be on the receiving end of a sermon denouncing perverse incentives and the waste of billions in public money on inefficient and indefensible subsidies for half-baked government boondoggles.

Better yet, start a conversation about sports stadiums. Suggest casually that a major league baseball team is a civic asset so valuable that it justifies whatever the cost to taxpayers of gaining it or keeping it might be, even if that cost ultimately runs into the hundreds of millions of dollars. Then get ready for a lecture. If there's one article of faith that unites economists and public policy analysts of all colors and creeds, it's that subsidies to sports teams are a scandalous example of welfare payments to millionaires that accomplish nothing for cities or their governments in the long run.

In the past decade, specialists in economics and public policy have written more than a dozen scholarly books attacking the sinister connections between cities and sports teams, and decrying the tragic inefficiencies they create. Whenever a new stadium-subsidy deal is announced, experts such as Andrew Zimbalist, Mark Rosentraub and Robert Baade turn up on sports pages all over the country, denouncing yet another foolish giveaway. One commentator has gone so far as to refer to the group as a "cottage industry."

Industry or not, the scourges of subsidies will be busy in the next few months as Washington, D.C., finalizes its plan to bring the Montreal Expos to the nation's capital and build a new baseball stadium for the team to play in. It is just the sort of arrangement every economist loves to hate. Regardless of who ends up owning the team, Washington's mayor

Originally published as "Ballpark Dreaming," *Governing*, Vol. 17, No. 11, November 2004, by Congressional Quarterly Inc., Washington, D.C. Reprinted with permission of the publisher.

is committed to spending $440 million on the stadium, to be located in an underused industrial neighborhood along the Anacostia River. To pay for the project, the city plans to issue 30-year bonds, repayable mostly through a surcharge on stadium tickets and concessions, and a special tax on D.C.'s largest businesses. Only about 14 percent of the cost — about $5.5 million per year — would be met by rental payments to D.C. from the team's owners.

As is typical of any big stadium deal these days, supporters of D.C. baseball touted the tangible benefits that the team and the new ballpark would bring to the city: jobs, economic growth, millions in new revenue from gate receipts and revitalization of a long dilapidated part of the community. "This is a really incredible day," Mayor Anthony A. Williams said in making the announcement. "America's pastime is coming back to this city and once again giving us the ability to dream great things."

Those are sweet dreams. What's wrong with them? Just about everything, an economist will tell you. For one thing, sports are a tiny part of any regional economy. Rarely do they represent more than 1 or 2 percent of the local job base. A new stadium and the low-wage service jobs it creates represent no more than a drop in the bucket. Fans do pay millions of dollars for tickets, hot dogs and beer, but most of that revenue simply replaces money they would have spent on other forms of recreational activity in the same vicinity.

And finally, economists say, new stadiums don't do much for the surrounding territory. Just ask the merchants around Pioneer Square in Seattle, which was a sleazy downscale neighborhood in the 1970s, before the multi-sport Kingdome was built, and was just as much of an embarrassment 30 years later, when the Dome was demolished and separate new facilities for football and baseball were erected to replace it, at a cost of $700 million.

On the jobs and revenue questions, I will give the economists their due. Sports promoters who glibly predict that a new stadium and/or franchise will bring in tens of thousands of jobs and as much as $100 million in net revenue are talking through their hats. A host of careful studies done over the past 15 years makes it pretty clear that no team has ever come close to accomplishing this. On these issues, I can't really challenge the views of Steven Reiss, one of the most prominent of the sports-subsidy critics: Reis says cities "continue to rely on unsubstantiated forecasts by well-paid consultants to support sports as a economic development tool."

When it comes to neighborhood revival, though, I don't think the answer is quite as clear. It's true that the Kingdome did nothing for downtown Seattle. Nor has the Ballpark at Arlington, where the Texas Rangers play, brought a lot of new life to the community around it. A new baseball stadium didn't save downtown St. Louis in the 1970s, nor is a new domed football stadium helping it much right now. Even a great facility and a playoff team can't accomplish an urban renaissance all by themselves.

On the other hand, there's good evidence — even if it's anecdotal rather than academic — to suggest that professional sports can be critical to inner-city renewal if it's part of a broader public plan. Anybody who walks up 16th Street in downtown Denver, past the restaurants and lofts of the revived LoDo district, and on to Coors Field at the end of the road, can't help but see how commerce, architecture and sports have joined together in a web of successful redevelopment. Camden Yards in Baltimore and Jacobs Field in Cleveland haven't brought any form of salvation to their seriously troubled cities. But they have helped to reclaim parts of them by bringing in millions of visitors. Do those benefits justify the enormous costs that taxpayers in

Cleveland and Baltimore are still paying off? I think that's an arguable question — one that cannot necessarily be answered by statistics on economic growth and job creation.

Where the economists clearly are right is in pointing out that the huge subsidies cities give sports owners are the result of an artificial scarcity the owners have created. There are 30 franchises in major league baseball. The owners refuse to make any more, and so any city that wants a team — or wants to keep its team — has to compete against every other aspiring host city in a rigged sellers' market. If baseball management wants to demand a $440 million stadium subsidy as its price for allowing the Expos to relocate to Washington, it can get away with that.

That's because no matter what the press releases say, cities that pay big money for teams and stadiums aren't making an economic investment. They're making an emotional statement about the kind of community they want to be. They want to be "major league," in every sense of the word. When St. Louis offered a subsidy that may eventually come to $700 million to attract the NFL Rams, one civic leader expressed the rationale in blunt terms: "Without them, we're a cow town."

When you lose a team, you lose civic self-respect. When you regain a team, you get some of it back. Even the economists understand the importance of that. And political leaders feel it even more keenly, if possible,

than ordinary fans. When the Chicago White Sox threatened to move to Florida in the early 1990s, Illinois Governor James Thompson promised that he would "bleed and die before I let the Sox leave Chicago." And they stayed, at a cost to taxpayers of $167 million.

That's pretty much the way it works. Economists and public policy analysts will keep doing studies that document the inefficiency of sports and stadium subsidies. Mayors and governors will continue to make lavish promises to the few available teams, and taxpayers will continue to foot the bill, accumulating long-term public debt in the hundreds of millions of dollars almost every time a deal is made. And they generally will pay it without complaining, even if they never voted for it.

If the economics of sports were more rational, there would be three times as many major league teams in every sport. The owners would pay for new stadiums with their own money, or they wouldn't build them at all. We would all get a few of our tax dollars back.

But sports cannot really be understood as a rational enterprise. As one of the most prominent subsidy critics, Mark Rosentraub of Cleveland State University, lamented a few years ago, "the men manipulating the smoke and pageantry of sports are presenting an illusion steeped in the culture and traditions of our society." It's not an illusion that shows any signs of disappearing.

CHAPTER 8

Boise Finances Multi-Use Facility for Community Events

Stephanie Worrell

Boise State University's latest marketing slogan is "beyond the blue," referring to the now infamous blue turf that covers the school's varsity football field. A $32.1-million expansion of Bronco Stadium, the facility that surrounds the field, has taken the slogan in the opposite direction of the fake blue grass — way up into the blue sky that usually hovers over the Treasure Valley.

The 83,600-square-foot project is being constructed on the west side of the stadium and includes luxury suites, expanded seating, club rooms, upgrades to the west concourse and other facilities — making the facility more than just a place to kick off on Saturdays during football season. It will become a multi-use, community facility that can be utilized year-round for special events, conferences and banquets. The expansion to the existing 30,000-seat stadium will increase capacity to 32,000.

"The expansion of Bronco Stadium is an important milestone in the ongoing portfolio of projects on the Boise State University campus," said James Maguire, Boise State University associate vice president of planning and

facilities. "It will serve as the cornerstone in the growth and development of the southeast area of campus. We have three additional projects in design right now."

To finance construction, Boise State University issued $28 million in bonds, and additional funds will be secured through the athletic department over the next several years.

Giant Structure on Stilts

The university contracted with Sandy, Utah–based Layton Construction to build the addition, and FFKR Architects of Salt Lake City designed the project. Work began in March 2007 and is slated to conclude in August 2008. Both firms came into the project with stadium design and construction experience. Layton has the University of Utah's Rice-Eccles Stadium and Brigham Young's LaVell Edwards Stadium — to name a couple — in its "stadium portfolio." Both firms also worked on facility expansion projects for those two facilities.

"Even though this isn't the type of proj-

Originally published as "Bronco Stadium Expands," *Pacific Builder and Engineer*, February 2008, by Associated Construction Publications/Reed Construction Data, Oak Brook, IL. Reprinted with permission of the publisher.

ect you see being built every day in a community, it's really fairly standard in terms of concrete and steel form construction," said Layton's project manager, Jeremy Hobbs. "But this project is unique in the fact that it's basically a giant structure on stilts. The tops of the two towers included in the facility expansion rise 69 feet above the existing structure."

Staging to construct what have been dubbed the "north" and "south" towers was 24 hours, seven days a week — and at the time of publication, was complete.

"It is amazing for people to see how fast the towers go up," said Hobbs. "A 25,000-pound forming system (provided and engineered by Scanada) was trucked in from New Hampshire and assembled on the site. A crew of about 22 guys worked around the clock, first on the north tower and then on the south. The towers went up at the rate of about 10 to 14 inches per hour, each taking between six to eight days to erect."

The form included three levels, and included four, 22-ton hydraulic jacks that climb on 2½-inch jack rods moving the entire 25,000-pound, three-level platform and workers upward at 1-inch increments. The upper level was used for landing rebar, concrete and embeds, and the second was used for placing concrete, driving the form and rebar placement. The third and lowest level was for concrete finishers to finish concrete as it came out at the bottom of the form.

Getting materials up to the site of construction was a challenge at times. A 275-ton hydraulic crane assisted with the lifting of materials while a temporary stair tower was used for access for the construction personnel. All of the concrete was wheel-barrowed and placed into the narrow formwork manually by the concrete crews.

The north tower, which spans 170 feet, utilized 1,130 cubic yards of concrete and 252,360 pounds of rebar. There are 34 doors

(includes elevators) and 860 concrete embeds. The south tower is the same height and uses about the same amount of concrete and rebar, but it has 29 door openings and 680 concrete embeds. Approximately 200 loads of concrete were trucked in — also 24-7 — per tower.

"Of course, the safety of our crews has been top of mind throughout the project," said Hobbs. "It can be a bit more challenging when you are working so high off the ground, but it is a daily, conscious effort for us and we've had no issues so far."

No Major Delays

Layton Construction boasts an annual volume of over $700 million. The company is ranked as the top commercial builder in the state of Utah by *Utah Business* magazine.

Other major partners and subcontractors working on the stadium expansion include:

- Lea Electric (Boise)
- DeBest Plumbing (Boise)
- YMC, Inc. (Meridian, Idaho)
- Boise Crane (Boise)
- Velocity Steel (Wilder, Idaho)
- GB Redi Mix (Boise)
- Materials Testing & Inspection, Inc. (Boise)
- Sommer Builders (Boise)
- Fought Steel (Portland, Ore.)
- REFA Erection (Portland, Ore.)

"Every effort has been made to use local Idaho partners, crews and materials," said Hobbs. "Our company makes it a priority to support and become part of the local community."

In terms of project challenges, Hobbs noted weather and staging as the only concerns to date. Abnormally cold weather and unusual amounts of snow in the months of November, December and January slowed progress a bit. But, no major delays are expected in the overall project timeline. Hobbs said he believes that crews will meet the August finish date.

"Staging a project when part of it must remain open for use is always complicated," said Hobbs. "We continued construction during the 2007 football season and one major bowl game, hosting thousands of fans on any given game day."

Temporary concessions, elevators, access ramps, and entrances were all part of the major logistical efforts that were coordinated prior to the season. A temporary, albeit smaller, press box also was constructed in order to serve media during the season.

"Layton has kept this project on time, through track meets, rain, snow, 100-degree days, and eight packed football games," said Lori Hays, Boise State University assistant athletic director for operations. "They helped us place porta-potties and keep the construction site clean and safe on game days. Their pride in their work and partnership with the community is obvious."

What's New

The new press box, which will provide state-of-the-art facilities for print and broadcast media, will feature high-performance glazing curtain wall systems designed for energy efficiency. Insulated metal panels will be used where glass is not installed.

New entrances will be opened at the ground level on the west side. Two elevator lobbies provide five elevators, with three in the north tower and two in the south tower. A new ticket office — slated to operate daily for tickets to other local events — will be opened on this level in a central lobby that also will house the Bronco Shop. An entry plaza with seating and landscaping is planned for the west side.

Design elements included enhanced views of the scenic Treasure Valley. For example, additional outdoor club seating will accommodate about 750. Patrons in these seats have the option of being indoors, with a window system that opens all the way in good weather. The sky suites and press box also feature windows that open completely when the weather allows.

An exposed steel structure running from the concourse to the loge level supporting the new press box will add creative aesthetic detail to a utilitarian structure. The narrow existing concourse level will be replaced with all new concession stands and additional restrooms. A full culinary kitchen will be going in on the ground level. The new concourse will span 40 feet wide.

With the towers complete, crews are beginning to pour slab on the metal decks and to rough-in electrical and mechanical. In February, the exterior shell, glass paneling and roofing will be added to the exterior.

Hobbs is confident that the stadium will be open for business in mid–August — just in time for the first game on 2008 Bronco football schedule.

"Upon completion of the stadium expansion, the assembly of space is going to be known as a true landmark because of visibility from the city," said Maguire. "The views of the mountains to the east are going to be striking. Bronco Stadium is going to be a remarkable structure, both from without and within."

CHAPTER 9

Boston and Other Cities Maximize Use of Inner-City Sports Facilities

David Nardone

Because urban land is at a premium, designers of athletic fields often must design, or redesign, existing sports facilities to maximize flexibility and allow for the greatest number of users. To this end, site planners are designing these fields as multiuse facilities to avoid the need to provide separate fields for different sports.

To best plan for a field that will accommodate a school's entire sports program, site planners need to create a comprehensive athletic field master plan that not only illustrates field layout, but also considers the sports schedule as it relates to seasons and league participation. For example, efficient planning and design can allow a field used for baseball in the spring to become a football practice field and field hockey facility in the fall through strategic configuration of the outfield. In highly populated areas, the most common and efficient fields are shared soccer fields and baseball outfields. These fields typically offer the most flexibility and often overlap one another because the baseball outfield can accommodate soccer and other sports.

When a plan calling for one field or overlapping fields is not enough, a master plan can achieve the most efficient use of land by mapping out the orientation of multiple fields. Careful planning will allow facilities designers to create the most fields possible within the designated space while still including adequate runout/buffer zones to ensure player safety. In addition, a master plan addresses the orientation of the fields in relation to the sun to minimize glare and prevent low sun angles from affecting players and spectators.

In dense urban neighborhoods, existing area constraints and infrastructure create additional obstacles for the planning of such site components as drainage. For example, to address stormwater compliance in an urban setting, underground stormwater storage facilities are often installed to work within the framework of an area's existing system.

In Boston, an urban athletic field redesign is underway for Teddy Ebersol's Red Sox Fields at Lederman Park, dedicated to Teddy Ebersol, NBC Sports chairman Dick Ebersol's 14-year-old son who died in a plane crash in November. The renovation is intended to revitalize and maximize the space of

Originally published as "The Minor Leagues," *Urban Land*, Vol. 64, No. 7, July 2005, by the Urban Land Institute, Washington, D.C. Reprinted with permission of the publisher.

the existing field complex, constructed in 1951 as mitigation for displacement of the Frederick Law Olmsted–designed Charlesbank, the first free outdoor recreational facility on Boston's historic Esplanade. The project is currently in the permitting stage, and construction is set to begin this summer. Last summer, 68 user groups applied for permits, indicating the high demand for access to the fields.

The redesign and dedication are a result of a public/private partnership. The land is owned and controlled by the Department of Conservation and Recreation (DCR) in the Massachusetts Executive Office of Environmental Affairs, while the project is privately funded by the Esplanade Association, Hill House, and the Red Sox Foundation. The existing complex consists of one large adult softball field, two youth-sized fields, and two tennis courts. From the current layout, the site designers identified three major components in their master plan — reorganization of the space, drainage, and lighting.

Because the tennis courts are in disrepair, their removal is considered essential to reorganizing the field space. Tennis is viewed as an inflexible sport because few people can use a court simultaneously. In addition, with their special asphalt surface and nets, courts cannot be used easily for other activities. Removal of the courts will allow the adult softball field to be moved to the south to create space for a fourth field. Moving the large field will also enable the second field to be expanded to create fields with legitimate youth baseball/adult softball dimensions. The orientation of the third field will then be adjusted to accommodate tee ball, youth baseball, and adult recreation leagues, thus maximizing the athletic field space and use. In addition, a grass area has been designated for tee ball to increase the number of children that can participate in baseball activities simultaneously. This newly opened space will also provide additional flexibility for youth and adult soccer leagues.

To accommodate the additional activity and maintain a high-quality playing surface, a drainage problem had to be addressed. The existing fields are too flat to move the surface water, and the soils are compacted, leaving the fields unplayable for days after a storm. Site planners have recommended that the surface be graded to allow stormwater to flow to several low points where it will collect in a drain line/storage system with controlled release into an existing drainage system. Keeping the surface water moving and providing storage will allow the fields to dry out in just hours.

Lighting is also proposed for the two larger fields. This will allow increased use, extending the hours that young people can participate in games and practices after school, while adult leagues can be accommodated in the evenings. Because the urban setting does not allow much space between the fields and surrounding high-traffic areas, a state-of-the-art lighting system has been designed to control glare and to have a negligible impact on abutting properties. In addition, to maintain the aesthetics of the area and to preserve an open park landscape, light poles will be installed at the park's perimeter along the tree line.

Synthetic turf was considered for the fields, but it was decided that only natural grass would be appropriate for the historic, natural landscape of the Esplanade and Charles River. Many urban areas, however, are switching from natural grass to synthetic turf because high levels of activity can make it virtually impossible to keep real grass alive. Synthetic turf fields can also eliminate the need for exposed detention basins because the drainage system can be designed to incorporate stormwater storage into the field. Although synthetic fields are initially more expensive to install — $8 to $12 per square foot, two to three times the cost of conventional grass fields — they pay for themselves over time by providing a more consistent playing surface, decreasing maintenance, and withstanding increased activity.

The recent renovation of Granger Field at Clark University in Worcester, Massachusetts, exemplifies how synthetic turf can maximize space and field use at an urban institution with extremely limited field space. Granger Field, previously all natural grass, was used heavily throughout the year, and as a result, the field quality was less than desirable. The university determined that an upgrade was essential to meet the athletic programs' needs. Previously, the site held six tennis courts, a baseball field with a multipurpose outfield, and a field-hockey field, none of which met NCAA regulations. The new design accommodated all these elements in a layout that allowed maximized field space exceeding NCAA layout criteria. The tennis courts were moved to the south end of the site and the synthetic baseball/multipurpose field was positioned in the center, providing space for a dedicated soccer field at the north end of the site.

To accommodate this multipurpose and high-level use, site planners recommended installation of synthetic turf. For Clark, the synthetic turf was designed specifically to better fit the needs of the field hockey and baseball programs. Because the synthetic field can accommodate increased activity, Clark now provides opportunities for greater community participation, including use by local high schools and other Worcester-area colleges. According to Clark athletic director Linda Moulton, the redesign allowed the university to "literally use every square inch of the property for athletic program space. Nothing is wasted."

Site planners need to ensure that no land is wasted when designing athletic fields in urban settings where space is limited. Through comprehensive master planning, reconfiguration of fields as multipurpose facilities, and installation of synthetic turf where appropriate, athletic facility directors can maximize efficient use of space and accommodate increased use of urban sports fields, providing benefits for any community.

CHAPTER 10

Chicago's Two Sports Stadiums Have Different Economic Impacts

Robert A. Baade, Mimi Nikolova, *and* Victor A. Matheson

The past 15 years have witnessed an unprecedented boom in stadium construction. By 2006, 89 of the 120 major league teams in the "Big Four" North American sports, football, baseball, basketball, and hockey, played in facilities built or significantly refurbished since 1990. These stadiums and arenas were constructed at a cost of more than $17 billion of which roughly $12 billion was provided by public sources (Matheson, 2006). The stadium building boom is not a uniquely American phenomenon. Germany spent over 1.4 billion euros building or rehabilitating 12 stadiums for the 2006 FIFA World Cup. At least 35 percent of this sum was provided by local, state, and federal taxpayers (FIFA, 2006).

Most economists have been critical of public funding of sports facilities. Numerous academic studies of stadiums and arenas, professional franchises, and major sporting events such as the World Cup, Olympics, and championship or All-Star games have uniformly found little or no gains in income, employment, or tax revenues as a result of professional sports. (See Siegfried and Zimbalist (2000) for an overview of such research). These economists speculate that spending on sports merely substitutes for other expenditures that would have occurred in the economy in the absence of sports. It is asserted, furthermore, that the crowds and congestion that accompany big games serves to displace non-sports activity. Finally, money spent at sporting events is less likely than other sorts of spending to remain and recirculate in the local economy (Matheson, 2006). Professional sports franchises, therefore, may enhance the quality of life in a host community without exerting a measurable impact on the economy. Teams may represent a nice cultural amenity for a city, but the direct economic benefits from professional teams do not seem to justify large taxpayer subsidies.

On the other hand, supporters of stadium construction suggest that professional sports franchises promote economic development even if the teams themselves do not directly provide many jobs or increased tax revenues to host communities. It has become increasingly common for sports boosters to defend taxpayer subsidies for stadiums by stating that sports infrastructure can play an im-

Originally published as "A Tale of Two Stadiums: Comparing the Economic Impact of Chicago's Wrigley Field and U.S. Cellular Field," *Working Paper Series*, Paper No. 06-14, August 2006, by the International Association of Sports Economists, Limoges, France. Reprinted with permission of the publisher.

portant role in the recovery of blighted areas by serving as an anchor for local economic redevelopment. Stadiums, it is said, promote the establishment of ancillary business such as bars, restaurants, and retail shops that capitalize on the crowds that arrive on game days. The economic studies apparently overlook these important neighborhood effects. The purpose of this report is to assess how and to what economic effect the location of a modern sports stadium in a neighborhood has had on host cities in the United States. The spatial implications are not trivial and have served in many instances to impede neighborhood development rather than promote it.

A Brief History of Integrating Stadiums into Cities in the United States

Earlier in the twentieth century, stadiums were woven into dense urban fabrics. Rather than the stadium defining and shaping an area, the stadium was viewed as subordinate to a larger urban design and function. The existing urban grid established the shape and location of many urban ballparks. The Baker Bowl, for example, home to Major League Baseball's (MLB) Philadelphia Phillies until 1938, was also known as the "Hump" because it was built on an elevated piece of ground to accommodate a railroad tunnel running under center field.

Professional sports in the United States have been undergoing an economic revolution inspired by a confluence of circumstances both inside and outside the industry. These changes have affected both the supply and demand for professional sports, which, in turn, have had implications for where and how professional sporting events are packaged and presented. Nowhere are these changes more apparent than in the design and location of stadiums

and arenas, and two developments in that regard should be noted. First, financial imperatives have worked to all but eliminate the multipurpose, circular stadiums built several decades ago in cities such as Cincinnati, Pittsburgh, and Philadelphia to host both football and baseball. More stadiums and arenas now exist in cities in the United States as a consequence.

Second, the pursuit of greater profit by individual teams has reversed the trend toward locating sports facilities in suburban areas where relatively cheap real estate made large tracts of land for parking for automobiles economically feasible. Stadiums and arenas have been migrating back to the cities with promises of fan spending spilling over into the commercial corridors of the neighborhoods through which fans flow to reach transportation centers or remote parking. Cities have used this promise of increased commercial activity to persuade fans to lend financial support to an aggressive city strategy to remake their centers into cultural and entertainment destinations. Cleveland, for example, has developed the Gateway complex, which includes both Jacobs Field for MLB and the Gund Arena for the National Basketball Association, to lure people back to its downtown. Atlanta, Baltimore, Denver, Indianapolis, Minneapolis, and Nashville, to name a few other cities, have opted for placing stadiums in or near the central business district in an effort to revitalize their cores.

Have the city promises of economic rejuvenation been realized? While some cities have realized a benefit, in other cases economic development has been retarded by the new playing facility. The City of Chicago provides an interesting case study on how a new stadium, U.S. Cellular Field (the new home of the MLB Chicago White Sox), has been integrated into its southside neighborhood in a way that may well have limited economic activity within that neighborhood. This economic outcome stands in stark contrast to Wrigley Field on the north side of Chicago which continues to experience a synergistic commercial relationship with its neighborhood.

Chicago: A Tale of Two Stadiums

Chicago is the home to two MLB teams, the White Sox and the Cubs. Both teams have been in existence for over 100 years, and each has strong ties to the Chicago community along with legions of die-hard fans. Until the White Sox won MLB's championship in 2005, the White Sox and Cubs had also shared a common bond of futility in the post-season with neither team having won the World Series since the 1910s.

The similarities end when one arrives at each team's respective stadium, however. Wrigley Field is a shining example of how a sports facility can integrate itself within a local neighborhood and provide positive economic spillovers to the nearby community. U.S. Cellular Field, on the other hand, provides the classic case of the sports stadium as a "walled fortress" that internalizes all economic activity in order to maximize revenues for the franchise at the expense of local economic development. Unfortunately for the proponents of sports-based development, the White Sox model is the path that is most often followed by team owners desiring new stadiums to replace aging or economically obsolete facilities, and the features that make Wrigley Field such a good fit for the local community are unlikely to be replicated at other stadiums.

Wrigley Field was built in 1914 on Chicago's north side, and is, along with Fenway Park in Boston, one of the two oldest remaining stadiums in MLB. The stadium is nestled into a neighborhood that is densely populated with restaurants and bars, retail shops, and residential housing. Wrigley is famous for the apartments bordering the stadium from which the occupants can look down into the stadium and watch games as they are played. Many of these buildings, in fact, actually sell tickets to non-resident customers for rooftop viewing.

Wrigley predated the automotive culture and the exercise of monopoly muscle by professional sports leagues in the United States, and almost no large parking lots are within easy walking distance of the stadium as a consequence. Fans either arrive by mass transportation or park on neighborhood streets. Local residents also do a brisk business selling spots in garages down back alleys.

The footprint of the stadium itself is also rather small. While Wrigley Field seats nearly as many fans as U.S. Cellular, its concourses and walkways (as well as its restroom facilities) are much smaller than those at the newly constructed U.S. Cellular Field. The smaller concourses significantly limit the variety and the number of vendors selling merchandise and food at Wrigley Field, translating into lower revenues for the Cubs' owners. The White Sox generate approximately 35 percent more in non-ticket revenue per fan in attendance than the Cubs.

U.S. Cellular presents a completely different picture. Built in 1991, the stadium itself is much larger than Wrigley Field. Modern sports teams rely much more on the sale of concessions and other paraphernalia for revenue than teams back in the day when Wrigley Field was constructed. Therefore, most modern stadiums like U.S. Cellular are designed to bring as much fan spending inside the stadium walls as possible. Of course, with expansive shopping, eating, and drinking options available within the stadium, fewer entrepreneurs have an incentive to locate businesses outside the stadium in order to cater to White Sox fans.

The other striking difference between Wrigley and U.S. Cellular is, of course, the availability of onsite parking around the White Sox' stadium. Massive parking lots surround U.S. Cellular Field on the south, west, and north while the stadium is bounded on the east by a major interstate highway. Like supplying expansive concessions services, supplying adequate parking also serves to increase the revenues of the team at the expense of local businesses. Because of the size of the parking lots, fans are dissuaded from walking to local bars and restaurants either before or after the game simply due to the physical distances involved.

One final unique quality differentiates Wrigley Field and the Cubs from the White Sox and, indeed, the rest of Major League Baseball. Most MLB teams play 5 to 6 games per week during the season including 3 or 4 weekday games. In order to accommodate the schedules of their fans, the vast majority of these weekday games are played at night. For example, in 2006 the White Sox, a typical team in MLB, play 81 home games of which only 26 are day games that start before 3:30 in the afternoon. On the other hand, the Cubs were the last team in the Major Leagues to add lights to their stadium, and they still continue to minimize the number of night games they host, playing 52 of their 81 games during the day in 2006.

Playing day games encourages the creation of local establishments in the neighborhood of Wrigley Field for several reasons. First, since baseball games usually last around 3 hours, during night games fans leave stadiums late at night limiting their interest in visiting local eating and drinking establishments (or at least limiting the amount of time they can patronize a bar). On the other hand, afternoon games discharge fans in the late afternoon or early evening leading to a huge flow of patrons towards neighborhood bars and restaurants.

Second, afternoon games allow the team to share the area with neighboring business without crowding out other activity. The congestion associated with 40,000 baseball fans will tend to crowd out other economic activity around a baseball stadium during home games. It is therefore difficult for restaurants or theaters in the neighborhood of a stadium to attract non-sports fans during games. Since these types of businesses tend to attract customers at night, sharing a neighborhood with a sports team that plays 50 or 60 night games per year, like the White Sox, frequently makes attracting patrons very difficult. The Cubs crowd out local business through night games only half as often as a typical MLB team.

Finally, playing games during the day allows fans to park on local streets and in personal garages while local residents are at work rather than necessitating the creation of large parking lots that detract from the creation of local businesses.

The neighborhood contrast between Wrigley and U.S. Cellular Field as it relates to economic development has broader application, and points, once again, to the influence of the automobile and the growing appetite for revenue made possible, at least in part, by the exercise of monopoly power by sports leagues in the United States. The contrast between Fenway Park's neighborhood and that of stadium neighborhoods in Cleveland and Seattle provides additional evidence of these realities.

Fenway Park and Stadium Neighborhoods in Cleveland and Seattle

Yawkey Way in Boston, the "street" that borders Fenway Park on the west, teems with pedestrian traffic on game day. Yawkey Way exemplifies the synergistic relationship between stadium and neighborhood in the same way that Waveland Avenue and Wrigley Field do in Chicago. Fenway Park, like Wrigley, was fit into the existing urban grid rather than redefining it. The neighborhood surrounding Fenway Park has been a participant rather than spectator to commercial activity induced by the MLB Red Sox. This commercial tradition has undergone modifications along with the stadium, but the essential commercial relationships have remained intact.

Newly constructed stadiums in the United States in recent times often have redefined the neighborhood in ways that would promote team commercial interests at the expense of the neighborhood. U.S. Cellular Field provides one example but is hardly unique. New stadiums have been constructed with the team's bottom line in mind, and the neighborhood's participation in economics, it is fair to say, are subservient to that aim. The parking-lot borders for U.S. Cellular Field represent not only an additional source of revenue for the White Sox, but they also provide a defense against what many perceive as a lack of safety in the area. Fans have been provided safe, convenient parking but an asphalt moat now exists that effectively separates the neighborhood and the ballpark.

New stadiums either through accident or design have appropriated revenues that in older stadiums were claimed by the neighborhood. The expanded food and drink options within the new stadium walls serve to diminish the importance of neighborhood restaurants and bars. The same can be said of the impact of "stadium stores" that sell team paraphernalia. There is no need to shop for a cap or pennant in the neighborhood when those items more conveniently can be purchased within the stadium's walls. While it may not be the intention of the team to take business away from

the community, the functioning of the new generation of stadiums does exactly that.

There are examples of how the team's commercial intent toward the neighborhood is not so benign. There are laws, for example, that prohibit the sale of souvenirs by vendors not associated with the team within a certain number of feet of stadiums in Cleveland, Ohio. Similarly the sale of "official" team paraphernalia without the explicit consent of the team is not allowed in many, if not all cities, in the United States. Explicit consent, of course, can be purchased, and the vendors then become partners in the team's commercial enterprise.

It should also be noted that sports does not enjoy a synergistic relationship with many other industries, and one key identified by many economists to urban growth, industry clustering, is impaired by the presence of sports. This outcome occurs in part due to the temporal-intensive nature of the sports industry. Sports events are occasional and seasonal, and stadium dead time is the standard. Game day, however, involves intensive use of public infrastructure by throngs of fans, which serves to crowd out other commercial activity during that time. The commercial interests that remain in the stadium neighborhood are those that are most compatible with sports, but parking and drinking establishments hardly constitute the backbone of a vibrant, growing urban economy. The economy of the neighborhood may actually be diminished to the extent that economic activity most compatible with the stadium replaces higher-growth, non-seasonal activity.

A survey of the commercial activity in Pioneer Square in Seattle as a consequence of the Kingdome (now replaced by two newer stadiums) being located there provides several important lessons with regard to the economic impact of stadiums on host neighborhoods. First, bars that had a sports theme and a location adjacent to the stadium derived substantial benefits. Sports bars/restaurants adjacent to the stadium reported as much as 1,700 percent in revenues on game days (Baade, 2000).

Second, the increase in the bar/restaurant business generally was inversely related to the establishment's distance from the stadiums. Unless the bar had a particularly compelling sports identity, three or four blocks walking distance from a stadium was sufficient to eliminate most of the positive economic impact. Proximity, however, is no guarantee of success. If the bar/restaurant was not on a main pedestrian thoroughfare, the impact was muted. For example, one restaurant less than two blocks away from the stadium, but removed from the constellation of bars frequented by fans after a game, attempted to build a clientele through sports promotions with no success and changed ownership four times in a couple of years due to a lack of business.

Third, the success of the sports bars/restaurants is highly sensitive to the success of the teams. Not only does a winning team attract more fans to the stadium, but apparently fans supporting mediocre or losing teams are in no mood to celebrate. Several sports bars that gushed about the positive impact of the Mariners and Seahawks sounded a much more sober note in describing the impact of the teams in years in which they did not compete for a championship.

Other businesses did not share the enthusiasm or the success of the sports bar entrepreneurs for the stadiums and its teams. Ethnic restaurants, art galleries, professional services, legal services, and most retail outlets reported a decline in their business. Some professional service establishments, including law offices, have considered changing their location because of the difficulties they encounter meeting clients on game days. The culprit cited by all firms adversely affected by the Kingdome was inadequate parking (Baade, 2000).

Conclusions and Policy Implications

Public subsidies for new sports stadiums in the United States have been justified on the grounds that they induce economic activity in their host neighborhoods. This article questions that proposition.

The type of economic development induced by stadiums may not be in the best economic interests of the neighborhood. Stadiums both old and new enhance to some degree bar/restaurant commercial activity. Modern stadiums, furthermore, are dependent on vehicular traffic, and the parking lots necessary to accommodate the heavy traffic flows on the occasional game day may diminish the prospects for neighborhood economic development through crowding out commercial activities that compete for scarce public space in the form of sidewalks, streets, and parking lots.

Finally, while teams ballyhoo the potential that a new sports facility for raising the economic profile of neighborhoods, the new generation of stadiums either through accident or design may actually diminish neighborhood economic activity through offering within their walls goods and services that compete with those offered by businesses in the stadium's environs.

Chicago's two professional baseball teams provide a compelling example of how new stadiums in serving the financial interests of their teams potentially dim the economic prospects for host communities.

References

Baade, R.A. (2000): The Impact of Sports Teams and Facilities on Neighborhood Economies: What Is the Score? In: W.S. Kern (ed): The Economics of Sports. Kalamazoo, Michigan: W.E. Upjohn Institute for Employment Research.

FIFA: Destination Germany: Venues (http://fifaworldcup.yahoo.com/06/en/d/) Accessed 1 August 2006.

Matheson, V.A. (2007): Economic Impact Analysis. In: W. Andreff and S. Szymanski (eds.): *The Elgar Companion to the Economics of Sports*. London: Edward Elgar Publishing.

Siegfried, J. and A. Zimbalist (2000): The Economics of Sports Facilities and Their Communities. *Journal of Economic Perspectives* 14(3), pp. 95–114.

CHAPTER 11

Corpus Christi Builds New Stadium for Minor League Team

Steve Bergsman

Minor league baseball has seen nothing but blue skies for the past decade, with unparalleled development of new stadiums.

Judged according to the size of the surrounding population, which baseball team does the best job of attracting fans to its home stadium — the New York Yankees, the Boston Red Sox, or a minor baseball team like the Round Rock Express?

Minor league baseball teams should not be dismissed just because their hometown might be a second- or third-tier city in terms of population. While major league baseball struggles with salary caps, television contracts, and team relocation, minor league baseball has seen nothing but blue skies for the past decade. Last year, minor league baseball experienced record attendance of about 40 million.

Part of the reason for this surge in popularity is the unparalleled development of new stadiums. Since 1990, about 100 new minor league ballparks have been built, reports Jim Ferguson, director of media relations for Minor League Baseball, the St. Petersburg, Florida–based association representing the

minor leagues, and one-third of those have opened since 2000. Four stadiums opened last year alone. These are significant numbers when one considers that there are only 176 official minor league baseball teams.

The impetus for the stadium building spree came first from the player development contracts negotiated in 1989–1990 by both the major and minor leagues, which established minimum standards for minor league ballparks. "At that time, there were few new ballparks built," explains Ferguson. "Most cities had old ballparks, and as a result of the new standards, the owners, whether it was a city, county, or sports authority, realized they were either going to have to put a lot of money into fixing up an old stadium or build a new stadium. The great majority elected to go into a new stadium."

A second driver of minor league stadium development soon arose — economic development. As the first new stadiums were constructed, attracting thousands of fans, other cities and team owners soon realized that these stadiums could be a boon for older downtown areas.

Originally published as "The Minor Leagues," *Urban Land*, Vol. 64, No. 7, July 2005, by the Urban Land Institute, Washington, D.C. Reprinted with permission of the publisher.

This past April, Corpus Christi, Texas, celebrated the opening of Whataburger Field, the new stadium home of the Hooks, a Class Double-A affiliate of the Houston Astros that moved to the city from Round Rock, outside of Austin.

"The stadium is located in the downtown area where there used to be some old port facilities and cotton warehouses that were torn down," says Corpus Christi city manager Skip Noe. "This will help us revitalize the area. We are a major tourist destination for the state due to our beaches, and we hope visitors might stay one more night to participate in minor league baseball."

The city bought the land on which the stadium was constructed from the Port of Corpus Christi, then built the structure. Capital for the development was obtained through a 15-year, one-eighth-cent sales tax hike that was approved overwhelmingly by voters, Noe says.

Whataburger Field has 5,050 fixed seats, 19 luxury suites, and two outfield berm areas that accommodate 2,000 more fans. While the stadium was designed to provide the atmosphere of an old ballpark, harkening back to the sport's golden age, it also pays tribute to the cotton industry and the warehouses that occupied the site in the 1920s. The look of the new facility is reminiscent of an old cotton warehouse, with an exterior consisting of brick and corrugated steel. The main entry features two large columns designed in the style of the structures that supported the warehouse roofs.

Corpus Christi was able to get a new minor league team because the team's owner, a group led by Reid Ryan, son of baseball legend Nolan Ryan, had so much success with its team in Round Rock. Before bringing the Express franchise to Corpus Christi, the team owners bought the Edmonton Trappers of the Triple-A Pacific Coast League and relocated the team to Round Rock.

"After six years, our average attendance was between 9,500 and 9,800 people a game," notes Jay Miller, president of the Round Rock Express. "The actual seating is 9,000, but we have an outfield berm — basically a grassy knoll — where we can sit as many as 4,000 people. The biggest crowd we ever had was 13,500."

Before the advent of minor league baseball in Round Rock, the city was best known as the home of computer company Dell Inc. Indeed, the stadium, which was built by the city, is called the Dell Diamond. The $25 million cost was mostly paid for by the team, but the city contributed $7.5 million from a hotel/motel tax for a broader project. "We built a convention center along with it," explains Round Rock city manager James Nuse. "We piggybacked with them." The 5,400-square-foot United Heritage Center, which has floor-to-ceiling windows overlooking the baseball field, became part of the project at the request of the city.

Because minor league baseball is family oriented, a number of the new ballfields offer other activities. For instance, the Dell Diamond includes a swimming pool, a basketball court, and a climbing wall. "You don't have to be a baseball fan to come to the game, there is so much else to do," says Miller. The stadium has also been an economic driver, helping to boost the number of hotel rooms in Round Rock to 2,200 rooms from 400, adds Nuse. With 10,000 people coming to the area to watch baseball, says Miller, "we are the biggest attraction. We get a lot of people from Houston and Arlington who rent motel rooms, as we also host the high school state playoffs."

All that means income for the town. "We have a terrific return on investment. It is through the roof for what we had to put into the deal," says Nuse. "Our $7.5 million is paid for out of the hotel occupancy, so it doesn't come out of the taxpayer's pocket. It comes from people coming in from out of town."

The Round Rock Express plays about 70 home games, with an average attendance of 9,300 fans per game paying $10 for box seats and slightly less for other seating. According to Nuse, the vast majority of these people come from outside the area. Even if they do not stay the night, they might eat at a local restaurant or fill up their gas tanks at a local station. In response, ancillary development continues, with restaurants and bars opening near the field. "The team has really been a boon for the area," asserts Miller. "We put Round Rock on the map."

Also expecting a financial home run are the New Hampshire Fisher Cats in Manchester, the Double-A affiliate of the Toronto Blue Jays. Manchester ended up with a minor league team because an aggressive ownership group bought a team — the New Haven, Connecticut, Ravens — and moved it to town. The team's first year as the Fisher Cats was 2004, when it played in the city's renovated 91-year old ballpark, Gill Stadium — a stopgap measure as Manchester prepared the new stadium it promised to lure the team to town.

The new stadium opened this year on the banks of the Merrimac River in downtown Manchester with 6,500 seats, 32 luxury suites, and a deck that looks over the river. The project was part of a $100 million downtown development effort that includes a new hotel. According to the local newspaper, the city borrowed $27.5 million, which will be repaid from rent the team pays and new property taxes generated elsewhere on the riverfront. The $27.5 million also covered renovations to Gill Stadium.

"This is a city-owned ballpark; the city donated the land," says Shawn Smith, president and general manager of the Fisher Cats. "It is bonded money and we have to pay it back over a 25-year lease." The same ownership group also owns the Single-A Lowell, Massachusetts, Spinners, an affiliate of the Boston Red Sox.

In one regard, construction of the new stadium was a true redevelopment project: the land on which the stadium was built had been vacant for more than 40 years, notes Smith. "It was actually a contaminated site. It took a lot of money and time to bring this vacant spot back to life."

In its first year at the old stadium, the Fisher Cats drew about 3,200 fans per game, which Smith considered a strong turnout. For its first year at the new stadium, Smith expects to attract an average of 4,100 fans per game. "We're looking to bring 300,000 people through the gates this year."

Stadium deals do not always go smoothly, even in cities that have a history of minor league baseball. In Nashville, owners of the Sounds, a Triple-A affiliate of the Milwaukee Brewers, were hoping to get the city to issue bonds for construction of a new stadium. Although the residents of Nashville "were fairly supportive" of the funding mechanism, according to Sounds general manager Glenn Yaeger, the city ultimately decided against taking on any risk.

That forced the team to be more creative. It brought in an equity partner to create a wider development with the stadium as the focus. "We had to go out and find financing on the project," says Yaeger. "We really wanted to create a neighborhood community around the ballpark. It was a way to position the project and meet some of the financing requirements that were restricting our ability to move the project forward. In other words, we needed to try and create some value from the ballpark development to help us pay for it. There was no public assistance."

The project is to be built near downtown on a 16-acre site that was once home to a trash-burning power plant. The development will cost about $100 million —$43 million for the stadium and $57 million for private development of residential and retail space.

"We are hoping to expand the property to 35 acres," says Phil Struever, chief executive of Baltimore-based Struever Bros. Eccles & Rouse, the Sounds' development partner. "On the first 16 acres, we will do 700 units of housing, 220,000 square feet of office, and 50,000 square feet of retail. With the larger plan, we are hoping for 1,500 to 2,000 housing units, 500,000 square feet of office, and 250,000 square feet of retail." In terms of density, diversity of use, and activity, "ballparks can be a wonderful contributor and component of a neighborhood," he adds.

Yaeger expects the new stadium to attract more fans. "Right now, we draw 400,000 fans in a substandard facility in a less-than-ideal location," he says. "Based on the data of teams that have built ballparks downtown, we expect our attendance to go to 700,000 to 800,000 with the new ballpark."

Although some recent studies, in particular one by a group from Western Michigan University, show that attendance at new minor league stadiums has a classic life-cycle curve of initial growth, stability, and then decline, that fact has not stopped many developments. The same study, Build It and They Will Come. But Will They Come Back Again? Lessons from Minor League Baseball, also notes that annual attendance, which hit about 40 million in 1949, dropped to 10 million by 1964 only to climb back to about 40 million this decade. In addition, the study reported, more than half the teams are competing in stadiums less than 12 years old.

"Most cities feel that having a minor league baseball team is a quality-of-life issue, and for some, it's about economic development," says Ferguson. "But baseball is still the reason why people come. The main thrust is, come out to the ballpark and we will entertain you."

CHAPTER 12

Denver and Other Cities Should Use Social Benefits to Justify Financing of Sports Facilities

Gerald A. Carlino *and* N. Edward Coulson

Are the large public expenditures on new stadiums a good investment for cities? Does hosting a major sports team have benefits? Although public subsidies for professional sports teams are controversial, the answer to these questions may well be yes. In this article, Jerry Carlino and Ed Coulson report the results of their 2003 study: When quality-of-life benefits are included in the calculation, building new stadiums and hosting an NFL franchise may indeed be a good deal for cities and their residents.

Rapid population growth in many metropolitan areas in the United States has made them economically viable locations for professional sports franchises such as those of Major League Baseball (MLB) or the National Football League (NFL). But since all four of the major sports leagues tightly control both the creation of new franchises and the relocation of teams, cities' demand for teams far exceeds the supply.[1]

As a result, the price cities have to pay to get teams has gone up. Cities have offered favorable stadium deals in their efforts to retain or attract teams. Partly as a result of this fierce competition for teams, "America is in the midst of a sports stadium construction boom," as noted by Roger Noll and Andrew Zimbalist. Professional sports teams are demanding — and receiving — subsidies from local governments for the construction or restoration of sports stadiums. According to Raymond Keating, the total cost of 29 sports facilities that opened between 1999 and 2003 is expected to be around $9 billion. Keating found that taxpayers' money financed around $5.7 billion, or 64 percent, of this $9 billion.

The boom in stadium construction coupled with the increased public support for these facilities raises the question: "Are subsidies to sports teams a good investment for cities?" The answer has been controversial.

Often, subsidies are justified by claims that attracting or retaining sports teams more than pays for itself in increased local tax revenue by creating new jobs and more spending. More recently, local officials have come to

---

Originally published as "Should Cities Be Ready for Some Football? Assessing the Social Benefits of Hosting an NFL Team," *Business Review*, Second Quarter 2004, by The Federal Reserve Bank, Philadelphia, PA.

view a downtown stadium project as an important part of the revitalization of the central city's urban core. Advocates of this approach point to Jacobs Field in Cleveland, Coors Field in Denver, and Camden Yards in Baltimore as models of how stadium-based development can work. However, independent studies by economists often indicate that taxpayers may not be getting such a good deal. Most studies that have attempted to quantify the creation of jobs, income, and tax revenue have found that the direct monetary impact felt by a city hosting a sports team is less than the sizable outlay of public funds. Yet civic leaders continue to make the case for professional sports and the beneficial role they play in the community.

Recently, economists have pointed out that previous studies missed a basic point: Professional sports teams add to residents' quality of life in cities that host teams. It's possible that people obtain benefits from having a local sports team even if they never go to a game. They root for the local athletes, look forward to reading about their success or failure in the newspaper, and share in the citywide joy when the home team wins a championship.

Economists have long studied the effects of an area's quality of life on wages and the cost of housing. Past studies have found that people are willing to pay indirectly for local amenities, such as good weather, scenic views, and nearness to the ocean, in the form of higher rents and lower wages. Similarly, if people benefit from having a professional sports franchise in their community, they are presumably willing to pay for it — if not directly through the purchase of tickets, then indirectly through an increased willingness both to pay more for housing in the area and to accept lower wages.

We did a study in 2003 in which we looked at the quality-of-life benefits residents receive in cities that host an NFL team. We found that once quality-of-life benefits are included in the calculus, the seemingly large public expenditure on new stadiums appears to be a good investment for cities and their residents.

The Political Economy of Sports Franchises

Professional sports teams play in facilities heavily subsidized by local governments. Typically, cities use general revenue bonds to finance their share of the cost of a stadium. These bonds are paid off through a variety of sources, for example, ticket surcharges, taxes on hotel rooms and car rentals, and state lottery proceeds. These stadiums are usually publicly owned and leased to teams. A city derives revenue from publicly built stadiums in a number of ways. Chief among them are rental payments made by teams; the local government's share of parking, concessions, and luxury boxes; property taxes on the stadium paid by the team; and rent received for non-sports activities, such as concerts.

On the cost side, the city must account for depreciation and maintenance of the stadium, and the city's share of the cost of providing utilities, refuse collection, and police, fire, and rescue services. In addition, municipalities must account for what economists call opportunity costs: local governments' spending on stadiums lowers spending for other worthy projects or programs. For example, suppose the annual cost of a stadium in City A is $20 million a year for the next 30 years. If an entry-level teacher's salary (including benefits) runs about $60,000 annually, one measure of the opportunity cost of the stadium is the 333 teachers that could have been added to the city's school system. Indeed, to keep the Cincinnati Bengals from making good on a threat to move to Baltimore in 1995, local officials agreed to a $540 million deal for two new stadiums (one for the Reds, too). Although the action might not have been linked to the stadium-funding bill, *The Economist* noted that shortly before the vote on the stadium-funding bill, Cincinnati laid off 400 staff members from its school district, including 200 teachers.[2]

In principle, cities could set rental payments to cover all the costs associated with constructing and operating municipal stadiums. In practice, since all four major sports leagues exercise considerable control over the geographic mobility of established teams as well as over the creation of new franchises, cities do not set rental payments in this way. In the intense competition for teams, cities have offered favorable stadium deals in their efforts to retain or attract sports franchises.

Numerous independent studies by economists have shown that any revenue cities receive typically fails to cover costs because of favorable clauses in the lease regarding rent; the teams' share of parking, concessions, and luxury boxes; and partial or full forgiveness of property taxes. For example, according to Michael Leeds and Peter von Allmen, the NFL's Baltimore Ravens pay no rent, while MLB's Chicago White Sox pay $1 a year for the use of New Comiskey Park. In examining 25 sports facilities built between 1978 and 1992, James Quirk and Rodney Fort calculated that the annual subsidy to professional sports teams averaged $9.2 million (or $12.3 million in 2002 dollars). Even then, the annual subsidy is underestimated because data were not available for investments made to facilities subsequent to original construction. Quirk and Fort also estimated that the annual subsidy jumps to $20 million ($29 million in 2002 dollars) for the average stadium when investments subsequent to original construction are included in the calculus.[3]

The Economic Development Rationale and Evidence

The question becomes: Why do local governments provide such large subsidies to professional sports teams? One justification for the subsidy has been that sports teams increase employment and income and promote growth of the local economy. Obviously, public investment in stadiums can be beneficial, but how do we evaluate a new sports facility's contribution to local economic growth?

To address this question, most proposals to use public funds for building stadiums are accompanied by an economic impact analysis. These studies attempt to evaluate the costs and benefits of a new stadium.

The costs and benefits fall into four broad categories: direct benefits, indirect benefits, construction costs, and operating expenses. Direct benefits stem from new spending that a team generates for the city. This includes spending by fans in local restaurants and hotels and for souvenirs and spending by players and other team employees and the team's spending for local goods and services.

These direct expenditures by teams, their employees, and their fans become income for other city residents, who then re-spend part of this income when purchasing other local goods and services. This re-spending process, which continues through second, third, and subsequent rounds, is the indirect benefit. Since direct expenditures lead to indirect expenditures, the direct expenditures are said to have a "multiplier" effect on the local economy. Thus, for example, if a dollar of direct spending resulted in an additional dollar of indirect spending in the local economy, total spending in the local area would be $2 and the multiplier's value is 2.[4] According to Joseph Bast, impact studies have used multipliers with values as high as 3.

One potential shortcoming of impact

studies is that they are often commissioned by proponents of the stadium projects, such as teams themselves, and conducted by accounting firms or local chambers of commerce. According to Noll and Zimbalist, the authors of impact studies tend to make very favorable assumptions about the income and number of jobs generated and how much of this income stays in the local economy. In addition, they may make unrealistic assumptions regarding construction and operating costs and fail to account for the opportunity cost of the funds tied up in these projects; therefore, the net benefits of stadium projects can be vastly overstated depending on the assumptions made.

For example, in its analysis of the new stadium being built for the NFL's Baltimore Ravens, the Maryland Department of Business and Economic Development estimated an annual economic benefit to the Baltimore metropolitan area of $111 million and the creation of almost 1400 new jobs. According to Leeds and von Allmen, independent analysis found a much smaller impact on annual income ($33 million) and jobs (534). In general, independent studies by economists suggest that the value of local multipliers is at most 1.25, less than one-half of the value suggested in some impact studies.

Because of the difficulties in using "multiplier analysis" to assess the economic impact of professional sports teams, economists have used other sorts of calculations to study this impact. These studies have attempted to measure the local impact of hosting a team using three different methods. First, some studies have compared the growth rates of income or employment in cities and metropolitan areas that have teams with growth rates of these variables in cities that do not have teams. For example, in a 1994 study, Robert Baade found no significant difference in per capita personal income growth during the period 1958 to 1987

between metropolitan areas with major league sports teams and those without.

Another way to measure teams' impact on the local economy is to compare growth before and after the acquisition of a new major league team. In a 1997 study, Baade and Sanderson looked at the impact on employment and output in 10 metropolitan statistical areas (MSAs) that had acquired new teams between 1958 and 1993. They found that while certain sectors closely related to professional sports do show some employment gain, aggregate employment shows little impact from the existence of sports teams.

A final way is to measure the impact of a specific team (such as the Baltimore Orioles) on economic development in a specific location (Maryland). For example, in a 1997 study Bruce Hamilton and Peter Kahn found that even at Camden Yards — widely believed to have been a good investment for Baltimore — public expenditure cannot be justified on grounds of local economic development. They estimate that Maryland and its municipalities lose about $9 million annually on Camden Yards.[5] They report that the stadium generates enough revenue to cover capital and maintenance costs, but under the conditions of the lease, the team's owners keep most of this revenue.

Regardless of the method used by independent researchers, the bottom line is that subsidies to sports teams appear to be much greater than the economic benefits they generate for cities. Findings such as these led Siegfried and Zimbalist to conclude that "few fields of empirical research offer virtual unanimity of findings. Yet, independent work on the economic impact of stadiums and arenas has uniformly found that there is no statistically significant positive correlation between sports facility construction and economic development."

Moreover, economists have pointed out

that local spending related to professional sporting events may result in less spending on other recreational activities. While the attraction of a new team to a city or the construction of a new stadium may lead to entirely new spending in the local economy, it's more likely that much of the local spending by fans is redirected from activities occurring elsewhere in the local economy. Since households have limited budgets for and time to spend on leisure activities, sporting events may merely shift the timing and location of spending within the metropolitan area but leave aggregate spending unchanged.[6]

One exception would be if sports events attracted a large number of "out-of-town" fans, thus bringing new spending into the region. According to Noll and Zimbalist, these types of fans account for only 5 percent to 20 percent of all fans attending major league sporting events. Siegfried and Zimbalist point out that there is considerable evidence that out-of-state fans do not come to town because of regular season sporting events. They are in town for other reasons, such as a business trip or a visit to family and friends. Thus, if they had not attended a regular season game, they would have spent money on other types of leisure activities the region has to offer.

These findings pose the question: Is there an economic justification for subsidizing professional sports teams in an era in which local governments' budgets are under intense pressure and given the sizable opportunity cost associated with these types of projects?

External Benefits to the Rescue

The subsidies granted to professional sports teams, in some sense, suggest that civic leaders and residents view professional sports teams as valued assets of a city. Frequently, civic leaders speak of the intangible benefits of hosting major league sports, such as civic pride. A typical statement expressing these sentiments comes from Philadelphia's mayor, John Street: "We are incredibly fortunate to be the home of great professional sports franchises. They enrich our community, fortify our tax base, and provide major support for the region's future economic growth. And then there are the intangible benefits: These Phillies [Philadelphia's major league baseball team], if we give them our full support, will bring us together [and] solidify a sense of community with civic pride as they drive toward the pennant."

Similarly, economists have noted that professional sports teams contribute to the *quality of life* in an area by increasing the satisfaction or happiness of residents in general, not just those who attend games. As we noted earlier, it's likely that many city residents get pleasure from the presence of local professional sports teams even when they neither attend games nor pay for sports programming on cable TV. Mayor Street's words speak to the "civic pride" that can result from a successful franchise. Therefore, perhaps residents should think of a professional sports team in the way they think of a new art museum or new symphony hall or, indeed, an environmental resource such as an old-growth forest: It's a commodity from which they receive enjoyment just by having it around.

The interest that professional sports franchises generate suggests they are far more important than these other public goods. In the controversial words of Art Modell, owner of the Cleveland Browns-Baltimore Ravens franchise[7]: "The pride and the presence of a professional football team is far more important than 30 libraries" [quoted in Leeds and von Allmen 2002].

So teams create value for local residents that owners of sports franchises cannot capture. That is, the team can't charge a fan for just being a fan. But that doesn't make this "external benefit" any less real. If the value of these external benefits is large enough, they alone might justify the subsidies that local taxpayers grant to teams. But because no one is excluded from enjoying the external benefit generated by local sports team, it becomes difficult to know how much this matters to people, precisely because you can't charge them for the privilege of being a fan. While these benefits are hard to measure in dollar terms, economists have made significant strides in quantifying the value residents place on similar types of quality-of-life benefits, such as clean air, scenic views, nearness to the ocean, or good weather.

Measuring the External Benefit

The value of a city's special traits, such as good weather or the existence of professional sports teams, is determined by what people are willing to pay in order to live there. This amounts to the sum of what people are willing to pay for each local characteristic that either adds to or reduces the quality of life in an area. The trick is to determine the prices of these local amenities, or traits, since they are not bought and sold in markets.

Even though there is no explicit price for local amenities such as the presence of an NFL team, there is an *implicit* price. Suppose you are considering moving to either City A, which has an NFL team, or City B, which does not. Other than their NFL status, these cities are alike in all other aspects. Because the presence of an NFL team is something you value, you are willing to pay some extra amount, say, $1000, for having a team in your city.

There are two ways in which you could pay your extra $1000. One is by bidding up land prices, and ultimately rents, in City A relative to City B. But it is not necessarily the case that you will ultimately pay $1000 more to rent a house in City A. Part of the cost of living in a city with an NFL team could be paid in the form of lower wages than you would have accepted in City B. What must be true is that rent and wage differentials sum to $1000. Thus, the extent to which land rent is higher and wages are lower is the extent to which the amenity value of an NFL team is capitalized into local land markets and local labor markets. Put differently, since NFL status is the only difference between the two cities, a household's willingness to pay the extra $1000 to live in City A must be due to the difference in NFL status.

Measuring the Amenity Value of the NFL

Economists have developed statistical techniques to measure the variation in rents and wages that are attributable to each of the local area's traits, and economists have used these estimated implicit prices of amenities to rank areas according to their attractiveness. In our 2003 study, we argued that if people like having professional sports teams in their community, they are presumably willing to pay for it — if not directly through the purchase of season tickets, then indirectly through an increased willingness to pay for housing in the area and an increased willingness to accept marginally lower wages.

Bruce Hamilton and Peter Kahn first broached the idea that differentials in local wages and rents may provide a basis for valuing the social benefit of sports teams. They argued that while such differentials may exist, correlations between the presence of sports teams and wages and rents will surely be confounded by the correlation between these variables and city size (and perhaps other city-specific characteristics).[8] For example, because rents tend to increase with city size and large cities tend to host NFL teams, isolating the effects of an NFL team's presence on rents may be difficult.

In our study we confronted this issue in a number of ways. We focused our attention on NFL football franchises in the 1990s, since there was movement and expansion of NFL teams in both moderate-size cities (Jacksonville, Nashville, and Charlotte) and exit of franchises in larger metropolitan areas such as Los Angeles and Houston, the nation's second and fifth largest metropolitan areas, respectively. We assume that the movement and expansions will weaken the correlation between city size and NFL teams sufficiently to facilitate estimation of an NFL effect. Still, only eight of the 32 cities had a change in their NFL status between 1993 and 1999, the period of our study, making it hard to identify an NFL effect in local wages and rents.

In addition to looking at the recent movement to moderate-size cities, we focused our attention on NFL football franchises, for two more obvious reasons. The first is the preeminent attention the NFL receives among all sports in the United States. If any professional sport generates a measurable differential in wages and rents across cities, football is likely to be the one. Moreover, the most serious rival for that attention, Major League Baseball, has had very little expansion in recent years and no franchise movements since the early 1970s. The NFL, on the other hand, has had a bit more expansion and substantially more franchise movement.

Perhaps more important, the location of NFL franchises probably has less to do with city-specific characteristics, such as population size and growth, than in any other major sports league. Most of an NFL franchise's revenue comes from an egalitarian split of the national TV contracts, and even locally generated stadium ticket revenue is split more equitably (60 percent to the home team, 40 percent to the visiting team) than in other sports leagues. In contrast, baseball team revenue is far more heavily weighted toward local sources, particularly local TV contracts.

In our study, we estimated the change in rents and wages resulting from a change in NFL status between 1993 and 1999. We estimated two equations: one for wages and another for rents. We found that the presence of an NFL team raises annual rents, on average, 8 percent. We also found that wages were about 2 percent lower in cities that host an NFL team, but the differential was not statistically significant. Perhaps the demand for labor adjusts more rapidly than the supply of housing, and this more rapid adjustment tends to ameliorate the effect on wages. In addition, if the NFL amenity makes workers more productive, the demand for labor could also increase, and the effect on wages would be ambiguous. In what follows, we will focus only on the rental premium.[9]

Cost-Benefit Analysis

Since the 53 cities in our sample had, in 1999, an average monthly rent of $500, the finding of an average rental premium of 8 percent implies an NFL amenity premium of about $40 a month per housing unit, or $480 annually, on average, in cities hosting NFL teams. In 1999, there were approximately 290,000 households in a typical central city, so $480 per household implies that the aggregate amenity value to a city that hosts an NFL team is, on average, about $139 million per year (or about $184 per person).[10]

How do the estimates of the amenity value of hosting an NFL team compare with the subsidies? Earlier we pointed out that James Quirk and Rodney Fort calculated that the annual subsidy to professional sports teams, including investment subsequent to the original cost, averaged $20 million in 1989 dollars (or $27 million in 1999 dollars).[11] The annual quality-of-life benefit of $139 million found in our study is substantially larger than the annual subsidy, suggesting that these subsidies were good investments for the typical city. Our study showed that the quality-of-life benefit to households easily exceeds the subsidies granted in all cities that hosted an NFL team during the 1990s.

Cost-Revenue Analysis

While the finding that the aggregate value of the quality-of-life benefit may justify the subsidies is good news for city residents, public officials may be more concerned with the impact these subsidies have on local budgets. Our results suggest that team subsidies can also potentially pass the cost-revenue test. This means that if cities could effectively appropriate through taxation the rise in property values that resulted from the local team's existence, any such subsidy has the potential to be self-financing. This is because higher rents imply higher housing prices for cities that host NFL franchises. The higher property values will lead to increased tax revenues for central cities when properties are reassessed.

Consider our representative city once again. In 1999, the median price of a house across the cities in our sample was $123,433. If 8 percent of this value reflects an NFL premium in these cities and if we use the average property tax rate of 1.75 percent, available for 50 of the 53 cities in our sample, that means the NFL premium yields property tax revenue of just under $173 per year per household.[12] This could potentially be worth about $50 million a year in tax revenue for our representative city with 290,000 households if it hosted an NFL team. The potential increase in property tax revenue of $50 million associated with hosting an NFL team is almost twice as large as the $27 million annual subsidy reported by Quirk and Fort, suggesting that, on average, these subsidies are good investments for cities. Those who benefit from the team in terms of higher property values would be pay-

ing for its subsidization. If the city could not effectively design a property tax in this way, the stadium subsidies would come out of general funds. In that case, subsidies may crowd out other expenditures that may have even greater benefits. Thus, our results do not constitute a blanket endorsement for stadium subsidies.[13] We found that the potential increase in property tax revenue exceeds the known subsidies granted to NFL teams in 22 of the 25 cities that provided stadium subsidies.[14]

Other Studies

While these estimates of the benefits may appear large, they are broadly consistent with estimates found in other studies that have quantified the benefits for various types of amenities. For example, Joseph Gyourko and Joseph Tracy found that the annual value for just *one* extra sunny day is $7 per year per household, and Glenn Blomquist, Mark Berger, and John Hoehn found an annual value of $12.[15] Based on these studies, Jordan Rappaport and Chad Wilkerson estimated that a metropolitan area with 2 million people should be willing to pay between $14 million and $24 million a year for just one additional sunny day. While direct comparisons are always difficult, Rappaport and Wilkerson's numbers, along with ours, suggest that the addition of an NFL franchise makes up for a week or so of cloudy days.

In their study, Rappaport and Wilkerson also noted that cities' aggressive bids to replace teams further supports the view that the external benefits associated with hosting an NFL team may exceed the cost of doing so. They point out that of the six cities that have lost NFL teams since 1980, "all but Los Angeles subsequently allocated considerably more public financing to attract a new NFL team than it would have cost to keep their old team." For example, voters in St. Louis approved $280 million in public funds to build a new football stadium after the Cardinals departed for Arizona in 1987. St. Louis voters declined to allocate $120 million toward a new stadium when the Cardinals were playing in St. Louis.

In February 2000, Bruce Johnson, Peter Groothuis, and John Whitehead conducted a survey of residents of the Pittsburgh metropolitan area, asking them how much they would be willing to pay in higher taxes to keep the NHL Pittsburgh Penguins from leaving the city.[16] The average response was $5.57 per household per year. Since there are almost 960,000 households in the Pittsburgh metro area, Johnson and his co-authors report that this gives an aggregate quality-of-life value of almost $5.2 million per year — a present value of $66 million if we use an 8 percent interest rate and assume a stadium life of 30 years.

According to Rappaport and Wilkerson, between 1994 and 2000, the average public contribution to NBA/NHL sports arenas was $84 million. The quality-of-life benefit of $66 million represents only about 80 percent of the average subsidy. While the $5.2 million annual quality-of-life benefit associated with hosting the Penguins seems small, the external benefit is likely to be much larger for other professional sports, such as football. In the United States, hockey continues to have the smallest fan base of the four major league sports. According to Rappaport and Wilkerson, in 2001, nine of the 24 NHL teams (38 percent) did not have local network television contracts. They also point out that ratings for televised NHL games are only half those of NBA games.

The evidence provided in our study combined with the high valuation placed on other quality-of-life characteristics found in other studies and the increased willingness to expand public funding for new NFL stadiums, even after a city has lost a team, substantially demonstrates that the quality-of-life benefits associated with hosting an NFL team may justify the seemingly large public expenditures.

Still, assessing the benefits and costs associated with sports teams is a complex problem. Despite our careful attempt to control for the many local factors that could affect rents, it's possible that our estimate of the implicit value of an NFL amenity is overstated because we failed to control for some factor that is positively correlated with both the presence of an NFL team and rents. If our estimate of the implicit price of an NFL amenity is overstated, our estimate of the benefits used in the cost-benefit analysis is overstated.[17] On the cost side, while the dollar amount to build a stadium is known, the opportunity cost of funds may be harder to estimate.

Conclusion

Public officials and civic boosters are often criticized for encouraging the provision of subsidies to sports franchises. But if the subsidization we discuss in this article is so politically unpopular, it is doubtful that officials would be so much in favor of it. But as we have argued, the debate over public subsidies to stadiums has focused on job and income creation in the cities in which the facilities are built. Although on that score stadium subsidies appear to be a bad idea, the range of potential effects goes beyond those involving income and job creation. While large public expenditures on the construction of new sports stadiums are, and will continue to be, controversial, our findings suggest that sports are popular, and once the quality-of-life benefits are included in the calculus, public spending on new stadiums may be a good investment for central cities and their residents. This, of course, is not the same thing as recommending that cities immediately decide to fund stadiums if only because the opportunity cost of appropriating such funds is the elimination of other, possibly more worthy programs, such as building new schools.

Notes

1. The other major sports leagues are the National Hockey League (NHL) and the National Basketball Association (NBA). Visiting Scholar Ed Coulson is a professor of economics at the Pennsylvania State University, University Park, Pennsylvania.

2. "Footloose Football," *The Economist*, September 9, 1995, p. 90. *Business Review* Q2 2004 9 www.phil.frb.org

3. John Siegfried and Andrew Zimbalist point out that the escalating costs of recent stadium construction suggest that the average subsidy has surely grown since 1992.

4. Jordan Rappaport and Chad Wilkerson provide summary details for a representative sample of recent stadium impact studies. 10 Q2 2004 *Business Review* www.phil.frb.org

5. According to Hamilton and Kahn, the cost to the Maryland Stadium Authority for operating the stadium is approximately $20 million annually ($14 million in real interest and depreciation and $6 million in maintenance). The Maryland Stadium Authority receives approximately $6 million in rent annually from the Orioles and another $5 million in admission tax revenue; therefore, it incurs a deficit of approximately $9 million per year.

6. The shift in spending may be meaningful to an area's central city if sports fans who spend money because they are attending games would have patronized suburban establishments in the absence of a game. *Business Review* Q2 2004 11 www.phil.frb.org

7. In validating the bonds to construct Raymond James Stadium in Tampa, home to the NFL Buccaneers, the Florida Supreme Court described the public benefits of stadium construction in *Poe v. Hillsborough County.* The court explained: "[T]he Court finds that the Buccaneers instill civic pride and camaraderie into the community and that the Buccaneer games and other stadium events also serve a commendable public purpose by enhancing the community image on a nationwide basis and providing recreation, entertainment and cultural activities to its citizens."

8. See also the article by Rappaport and Wilkerson. 12 Q2 2004 *Business Review* www.phil.frb.org

9. Our study uses regression analysis in which we relate the level of rents and the level of wages in a city in each of two years to whether the city had an NFL franchise in 1993 or 1999. We control for city-specific traits that did not change between 1993 and 1999, such as nearness to an ocean, and we controlled for a variety of city characteristics that did vary between the two years, such as city size, city population growth, the rate of crime, local fiscal variables, and so forth. In addition, we also controlled for a large number of individual housing characteristics, such as number of rooms and age of the unit, and a random effect that controls for individual characteristics that do not vary over time. The implicit price of a professional sports franchise is measured by the coefficient of a dummy variable indicating the presence of an NFL franchise in the particular city and year. Given the existence of city-specific traits, the identification of this NFL effect comes from league expansion and franchise movements into and out of cities over the years between the two panel observations. As indicated in this article, eight of these cities had a change in NFL team status between 1993 and 1999. Six cities (Baltimore, Charlotte, Jacksonville, Nashville, Oakland, and St. Louis) did not have an NFL franchise in 1993 but had gained one by 1999. Two cities (Houston and Los Angeles) hosted an NFL team in 1993, but not in 1999. Twenty-four cities hosted an NFL team in both 1993 and 1999.

10. The average central city in our sample had a population of 753,705 in 1999. According to the *Statistical Abstracts of the U.S.*, there were 2.6 people per household in 1999, suggesting there are almost 290,000 households in a typical central city.

11. Interestingly, in their 2000 study that examined the 1995 budgets for eight cities, Donald Alexander, William Kern, and Jon Neill found an annual stadium subsidy in the range of $22 million to $29 million, depending on the city under consideration. *Business Review* Q2 2004 13 www.phil.frb.org

12. We were limited to 50 of the 53 cities in calculating the potential increase in property tax revenue, since the property tax rate was not available for three cities. The median house price of $123,433 is based on the 50 cities for which property tax rates are available.

13. The cost-revenue analysis we have presented here is for an average, or representative, city. Of course, the costs and revenue associated with hosting an NFL team will differ widely across cities.

14. The 8 percent increase in rents is an average effect across the 53 cities comprising our study. In addition, we assume that the effect on rents is the same for cities that gain a team as for those that lose one. In the long run, the supply of housing may increase and rents and housing prices may go up by less than the initial increases. Still, the greater number of housing units will lead to increased property tax revenue without the need to reassess housing values for tax purposes.

15. The annual values are expressed in 1999 dollars.

16. At the time of the survey there was some concern that the Penguins could not survive in Pittsburgh. The Penguins declared bankruptcy in October 1998. In addition, they continue to play in the oldest

arena in professional hockey, and Pittsburgh is a relatively small market.

17. To see if our findings hold up under scrutiny, we performed a variety of tests. For example, we controlled for the presence or absence of museums, another recreational amenity, and found that this variable was not statistically significant, regardless of whether the NFL variable was included in or excluded from the regression. We also found an 8 percent rental premium associated with NFL status, regardless of whether city population size was included in or excluded from the regressions. In addition, baseball added two teams during our sample period (one in Phoenix and one in Tampa Bay) that started playing in 1998. After controlling for the addition of these new teams, we found the quality-of-life premium associated with hosting an NFL team fell slightly below the 8 percent effect on rents reported in this article. The decline, however, does not appreciably affect the findings and conclusions reported here. *Business Review* Q2 2004 17 www.phil.frb.org

References

Alexander, Donald, William Kern, and Jon Neill. "Valuing the Consumption Benefits from Professional Sports Franchises," *Journal of Urban Economics*, 48, 2000, pp. 321–37.

Baade, Robert A. ""Stadiums, Professional Sports, and Economic Development: Assessing the Reality," The Heartland Institute, Heartland Policy Studies 62, 1994.

Baade, Robert A., and Allen Sanderson. "The Employment Effect of Teams and Sports Facilities," in Roger Noll and Andrew Zimbalist, eds., *Sports, Jobs and Taxes*. Washington, DC: Brookings Institution Press, 1997, pp. 92–118.

Bast, Joseph L. "Sports Stadium Madness: Why It Started, How to Stop It," The Heartland Institute, Heartland Policy Studies No. 85, February 1998.

Blomquist, Glen, Mark Berger, and John Hoehn. "New Estimates of the Quality of Life in Urban Areas," *American Economic Review*, 78, 1988, pp. 89–107.

Campbell, Harrison S. "Professional Sports and Urban Development: A Brief Review of Issues and Studies," *Review of Regional Studies*, 29, 1999, pp. 272–92.

Carlino, Gerald A., and N. Edward Coulson. "Compensating Differentials and the Social Benefits of the NFL," Federal Reserve Bank of Philadelphia, Working Paper 02-12/R, June 2003 (forthcoming in *Journal of Urban Economics*).

Gyourko, Joseph, and Joseph Tracy. "The Structure of Local Public Finance and the Quality of Life," *Journal of Political Economy*, 99, 1991, pp. 774–806.

Hamilton, Bruce W., and Peter Kahn. "Baltimore's Camden Yards Ballpark," in Roger Noll and Andrew Zimbalist, eds., *Sports, Jobs and Taxes*. Washington, DC: Brookings Institution Press, 1997, pp. 245–81.

Johnson, Bruce, Peter Groothuis, and John Whitehead. "The Value of Public Goods Generated by a Major League Sports Team: The CVM Approach," *Journal of Sports Economics*, 2, 2001, pp. 6–21.

Keating, Raymond. "Sports Park: The Costly Relationship Between Major League Sports and Government," Policy Analysis No. 339, The Cato Institute, 1999.

Leeds, Michael, and Peter von Allmen. *The Economics of Sports*. Boston: Addison Wesley Publishers, 2002.

Noll, Roger, and Andrew Zimbalist. *Sports, Jobs and Taxes*. Washington, DC: Brookings Institution Press, 1997.

Quirk, James, and Rodney Fort. *Pay Dirt: The Business of Professional Team Sports*. Princeton: Princeton University Press, 1992.

Rappaport, Jordan, and Chad Wilkerson "What Are the Benefits of Hosting a Major League Sports Franchise?" Federal Reserve Bank of Kansas City *Economic Review*, First Quarter 2001, pp. 55–86.

Rosentraub, Mark S. *Major League Losers: The Real Cost of Sports and Who's Paying for It*. New York: Basic Books, 1997.

Siegfried, John, and Andrew Zimbalist. "The Economics of Sports Facilities and Their Communities," *Journal of Economic Perspectives*, 14, Summer 2000, pp. 95–114.

Street, John. "Go, Phillies," Weekly Radio Address, August 18, 2001.

CHAPTER 13

East Rutherford, Other Cities, Receive "Naming Rights" Revenues from New Sports Stadium

Howard Bloom

In a naming rights agreement that defies economic logic, Barclays Bank and the New Jersey (soon to be Brooklyn) Nets last week announced a $400 million, 20-year agreement for the Nets new arena. Scheduled to open in time for the 2009-10 NBA season, the $637 million arena is part of the $4 billion Atlantic Yards project. Even as the announcement was being made Thursday, protestors were seen demonstrating outside the Brooklyn Museum against the redevelopment real estate project.

The Atlantic Yards, planned for a 22-acre site near Downtown Brooklyn, includes 6,400 rental apartments and condominiums, office towers and a boutique hotel, in addition to the arena. The project was approved by the state last month. The arena serves as the centerpiece for the Atlantic Yards project. Bruce Ratner paid $300 million to buy the Nets in 2003; it's unimaginable to think that less than four years later the Nets (who have never been considered one of the NBA's marquee franchises) would secure a record arena naming rights sponsorship agreement.

According to a *New York Times* report: the protestors were accusing Barclays of participating in the state's attempt to use eminent domain to condemn property for the project. They also said Barclays profited from the slave trade yet is aligned with Bruce Ratner, who is marketing his team to African-American fans. A company spokesman said Barclays had not been involved in slavery.

This was the first and it won't be the last time the controversial real estate project, with the Nets arena seen as a key to the entire project, has drawn critical attention. Two weeks ago on January 10, a group of tenants currently residing on the land earmarked for the $4 billion project filed a lawsuit against the Empire State Development Corporation, the state agency that is prepared to seize properties on behalf of Forest City, Ratner's Company (the Nets are owned by Bruce Ratner) for the project. The Empire State Development Corporation is prepared to cite "eminent domain" (the power of the federal or state government to take private property for a public purpose,

Originally published as "Location, Location, Location: The Sports Naming Rights Bar Is Raised Again Thanks to the Big Apple," *Sports Business News*, January 27, 2007, by the Sports Business News, Ottawa, Ontario, Canada. Reprinted with permission of the publisher.

even if the property owner objects). Protestors, seizing land and upset populous — nothing was going to bother anyone associated with last week's momentous announcement.

"Barclays is thrilled to partner with the Nets in this exciting endeavor. We are delighted to put our name to a development that will be a visual and economic landmark in the renaissance of Brooklyn," said Robert E. Diamond, Jr., President, Barclays PLC. "This opportunity brings together economic prosperity for Brooklyn and the chance to participate, in a unique way, in the cultural and sporting life of New York."

In addition to the agreement, Barclays has also agreed to partner with the Nets in the Nets-Barclays Sports Alliance, a non-profit organization whose goal is to promote athletics, education and personal development among young people in Brooklyn. The alliance will, as its first objective, repair and renovate basketball courts and other sports facilities throughout the borough, as well as sponsor amateur athletic tournaments and clinics for Brooklyn's youth.

This initiative mirrors the Barclays Spaces for Sports program in the UK, which helps local communities transform neglected land into the sporting facilities they want — from skateboard parks to soccer fields or multi-use game areas. So far Barclays has opened more than 100 community sports sites across the UK.

"We are very proud to be a partner with Barclays, a prestigious company that exemplifies and shares our commitment to excellence, leadership and success," said Bruce Ratner, President and CEO of FCRC and Chairman of the Nets. "We believe this partnership marks an important moment in Brooklyn's history and its place on the international stage. With this essential investment in Atlantic Yards and the borough, we are now one step closer to our goal of bringing thousands of

jobs, mixed-income housing, and, of course, a world-class arena and franchise to Brooklyn."

"We are excited that one of the most respected global financial services companies has chosen to partner with an NBA team to demonstrate its commitment to the United States market as well as its desire to make a difference in the communities where it operates," said NBA Commissioner David Stern.

"This partnership is a defining moment for the Nets business and brand," said Brett Yormark, President & CEO of Nets Sports and Entertainment. "It truly strengthens our position as a leading sports and entertainment franchise. We could not be more pleased than to have a partner as distinguished and well-respected as Barclays."

Sports are a significant part of the Barclays worldwide sponsorship portfolio, which includes the Barclays, the PGA Tour event at the Westchester Country Club scheduled for August 20–26 this year. In addition, Barclays sponsors the Barclays Scottish Open golf tournament at Loch Lomond, the Barclays Singapore Open golf tournament and the Barclays Premiership, the world's leading soccer league.

How big a dollar deal is this? Consider the most expensive arena naming-rights deal before the Barclays Center, the 20-year, $182 million Philips Arena deal in Atlanta. And that deal was made in 1999. Earlier this month Prudential Insurance put their name on the New Jersey Devils arena set to open in Newark in September. The Prudential Center moniker will cost Prudential an estimated $105 million over the lifetime of the agreement, making the $400 million Barclays agreed to pay the Nets that much more remarkable. Geographically the two facilities will be within 20 miles of each other. Either Prudential is getting a great deal or Barclays paid far too much.

And let's remember the New York Mets

and Citigroup announced a twenty-year naming rights agreement that will be worth at least $20 million annually, be for a term of 20 years, and include an option to extend the agreement to 35 years. Over the life of the agreement, the Mets stand to generate between $400 and $650 million from the sponsorship agreement. The Mets/Citigroup agreement obliterated the $10 million annual fee Reliant Energy pays the Houston Texans to call the home of the Texans Reliant Stadium.

Last year there were 13 major arena/naming naming rights agreements for the "Big Five" sports (Major League Baseball, the NFL, NBA, NHL and MLS) negotiated. The sum for those 13 sponsorship agreements naming rights deals in North America was more than $4.5 billion; 2007 has offered an impressive start with the Nets and Devils agreements with more than $505 million.

"To have an international investment bank without a major local presence to invest the way they are in the image of Brooklyn and the image of New York just is a remarkable vote of confidence," New York City's deputy mayor for economic development, Daniel L. Doctoroff said. "The idea of using Brooklyn and New York to build a global brand is one that we think is a very wise investment."

Barclays' lack of market awareness in the United States played a key role in the Nets search for a major corporation who might be interested in paying significant dollars for their arenas naming rights. Brian Schecter, an analyst who tracks naming rights for Kagan Research told the *New York Times* the deal made perfect senses.

"It strikes me as a nice price tag," he said. "What makes this deal even more lucrative is that it's basically a basketball-centric arena." (Philips Arena is home to both the NHL's Atlanta Thrashers and the NBA's Atlanta Hawks.)

Brett Yormark, the president of Nets Sports & Entertainment, made it clear in seeking a major sponsor for the Nets new arena he targeted Barclays as a possible naming rights buyer, with a New York–based fashion company, a bank and two telecommuncations corporations. With the arena's projected cost now pegged at $637 million the $400 million will go a long way towards paying a significant share of the arena's capital construction costs.

"We said: 'Who needs a game changer here? Who's got a footprint here, but isn't big enough?' and Barclays was on the list," he said in a *New York Times* report. "As we scouted financial institutions we saw Barclays needed a game changer, that they don't have as big a presence or brand recognition here as in the U.K. And we saw that it got involved with the Barclays Classic in Westchester."

As big and important as the Nets agreement with Barclays will be, many believe Wasserman Media marketing, the naming rights for the yet to be built Giants/Jets stadium located in The Meadowlands, minutes from the heart of Manhattan, will negotiate the biggest stadium/arena rights deal ever.

The 82,500-seat New Meadowlands Stadium, scheduled for completion in time for the 2010 football season, will be located just north and east of the site of the current Giants Stadium at the Meadowlands Sports Complex in East Rutherford, N.J. The Giants and Jets ownership families have formed a joint venture to build the new stadium as 50-50 partners, working together to create the NFL's premier sports and entertainment facility. The new stadium is being 100 percent privately financed by the two joint venture partners.

"The New Meadowlands Stadium arguably represents the most unique opportunity in the nascent history of naming rights," said Casey Wasserman, Chairman and CEO of WMG. "Combining the power of the NFL and its reach with two of the greatest sports teams creates an unparalleled platform for a marketer to align itself with the most prominent media, entertainment and sports destination in the world."

New York Giants Chairman Steve Tisch said, "Our overall objective is to create a strong identity for the stadium and environs as a world-class sports and entertainment facility. Wasserman Media Group has the experience and background to help us explore all the alternatives we have and to make the important decisions about how best to achieve our goals by associating ourselves with dynamic and exciting sponsorship, marketing and naming partners."

Woody Johnson, Chairman and CEO of the Jets, said, "This marks another important step as we work to build the premier football stadium and entertainment complex in the NFL. Wasserman Media Group will expand and enhance our vision to make the New Meadowlands Complex the most innovative and memorable spectator environment in professional sports. We welcome them as partners in this process and look forward to working together in the coming months and years."

John Mara, President and CEO of the Giants, said, "We look forward to establishing mutually beneficial affiliations and relationships that will serve to enhance the prestige and image of what promises to be a truly extraordinary facility. We expect to secure a naming partnership arrangement that reflects the unique nature of the opportunity."

New York Jets President Jay Cross said, "Designed from a fan perspective, this facility will transform the game day experience for our fans through cutting-edge technology and new amenities. We look forward to engaging potential sponsors and marketing partners who are as excited as we are about a project which will boast the best entertainment experience in the NFL."

"Given the strength and heritage of the Jets and Giants, coupled with the appeal and size of the market they serve, we anticipate there will be monumental interest in this historic opportunity," said Jeff Knapple, President, WMG Marketing. "We look forward to helping the teams realize the potential for a select partner to fully utilize this extraordinary marketing platform."

It's easy to appreciate why everyone associated with the selling of the Giants/Jets stadium naming rights believe they have the Holy Grail of corporate sports naming rights to sell. It begins with an opportunity to showcase your company's name a minimum of sixteen days each year on national television. It's reasonable to expect either the Giants or Jets to host playoff games on a regular basis, bringing even more value to whatever company agrees to spend hundreds of millions of dollars in a long-term agreement. It's likely during the lifetime of the stadium the United States will host at least one World Cup and with a state-of-the-art facility located in the shadow of Manhattan. In all likelihood the World Cup final (the most watched event in the world) will be played there.

The Yankees, who broke ground on their $800 million stadium in August, have no plans to sell the naming rights for the new Yankee Stadium. Give George Steinbrenner credit, it's another example of how he does business, and realizes what the Yankees brand name is worth. The Yankees would have been able to sell the naming rights to their new stadium for more than $10 million a year. However, renaming Yankee Stadium with a corporate name would sully the Yankees brand, taking away from the big picture philosophy Steinbrenner has always had during his stewardship as Yankees owner.

The new Yankee Stadium has been designed to generate tens of millions of dollars annually in corporate sponsorship naming rights fees. Each gate at the new Yankee Stadium will have its own lead (title) sponsor. The Yankees brand will drive decision makers to buy parts of the stadium for millions of dollars. Assuming the Yankees can meet their goals of what amounts to a series of "mini-naming rights deals," and there is no reason to believe they won't, the Yankees will easily surpass $10 million in annual corporate naming rights.

The variable in the three recent stadium/arena New York area agreements is the yet-to-be-signed multi-million annual for the Giants/Jets stadium, and the Yankees knowing full well the tens of millions of dollars they'll be able to generate without giving up the sanctity of the Yankee Stadium name is the New York market. There is no bigger or more important market. It's a marketing and sponsorship selling advantage New York–based sports franchises have, that other markets know all too well they do not have.

"I think the Jets and Giants right now are licking their chops," Michael Kelley, a senior VP for the Bonham Group, a consulting firm with vast experience in naming rights told *New York Newsday*.

Best guess? "With people seeing 20 million for the Mets and Nets, they could get up to 30 million," he said. "The question is who can afford that? There's a small handful of companies that can."

Deep pockets are a must. Said Kelley: "All these numbers have been blowing the cap off what everyone thought they'd go for."

Jeff Knapple, the president of WMG Marketing said to the *New York Times*: "We've watched with a keen eye toward what the Mets and the Nets have done. It's an indication of the power of the New York marketplace and its position in the nation and the world."

Knapple negotiated the most expensive arena naming-rights deal before the Barclays Center, the 20-year, $182 million Philips Arena deal in Atlanta.

"Philips was a massive leap above Staples Center, and it's held for seven, nearly eight years," he said.

The key isn't the teams that are playing in the facilities, the key isn't the leagues or the number of teams using those facilities, and it really is location and timing. Yormark, the Nets President, did his homework and found Barclays, a British-based company who believes they can generate greater market awareness through a sports naming rights agreement. Is it possible, if not likely probable Barclays may be involved in helping to provide some of the financing for the $4 billion Atlantic Yards project? If nothing else the awareness could serve as a catalyst to the many businesses looking to find a bank to help put together their needed financing.

The New York market had, until 1996, barely entered the naming-rights world except for the Continental Airlines, 12-year, $29-million deal to rename Brendan Byrne Arena in the Meadowlands. Now, a combined $800 million is going to the Nets and the Mets. And in a deal announced earlier this month, Prudential Financial will spend $105.3 million to name the Devils' new arena in Newark for 20 years. In less than two months three separate stadium/arena naming rights agreements in the Greater New York area have generated close to $1 billion in sponsorship fees. That's the power of location, location, location.

CHAPTER 14

Evansville Mayor Uses Advisory Board to Analyze Need for New Stadium

Roberts Stadium Advisory Board

The following represents the Roberts Stadium recommendations report from the City's Advisory Board to the Honorable Jonathan Weinzapfel, Mayor, City of Evansville, Indiana.

The final report states that "Utilizing all of the information at our disposal, the Roberts Stadium Advisory Board recommends that a new, high quality, multi-purpose sports and entertainment venue be built downtown." The complete report, dated May 19, 2008, from the advisory board to Mayor Weinzapfel is highlighted below.

The Roberts Stadium Advisory Board convened for its first meeting on June 27, 2007. Our mission was to provide feedback to the City regarding the future of the 51-year-old Roberts Stadium. Since then, we have conducted six Board meetings and have received a great deal of feedback from the public. We also received the results of the Market, Financial, Funding and Site Analysis report from Tom Chema of The Gateway Group.

On May 7, 2008, Dr. Sue Ellspermann joined the Advisory Board to facilitate a meeting at which we were to reach our recommendations to the City about Roberts Stadium. With Dr. Ellspermann's assistance, the advisory board developed a list of 45 Key Facts.

1. Roberts Stadium was renovated in 1990 at a cost of $16.2 million. It seats 12,232 people, has 15 corporate suites, and no club seating.
2. Roberts Stadium is a textbook "destination site." Destination site venues have not proven to be successful in stimulating ancillary economic development.
3. The problem with Roberts Stadium is that the floor is too small, there is no permanent ice making plant, the truck docks and marshalling areas are undersized for today's events, and the rigging is significantly under capacity for modem acts, concerts, and other events.
4. Roberts Stadium has served the community well for 50 years, but it is functionally obsolete. It cannot be brought up to today's standards due to the inability to "raise the roof" (as they did in Ft. Wayne), which also prevents the expansion of the stadium floor.
5. Renovation would be very expensive and impractical even if you didn't try to raise

Originally published as *Final Report of the Roberts Stadium Advisory Board*, May 20, 2008, addressed to Mayor Weinzapfel, and published by the City of Evansville, IN.

the roof. The estimated cost to increase the floor size, rigging capacity, truck docks, and add permanent dock space would be approximately $50 million.

6. According to the consultant's analysis, a downtown location is the only one that would help generate revenue equal to or greater than the cost of a new facility. A downtown location appears to create economic spin-off like retail shops and other businesses.

7. The consultant has determined it will cost approximately $92 million to build a 10,000 seat arena located downtown. A new arena will require a minimum of 3.5 to 4 acres and approximately 4,200 parking spaces within 2,000 feet of the entrances (2 to 3 blocks).

8. Downtown Evansville has a total of 8,300 parking spaces available. There are 2,418 private garage spaces; 2,417 spaces in private surface lots; 1,579 spaces in city garages, and 1,886 metered spaces.

9. The consultant has determined that potential funding sources for a new 10,000 seat arena downtown include: naming rights ($14 million), revenue bonds ($6 million), federal transportation support ($2 million), gaming revenue ($15 million), Transportation Improvement Program (TIP) ($32.5 million), Community Revitalization Enhancement District (CRED) ($.75 million), New Markets Tax Credits ($18 million), Food and Beverage Tax ($15 million), and Innkeepers Tax ($8 million).

10. The consultant readily stated that the funding sources presented were merely estimates, plus he did not provide a multiyear projection of revenues and expenses, debt service, and maintenance reserves. The cost of site acquisition is also likely to differ from the assessed value. It would, therefore, be appropriate to have a detailed financial forecast prepared by a firm or firms having significant expertise and experience with various funding sources and revenue/expense projections.

11. The public input and media coverage of the process to date has been very beneficial with the apparent preference of the community being a new facility downtown.

12. A major concern seems to be downtown parking and traffic flow.

13. Many citizens prefer an 11,000 seat arena, if it is economically feasible, because the city needs to prepare for growth 10 to 20 years into the future. We need the range of costs for both a 10,000 seat and an 11,000 seat arena.

14. Many citizens feel a new hotel next to an arena will be economically beneficial to the project.

15. Many citizens seem to prefer a new arena built near The Centre on the Executive Inn hotel site.

16. Most citizens do not want their property taxes increased in order to build a new arena.

17. Most of the markets that are comparable to Evansville, which have opened arenas recently, have more people living within 25 miles of their cities. However, Evansville is relatively strong when you compare the number of people living within 50 miles of the city.

18. The Evansville metropolitan area has an inventory of 425 corporations and branch offices. It ranks 4th among the markets analyzed for corporate inventory, and Evansville's inventory is significantly higher than the comparable market average.

19. The current average number of annual events at Roberts Stadium is fairly competitive with most of the comparable markets surveyed. The average number of annual events for the last three years at Roberts Stadium is 112.

20. "I believe the downtown area is a city's heartbeat and a thriving downtown often reveals a strong vibrant city. As a thirty-something Evansville native who returned home after living in Indianapolis and travelling fairly extensively, I believe that building an arena in downtown Evansville is the

catalyst Evansville needs to resuscitate its heartbeat. However, it has to make sense."

21. We should consider the loss of taxable revenue on a site where the owner is currently paying property taxes.

22. The average attendance at Roberts is 6,000 people for concerts; nothing close to the 11,000 seats that are being suggested for a new arena.

23. We have heard from many that this is a "once in a lifetime chance" to do it right. We should create a facility we will be proud of.

24. We should build for the future, not for the past (ex. the University of Southern Indiana growth).

25. We consistently heard from people that Evansville has momentum now. An arena is a key element in moving forward.

26. We should make sure this facility is not simply large, but also handles several different types of sports and events well (e.g., basketball, hockey, conventions, etc.).

27. The study saw The Centre as a place to function in tandem with an arena downtown (ex. exhibition space). An arena, The Centre, and hotels will be greater than the sum of their parts. We need to consider which location will result in the most potential economic development.

28. Many people question the revenue sources that came out of the study: Tax Increment Financing (TIF), parking, and Community Revitalization Enhancement District (CRED).

29. There may be other opportunities for use of Roberts Stadium that were not included in the study.

30. SMG (Evansville's entertainment and conference venue manager) does lose some concerts due to shortcomings of the current stadium.

31. The Mayor made it clear at the beginning of the process that the University of Southern Indiana (USI) and the University of Evansville (UE) would be instrumental in the development of this facility.

32. We think an arena should be used to help attract other events to our community: soccer, football, etc. We could be a capital for regional sports, collegiate sports and entertainment.

33. The negotiation process for some downtown sites will be easier and less costly than others (ex. fewer land owners).

34. There are 60–75 activities listed in a previous survey that Roberts Stadium was not able to accommodate (ex. automobile shows).

35. We should figure out how to involve the University of Southern Indiana (USI) in a new arena without being a detriment to the University of Evansville (UE).

36. We hear, "It would be wonderful if the $14 million of corporate sponsorship came in early in the process."

37. Some of the funding in the study is already dedicated to other budgeted items (i.e. Food and Beverage Tax goes to the Convention and Visitors Bureau).

38. We believe an arena will be an economic stimulator for the community.

39. We don't think we have exhausted the potential uses for Roberts Stadium beyond the recommended water park. This should be explored as part of the process.

40. We have heard that whatever happens to Roberts Stadium, it needs to pay for itself.

41. There is nothing that says Roberts Stadium could not be redeveloped and those profits used to support the cost of a new arena.

42. We could donate Roberts Stadium to the Evansville Vanderburgh School Corporation (EVSC), the University of Southern Indiana (USI), the University of Evansville (UE), and the Diocese of Evansville.

43. We heard from many people that the seating should be comfortable.

44. We think "optimal size" needs to be 10,000 to 11,000 seated comfortably. Arena size would depend upon our ability to finance, events we could attract, and looking to the future.

45. The process of designing and building a new arena should include the participation of the entire community. After reaching that list of 45 Key Facts, a multi-part recommendation was crafted and refined by the Board until we reached a consensus. Those recommendations are as follows:

• Utilizing all of the information at our disposal, the Roberts Stadium Advisory Board recommends that a new, high quality, multi-purpose sports and entertainment venue be built downtown. It should comfortably seat approximately 9,000 to 11,000 people. An arena should also factor in future needs of the City.

The decision to build should be contingent on:

• Assurance of adequate funding. Total overall funding should exceed the cost.
• Confirmation from businesses to purchase naming rights and/or purchase suites for a multi-year period, even though the City may not have commitments for the entire $14 million as estimated by Gateway.
• Engage well-qualified financial experts to prepare detailed, multi-year financial projections to confirm the viability of this project over the long-run without negatively impacting property taxes.
• Confirmation that land can be acquired at an affordable price.
• Negotiation of a multi-year contract with the University of Evansville (UE) that does not significantly increase the cost of use of the arena and meets the Missouri Valley Conference (MVC) scheduling requirements.

• Engage an architectural and engineering (A&E) firm to prepare cost estimates.
• The site and building should enhance the image of the City, and provide other retail and economic opportunities.
• Invest in an economic impact study and build the arena in a location that leverages potential impact.
• Address parking and traffic concerns.
• Fully consider the best possible community use for the current Roberts site.

Additionally we recommend:

• Cases for the Corridor of Champions should be designed and built into the new facility. The Roberts Stadium Foundation has committed to updating and maintaining this important tribute to local sports.
• Additional study should be done on attracting a professional hockey franchise. Permanent ice would lend itself to additional entertainment options. If the potential benefit outweighs the cost, permanent ice should be included in the facility.
• Continue to explore expanded use by the University of Southern Indiana (USI) and other area groups.
• We encourage the participation of local skilled trades, minorities, women, and vendors.

The Roberts Stadium Advisory Board has been proud to serve the City. We hope our recommendations will be seriously considered as the potential is assessed for a new arena in Evansville. The report ended with the following closing "Sincerely, Roberts Stadium Advisory Board."

CHAPTER 15

Fargo and Other Cities Ponder the "Public Good" in the Taxpayer Financing of New Sports Facilities

Ronald A. Wirtz

In today's sports-saturated culture, major cities and their states have spent a significant amount of political and financial capital to build new homes for major league sports teams. Since 1990, more than 50 new stadiums and arenas have been built, and another 20 are in either planning or construction phases. The vast majority are mostly or entirely financed with tax dollars.

On the surface, "the stadium issue" would appear to be a fairly minor one for the Ninth District, save for the Twin Cities, where innumerable stadium proposals have surfaced regarding Minnesota's Vikings and Twins, and a new arena welcomed hockey's Minnesota Wild for its inaugural season. With no other cities over 100,000 people, the rest of the Ninth District would seem to be far removed from the stadium debate. But, in fact, numerous district cities are investing millions in stadiums and multiuse arenas for quasi-professional or college teams and to bring other entertainment to town.

To be sure, the stadium issue plays out a little differently between major metropolitan areas and the likes of Fargo, N.D. For starters, "you don't have millionaire ballplayers and billionaire owners" of teams, said Pat Zavoral, Fargo city administrator.

But aside from a lack of zeroes, the stadium issue still boils down to many of the same core arguments. Teams still seek public assistance to improve their profitability. City officials, worried about the national or regional persona of their community, argue that the presence of a professional or college sports team and the ability to host concerts and other entertainment provides economic and civic benefits well worth the public investment.

Apples and Oranges and Apples

Though outside the mainstream sports leagues, Ninth District cities nonetheless have a grab bag of sporting options available to them. Currently, there are at least seven minor and quasi-professional sports leagues with up-

Originally published as "Pitching for the Minor Leagues," *FedGazette*, March 2001, by the Federal Reserve Bank, Minneapolis, MN.

wards of 30 franchises playing or scheduled to play in Ninth District cities. Teams, and even entire leagues, are often footloose, sometimes not playing for more than a year in a particular location as they look for stronger fan bases and financial viability.

Player salaries in these bus leagues — defined merely by the common means of travel — can make teams easy to start up and shut down. Indoor football players earn a paltry $200 a game. Players in the Continental Basketball Association (CBA) earned $400 to $500 per game, or about $25,000 a year until the 55-year-old league recently shut down.

Given the volatility of franchises, one might think teams have little or no bargaining power with cities. Most cities have hosted numerous teams in different sports over the years, but a handful are making stadium improvements directly connected with local professional teams.

Last summer, Sioux Falls, S.D., spent about $4 million on a makeover for Sioux Falls Stadium, home of the Northern League's Canaries. The league is unaffiliated with Major League Baseball (MLB) but has gained a solid following, thanks in part to the likes of Ila Borders, a southpaw pitcher and the first woman to don a professional baseball uniform, and short playing stints by former big-leaguers Daryl Strawberry and Jack Morris.

The Canaries pitched in a little over $1 million and "assumed a lot of operating costs" that were previously paid for by taxpayers, including the lighting bill and field maintenance, according to Dean Nielsen, city chief of staff. Sioux Falls also spent about $1 million retrofitting a local arena for use by the Stampede of the U.S. Hockey League. The team will pay back — interest free — about $700,000 over the next 10 years, Nielsen said.

Another Northern League franchise, the Redhawks, got a brand new stadium when the team came to Fargo. The city built Newman Outdoor Field in 1996, leveraging an earlier proposal for a new baseball stadium by North Dakota State University (NDSU). The city spent $3 million on the field, and local businessman Harold Newman paid $1.5 million for naming rights to the 4,600-seat facility, according to city officials. In Missoula, Mont., the city has committed $1 million in infrastructure improvements to complement a $5 million private investment for a new playing field for the Missoula Osprey of the Pioneer League, a rookie league with MLB affiliation. Up the road, Great Falls voters will likely get a chance this spring to vote on a $12 million multifield complex that will include a new home for the Great Falls Dodgers, also of the Pioneer League. About 30 percent of the project is expected to be privately financed, according to a team official.

It might not be coincidence that most of the stadium projects have involved baseball, if Fargo's experience is any indication. Zavoral said the city has played host to "seven or eight" professional hockey teams in the past 20 years. Last year the city had an indoor football team, "and they had a hell of a time," he said. The Beez, an International Basketball Association (IBA) franchise, has been in town for three years but has an average attendance of only 700, when 1,700 is the break-even point, Zavoral said.

In contrast, the baseball Redhawks have averaged better than 4,000 in attendance since coming to town in 1996, in part because neither college nor high school teams compete for fans' attention in the summer. The Redhawks, Zavoral said, "gives them another thing to do in the summer."

Stadium Version of Multitasking

Many cities have pursued multipurpose arenas — domes built for the expressed purpose of drawing entertainment to the community, sporting and otherwise. Fargo built the Fargodome in 1992 in part for the NDSU football team, but designed it to also host concerts, other sporting events and conventions.

Other cities are following suit. Grand Forks, N.D., has not one, but two, multiuse facilities in various stages of construction. After several unexpected setbacks — including flood-related delays, a collapsed roof and cost creep from $49 million to $78 million — the Alerus Center finally opened in February, boasting a 13,000-seat arena and convention facilities. The facility is being paid for by local sales taxes, save for a $3 million naming rights fee being paid by Alerus Financial of Grand Forks.

Following closely on its heels is another $85 million arena that will be the new home of the Fighting Sioux hockey program at the University of North Dakota. The project is being financed through a $100 million donation by UND alumnus and casino magnate Ralph Engelstad. Although designed and intended mostly for hockey, arena officials have inquired about hosting other sporting events and concerts, according to local reports.

Other district cities are also using local college sports as the hook for new facilities. The city of Mankato, Minn., leveraged the popularity of college hockey to build a new $22 million arena for the jump to Division I by Minnesota State University-Mankato.

Not all such efforts have won over local voters. Community drives in St. Cloud, Minn., and Fargo for new college hockey arenas have fallen through in the last two years. In St. Cloud, voters rejected a proposal to build a $69 million events center, whose anchor tenant would have been the hockey Huskies of St. Cloud State University. "It was St. Cloud's answer to the Fargodome," said Chris Hagelie, city administrator. The state even pledged $25

million toward the project, provided the city could find local matching money.

In 1999, the city held a referendum on a $70 million package of community projects, which included $44 million in local money for the events center. Seeking an all-or-nothing vote, the proposal narrowly lost because of voter dissatisfaction with the events center, local sources said. "It was the anchor holding everything back," said City Clerk Greg Engdahl. "There's a bad taste in people's mouth now concerning stadiums. There's such a connotation attached to stadiums that people don't want to participate in."

That was obvious when the city held another referendum. This time it took out the events center, added a few other items, and put each item of the new $40 million package on the ballot and "they all passed by a large amount," Engdahl said. A similar referendum in Fargo to build a $48 million arena for a Division I hockey program at NDSU recently lost by a two-to-one margin, Zavoral said. Part of the reason was a feeling among voters that the project benefited the university more than the community, Zavoral said, and "a backlash on public support for arenas."

Contrast that to the local opinion of the Fargodome, constructed in 1992 after a local sales tax referendum to pay for the dome passed by a three-to-one margin, according to Zavoral. Today the Fargodome "has a good following and warm spot in the heart of the city," he said. "[Residents] think it's a raving success."

Swing and a Miss

Some of that voter pessimism likely comes from lessons learned the hard way, like in Rapid City, S.D. In 1987, the city got a CBA team — the Thrillers — from Florida and had great success for about the first four or five years, with average attendance better than 5,000 per game. "Through 1991-92, we did very well" with the team, said Brian Maliske, business manager of the Rushmore Plaza Civic Center, which includes a 10,000 seat arena that was home to the Thrillers.

But in 1993, the CBA salary structure went up as the league positioned itself as a feeder system to the National Basketball Association. Player and coaching salaries escalated quickly, "and that had to be passed on to fans," Maliske said. General admission seats went from the $4 to $6 range to $10 or $12, and "the fan base took a big dive downward," along with corporate sponsorship and other revenue sources.

By the 1994 season, average attendance dropped better than 60 percent to about 2,000 per game, he said. The team came to the city several times looking for financial help, first asking for a cut of the city-owned concessions, and as a last ditch effort, offering to sell the team (along with about $100,000 in debt) to the city. Both were turned down.

"They weren't being greedy. They were just in a tight spot," Maliske said. Nonetheless, Rapid City's love affair with the team quickly went sour. "They went from being the ticket in town to the disgrace of town."

The city later attracted an IBA team, but they "couldn't get that to work." Part of the reason was a "holdover of ill will" from the CBA team, Maliske said, adding that the city is actively keeping any other professional basketball teams out until the city "gets the taste out of its mouth."

Rapid City was also slated to be home to a new junior hockey team franchise last year. But a proposal for a small, $3 million, privately financed rink for the team morphed into a $7.5 million proposal for a multiuse facility, two-thirds of which would come from the city. Projected costs ballooned to almost $10 million because of multiuse modifications, and

disagreements surfaced over who would receive profits from the stadium. "The thing just blew up," Maliske said.

Adopt-a-Team

In the final debate, the stadium issue in smaller markets also involves a slightly different perception of what constitutes the public good.

For some, additional entertainment options provide value to the community. Tam Baker, a member of the Sioux Falls city council, said she supports the city's current involvement with minor league sports teams. "I believe they enhance the quality of life for our citizens. They allow people an outlet for their spare time," Baker said. "These activities provide family-type entertainment that I feel is affordable for many of the citizens."

Stadiums and arenas in smaller markets also have more potential to meet legitimate community needs outside of spectator events. For example, new hockey arenas usually offer ice time for residents and community teams.

That makes public control of these facilities critical, according to Art Fahey, director of the La Crosse Center, a multiuse facility in La Crosse, Wis. Giving up that control would likely mean sacrificing some community events, because a profit-driven facility would likely charge user fees that "are probably out of reach" of the high school basketball team or community groups. "We have to make concessions to those kinds of events."

When Missoula began negotiating with the Osprey baseball team for a new 3,500-seat stadium, the city made it clear that the stadium was first a civic place "and had to accommodate events in a way that benefited the community," said Geoff Badenoch, director of the Missoula Redevelopment Agency. "The bar was set quite high."

But aside from community access to the field, the team itself brings community value. "Missoula has a lot of different people, and people with not a lot in common find baseball," Badenoch said. "Minor leagues are not a sport. It's leisure. The focus is on family entertainment."

As a rookie league, most players are 21 or younger and earn just $850 a month. Many come from different countries trying to make it to the big leagues, but along the way become a part of the community — literally, by staying with families in town.

"These kids basically get adopted. [Missoulians] love these kids," Badenoch said. The players get their first taste of being in a fishbowl, too. "For many of the players, it's the first time they've signed an autograph." Badenoch said. "They fit well in the community."

CHAPTER 16

Frisco Focuses on Public-Private Partnerships for New Sports Complex

George A. Purefoy

When the small agricultural town of Frisco, Texas, experienced a population explosion in the mid–1990s, there were concerns along with celebration. Now recognized as having one of the fastest growing populations in the country by the U.S. census bureau, how could retail and commercial development keep pace? How could property taxes be kept low when the call for city services was increasing so drastically? And what kind of family entertainment options were needed to build Frisco into the kind of city that would keep citizens glad to live, work and play here? Besides these sustainability issues, the city and school district, along with most other organizations in Frisco, were growing out of their facilities.

The Frisco City Council faced these monumental issues at their 1996 summer work session. Recalling the city's "Live, Work, Play, and Grow" motto, they decided that the City of Frisco, then a town of 16,450, should pursue opportunities to host a professional sports franchise. A public-private partnership to build and operate a new minor league ballpark as part of a greater Sports Complex was the vehicle used to achieve this dream.

Partners in this massive undertaking include the Frisco Independent School District, City of Frisco, Frisco Economic Development Corporation (FEDC), Frisco Community Development Corporation (FCDC) and Southwest Sports Group. The centerpiece is the new Dr Pepper/7 Up Ballpark, home of the Frisco Roughriders, a Double A affiliate of Major League Baseball's Texas Rangers. The Stadium, which opened on April 3, 2003, surpassed ticket projections in its first two seasons.

The Sports Complex was completed later in 2003 with the opening of the Dr Pepper StarCenter. The StarCenter, which houses two NHL ice rinks, serves as the administrative offices and practice center of the National Hockey League's Dallas Stars. Additionally, the facility is the home of the Texas Tornado, a developmental hockey league, and Kurt Thomas Gymnastics Center.

Funding for the sports venues, including the parking, land, and infrastructure, totals $68 million and comes from a variety of public and private sources, with debt service at approximately $6 million per year. The Frisco

Originally published as "Frisco Sports Complex," *Nomination Form for Program Excellence Award for Outstanding Partnerships*, International City/County Management Association's 2005 Annual Awards Program, March 2005, by the Office of the City Manager, City of Frisco, Texas.

Sports Complex is located in Frisco's Tax Increment Reinvestment Zone (TIRZ), which contributes $2.4 million annually. The city's hotel occupancy tax, FCDC and FEDC each contribute $500,000 yearly for the public subtotal of $3.9 million. Operating agreements place all of the maintenance and operational costs on the private companies managing the facilities. Private funding comes from leases amounting to $1.7 million annually.

Outcomes

Benefits to the community are already being realized. The Frisco Rough Riders' first season attendance of 706,534 exceeded projections. Approximately 86 percent of season tickets were sold by opening day, and the stadium was named the Best New Ballpark of 2003 by Ballparks.com. The Frisco Rough Riders and the Texas Tornado are currently the champions of their leagues. A Frisco hotelier received the contract to provide lodging for visiting teams. The FISD and the City have access to the ballpark and arena for large events, athletics, and graduation.

Quality of life has improved, as residents have more entertainment options in closer proximity, and the project is accelerating development of an Embassy Suites Hotel and convention center, which will be complete by summer 2005. The new hotel is expected to have over 330 rooms, and the convention center is to be approximately 110,000 square feet. The Dr Pepper StarCenter regularly hosts regional ice skating competitions and is home to junior and adult hockey leagues and competitive ice skating clubs. Just south of the Ballpark, retail furniture giant IKEA is building its second Texas store in Frisco.

Despite all this improvement, there has been no additional tax burden on citizens. In fact, adding the sports facilities to the commercial mix of the city has contributed to the city's strong sales tax revenues and property valuation. Longer term, the city anticipates additional customers for the mall and retail developments, located just across the street from the ballpark, as well as additional corporate and retail growth, increased valuation of property taxes, and increased revenue from the hotel occupancy tax as the sports complex is completed and the city establishes itself as a tourism destination. Public-private partnerships are the key to achieving this economic impact and to establishing Frisco as a unique and sustainable community.

Lessons

At all times during construction of the Frisco Sports Complex and subsequent offshoot projects, an evaluation process has been in place to measure the partnerships outcomes. Every agreement between the partners can be evaluated and amended based on the outcomes from the first year of operation and subsequent years of operation as needed. The Frisco Sports Complex continues to grow and evolve. It has reduced costs to the citizens of Frisco while increasing service delivery of family friendly entertainment.

In great measure due to the success of the Frisco Sports Complex, Major League Soccer's (MLS) Dallas Burn, recently renamed FC Dallas, is relocating to Frisco and building a new 20,000-seat stadium with seventeen tournament fields, expected to draw one million visitors annually. The city is using experience cultivated from the sports complex as this project, called the Frisco Soccer and Entertainment Center, comes to fruition. This new public-private partnership between the City, FISD, Hunt Sports Group, Collin County, the Frisco Economic Development Corporation, and the Frisco Community Development

Corporation will help to keep school district taxes low, as the FISD was in the design process of an $18 million stadium for multi-purpose use. The school district was able to contribute $15 million to have access to a $65 million stadium and will avoid the estimated $500,000 maintenance and operations costs over the 40–50 year lifetime of the stadium, which are covered by Hunt Sports Group. The cost avoidance to the school district alone in this case amounts to tens of millions of dollars over time.

Public-private partnerships allow communities to realize dreams, establish economic sustainability, differentiate themselves, and promote improvements that could not be accomplished alone. The Frisco Sports Complex partnerships provide a shining example.

CHAPTER 17

Glendale and Other Cities Have Mixed-Use Facility to Create Sports District

Marc Hequet

Jon Froke, AICP, is juggling 30 major projects near the Glendale (Arizona) Convention Center. The local buzz isn't about conventions. It's about sports.

That's because sports venues are now mixed-use anchors. The two-year-old Glendale Arena, home of the Coyotes of the National Hockey League, is right next to the convention center, and Arizona Cardinals Stadium will open across the street in August. In the surrounding three square miles of this Phoenix suburb, four million square feet of commercial projects and 413 residential units are under construction. It's "a once-in-a-career" experience, says Froke, Glendale's busy planning director.

Comparable projects are under way in San Diego, St. Louis, and Columbus, Ohio. But all of them happened with some help from the cities involved. "Don't assume that things will spin off from the arena," warns Mark Barbash, Columbus's development director. "You have to plan for it."

His city's Nationwide Arena opened in 2000 for the NHL's Columbus Blue Jackets — but developer Nationwide Realty planned much more for the surrounding 95 acres. Now brick-paved alleys lead to restaurants, bars, a theater complex, and a music hall. The $540 million development includes one million square feet of office space and 500 housing units. People live and work in the district — even some who don't care for hockey.

In St. Louis, the Cardinals' new baseball stadium opens in April flanking Ballpark Village — 12 acres with 450,000 square feet of office, 400 residential units, an aquarium, the Cardinals' Hall of Fame, and shops fronting a one-acre plaza.

San Diego's Petco Park opened in 2004, triggering $1.8 billion in hotel, retail, and residential development in a rundown area next to the city's historic Gaslamp District. Padres owner John Moores agreed to develop 26 blocks as part of the baseball stadium deal. The city's finances are bogged down at the moment, but its development agency is sepa-

Originally published as "The New Fashion in Stadiums," *Planning*, Vol. 72, No. 4, April 2006, by the American Planning Association, Washington, D.C. Reprinted with permission of the author.

rately funded by tax increments — and the ballpark's neighborhood is thriving.

Other big projects are pending, including a new home in New Jersey for football's Jets and Giants and a $2.5 billion mixed use project in Brooklyn, New York, with an arena for the Nets basketball team.

Smaller markets welcome sports anchors, too. A renovated Lambeau Field in Green Bay, Wisconsin, is a prototype sports anchor. "You take an asset that only functions as an event-driven facility," says Amy Supple, "and it becomes the heart of the community." Supple is development manager with Hammes Company, a developer based in Madison, Wisconsin, that worked on Lambeau Field and Detroit's Ford Field.

Pittsburgh's new hockey arena may allow for the rebuilding of a neighborhood that was wiped out in the 1960s to make way for a hockey stadium and parking lot for the Penguins. The Pennsylvania Gambling Commission will decide whether to allow a casino next to the new arena. In any case, the existing arena would be demolished and a new arena would be built nearby, creating the opportunity for mixed income housing on the old arena site. "I've always seen this kind of healing that wound," says Don Carter, AICP, president of Urban Design Associates in Pittsburgh, whose firm is master planning the arena development.

Stadiums also attract tourists. Green Bay, with a metro area of 290,000, draws two million annually to Lambeau Field. And in Glendale, a new Cabelas — the big sporting good retailer — is expected to draw four million visitors to the city's sports district.

Traffic snarls are inevitable, but in Columbus, office workers and fans share arena district parking: Fans arrive for night games after workers depart for the day.

Still, who wants to live, work, or shop where sports nuts gather? Patrick Hassett,

AICP, Pittsburgh's assistant planning director, is looking for opportunities to locate residential developments near Pittsburgh's football, baseball, and hockey facilities. Steelers fans are rambunctious, while Pirates and Penguins fans are more family oriented, he says. Housing might be compatible with baseball or hockey, he concludes.

The surrounding neighborhood matters, argues John Collum, AICP, a senior project manager with San Diego's development agency. At Petco Park, the new stadium, a public park softens the edge. People can stroll up to the outfield wall and gaze on the field. "I don't know any other stadium that gets you that close," says Collum. On the other hand, the public park is closed on game days, except to paying fans.

How big should the master plan be? In Glendale, Development Design Group Inc. of Baltimore gained city approval for its master plan of the hockey arena and nearby commercial development. Then the city announced the Cardinals had chosen the abutting parcel for a football stadium.

So now the carefully planned hockey arena's loading dock faces its big new neighbor. "If we had known the stadium was going to go there, we would have altered the plan to embrace it," says Jim Baeck, DDG vice president. DDG has 12 sports-related projects in the pipeline, including minor league baseball parks.

Glendale is an extreme case, with $12 million in infrastructure, six miles of new streets, and $500,000 in traffic-monitoring equipment — all in preparation for the Cardinals, the Fiesta Bowl, the 2008 Super Bowl, and possibly the 2009 National Hockey League All-Star Game.

Has planner Froke forgotten anything? Yes. "What it's like," he says, "to have time off."

CHAPTER 18

Harrisburg and Other Cities Consider Public Ownership of Sports Teams

Charles Mahtesian

Paul Jadin can usually count on walking the corridors unnoticed at a mayors' conference. As chief executive of the nation's 199th largest city, with a population of barely 100,000 people, he is no match for the Daleys, Giulianis and Rendells of local government.

Except this year. In January, when the mayors held an emergency summit meeting in Cleveland to discuss sports franchise problems, Jadin suddenly found himself mobbed by admiring colleagues. He couldn't have been more popular if he was handing out block grants.

That was because, at a moment of widespread municipal panic about teams abandoning their cities, Jadin was the one mayor with nothing to worry about. He is the mayor of Green Bay, Wisconsin, the only town in America that hosts a major league franchise as a nonprofit corporation. In Green Bay, the owners can't run out on the fans because the fans are the owners. "Everyone there," Jadin said after the meeting, "would have loved to be in the position Green Bay is in."

At the time Jadin and his colleagues met,

Cleveland Mayor Michael White was struggling desperately to fight the departure of the Browns football team, whose owner, Art Modell, provoked a cataclysm of civic grief in November when he announced that he was taking the team to greener pastures in Maryland.

Modell's sweetheart arrangement with Maryland Governor Parris N. Glendening was written to provide the Browns with a spanking new $200 million stadium and a slew of other lucrative incentives sufficient to keep Modell rolling in cash for years to come. To many Maryland fans, Modell's move was only fair compensation for the treachery of Robert Irsay, the owner who packed up the Baltimore Colts and moved them to Indianapolis under cover of night more than a decade ago.

But Cleveland didn't see it that way—and neither did scores of cities all over the country whose mayors began wondering whether they might be the next victims of sports franchise greed. "If this can happen to Cleveland," Mike White warned, "then there is no city that is safe."

As the mayors' summit meeting took place, Cincinnati, Seattle and Tampa were all

Originally published as "Memo to Cities: If You Can't Bribe the Owner, Maybe You Can Buy the Team," *Governing*, Vol. 9, No. 3, March 1996, by Congressional Quarterly Inc., Washington, D.C. Reprinted with permission of the publisher.

facing the threat of losing their National Football League teams. The Chicago Bears were making noises about leaving their historic home for Gary, Indiana. The New York Yankees were considering a move to New Jersey, where the world champion New Jersey Devils hockey team had only recently pondered a move to Nashville, which was also in the midst of trying to lure the NFL's Houston Oilers.

Mayors threatened by all this franchise-hopping have advocated a variety of legislative measures to stop it. Daley of Chicago advocates a federal law to punish lease-breaking teams. Tampa Mayor Dick Greco has called for a 24-month notice period during which teams would have to stay put while the city presents a new deal or seeks a new franchise. Cleveland has explored seizure of the Browns under the powers of eminent domain, which would require the city to pay a fair market price determined by a court.

But given the difficulty of implementing any of these solutions, it is no wonder that so many mayors are showing interest in Paul Jadin and the Green Bay solution. Whether a city is home to a mighty NFL franchise or a lowly rookie league baseball team, the Green Bay model suddenly seems to offer a tantalizing way of keeping the home team home forever.

"We have this extraordinary phenomenon of these highly profitable, private monopolies whipsawing impoverished governments for more money," says New York Assemblyman Richard Brodsky. As far as he is concerned, the Green Bay option is no pipe dream. Brodsky is sponsoring a bill that would create a New York sports authority to sell bonds, buy a team and then offer team shares for public purchase. "The Green Bay Packers work fine, thank you," Brodsky says. "It is the only thing left."

The truth is that public ownership of sports teams is not only conceivable — it is ac-tually being done in quite a few communities around the country. Green Bay remains the only place to have accomplished it with a major league team, but experiments on a smaller scale are being launched in increasing numbers. "It's not as off-the-wall as it sounds," says Steve Resnick, an accounting consultant to minor league baseball franchises. "It potentially could be the answer."

That is the way Mayor Stephen Reed saw it in Harrisburg, Pennsylvania. The Senators of the Eastern Baseball League moved to Harrisburg only in 1987, and they were clearly popular with the fans. Yet by last summer they were on the verge of leaving for Springfield, Massachusetts, a city so desperate for baseball that it had already earmarked $14 million to construct a new stadium. The Eastern League had even approved the relocation bid.

Then Harrisburg, faced with the loss of a key component in its successful riverfront revitalization initiative, decided to try something desperately simple: a flat-out purchase of the team. Reed persuaded the city government to pay the Senators' ownership $6.7 million both for the franchise and for future civic peace of mind.

It was not a bargain price. The private owners had bought the franchise for $4.1 million only six months before. But as far as Reed was concerned, it was a sensible policy decision, similar to the city's recent bailout of a downtown hotel. Uneasy with the idea of municipal oversight, the city contracted out day-to-day baseball operations to Resnick, the franchise's former managing partner, at a cost of $200,000 over four years.

As bold as the tactic seemed to many, Harrisburg was not even the first place in the state to have tried it. Two hours away on Interstate 81, Scranton and surrounding Lackawanna County concocted the same idea several years before. In order to ensure occupancy of a new $25 million stadium that required regular debt service, the Lackawanna County government went out and purchased a baseball club to go along with it. The facility opened in 1989 with the Scranton/Wilkes-Barre Red Barons as the publicly held host club.

It was a controversial move at the time, but Lackawanna County Stadium now serves as anchor for a successful development project that has expanded to include a ski area and an adjacent office park. Ballpark attendance, as a proportion of local population, is higher than in any of the other nine International League cities; in seven seasons, the Red Barons have drawn 3.5 million fans. Despite the relatively limited market size, there is a waiting list for corporate luxury boxes. Perhaps more important, the whole venture has been a clear source of civic pride. "Nobody can jerk our team away from us," says Bill Risse, the county information officer. "We've built something that will be here for us and our children in the future."

Those are sentiments that come up not only in Scranton and Harrisburg but in most of the communities that have invested public money in sports franchises in the past decade — among them Indianapolis; Columbus and Toledo, Ohio; and Rochester, New York.

Of course, it is not the major leagues. Publicly owned minor league baseball franchises are practical in part because their budgets are so low. Normally, the team affiliates with a major league operation, and the major league club takes care of all the payroll and personnel costs. The gross operating budget of a minor league baseball team rarely exceeds a few million dollars, roughly the salary of a single journeyman player in the majors.

Sure, there's a big difference between the Scranton Red Barons and the Green Bay Packers. But could it happen somewhere soon in the major leagues? Perhaps.

Green Bay's bond with professional football dates back to well before the National Football League came into existence in 1921. In the league's early years, the Packers shared the field with the likes of Pottsville, Racine, Rock Island, Hammond and Duluth. But among all these undersized sports towns, only Green Bay survived. Public ownership is the reason.

Without the team, nearly everybody admits, Green Bay would be about as well recognized today as Pottsville or Hammond. With the team, Green Bay is able to make a plausible claim that it occupies a special place in the nation's consciousness. "Any human being you speak to on the face of the earth who hears the name Green Bay thinks first of the Green Bay Packers," says Mayor Jadin. "That is our identity."

There are more tangible benefits to Green Bay's arrangement. By design, ticket prices and concessions at municipally owned Lambeau Field remain among the most affordable in the NFL. In another unique arrangement, concessions are parceled out to local service organizations and charities, raising nearly $400,000 for groups that spend their Sunday afternoons pouring beer and cooking bratwurst.

During the football season in Green Bay, church services are scheduled around game times. Real estate agents don't bother scheduling open houses on Sunday afternoons. Halloween trick-or-treating hours had to be rescheduled last fall because they coincided with game time. "People grow up just knowing that life revolves around the Packers," says Nancy Nusbaum, county executive in surrounding Brown County. "They have no basis for comparison that this isn't normal."

The Packers were first incorporated in 1923, in a last-gasp move to save a team teetering on the brink of bankruptcy. The corporation was reorganized in the midst of the Great Depression and then bailed out one last time in 1951 with a stock sale. To prevent any one shareholder from gaining majority control, the new rules specified that no individual could buy more than $5,000 in shares. Today, 1,898 shareholders own a total of 4,634 non–dividend-paying shares.

The corporation is governed by a seven-member executive committee elected by an unpaid 45-member board of directors. A paid, elected president serves as chief executive officer. Football operations are handled separately by a general manager, as they are with other NFL teams. The Green Bay Packers Inc., which is exempt from state and local taxes though not federal taxes, posted a $1.9 million profit in 1994.

If the team is ever sold, the proceeds would go to the local Sullivan-Wallen American Legion Post 11, "for the purpose of erecting a proper soldier's memorial." It would be a lavish memorial indeed, since the team is now worth in excess of $100 million. "Some of those safeguards were set up to keep it here in perpetuity," says Packers executive Phil Pionek. "I don't believe the situation will ever come to pass that the team would leave."

About the only way Green Bay could lose the Packers would be if they became financially unable to compete in the NFL, an unlikely scenario but one that would be imaginable if the league were to abandon its various revenue sharing schemes and its salary cap. One owner, the Dallas Cowboys' Jerry Jones, is currently challenging the sharing arrangement for NFL Properties, the merchandising arm of the league. Given that as much as 86 percent of the Packers' revenue comes in shared form, the end of the system would be a disaster for them. The Packers would be unable to vie with larger-market teams and multi-millionaire private owners for the best free-agent talent. "If there wasn't revenue sharing," says Pionek, "I don't know how long we'd last."

For now, the status quo is working quite nicely in Green Bay. In fact, rather than en-

couraging his envious fellow mayors to take drastic action against unfaithful private owners, Jadin worries that mayoral efforts to impose a solution might inadvertently wreak havoc on Green Bay. One of several ideas now kicking around Congress is repeal of the antitrust exemption that enables major sports to control national telecasts and divide the proceeds. That would be a nightmare for the Packers' civic ownership arrangement. "Are they going to try to get some legislation that will end up impacting Green Bay's security?" the mayor asks, a little nervously.

All in all, the Packers' success as a publicly held big-league team is enough to make any community of 100,000 think about trying to copy it. Before they get started, however, mayors around the country need to know why only one such NFL franchise exists. Green Bay was grandfathered in.

League rules now require that one individual own at least 51 percent of any team's stock. This is ostensibly so that the team can speak to the league with a single and consistent voice. But the more obvious reason is because it is in the other owners' financial interest. The value of a franchise depends in large part on its freedom to move to more lucrative territory. Or, as Art Modell said to his fellow owners in January, "if this league allows the mayor to hold the Browns hostage, then every one of you are hostages, too."

"Having a community without a team that wants one helps all the other owners because it gives them leverage," says Art Johnson, a University of Maryland-Baltimore County professor who studies sports economics. "A municipal owner would not be interested in moving or using a team for leverage."

The National Football League can hardly be expected to repeal its private ownership provision voluntarily. On the other hand, it is not inconceivable that Congress might step in, particularly if franchise shifts continue to proliferate. But the more encouraging news for communities out to replicate Green Bay is that no major league in any other major sport — baseball, basketball or hockey — has such a provision. And below the big-league level, Scranton, Harrisburg and a number of other cities are proving that public ownership is perfectly compatible with profit and sound business judgment.

The largest obstacle, at any level, is the price tag. Green Bay residents paid only $5 a share when stock was first offered in 1923. By contrast, the last NFL franchise on the market sold for about $190 million.

In Cleveland's case, according to *Financial World* magazine, the Browns are valued somewhere in the neighborhood of $165 million. A high-end estimate for the Municipal Stadium renovation costs necessary to make the team profitable is $175 million. In an era of budget austerity, even the most profligate of cities should think twice before making a $340 million expenditure for an item that is, in essence, just a game.

Yet that is a close approximation of what the state of Maryland and cities such as Seattle and Nashville are currently prepared to do. Above and beyond the $200 million rent-free Baltimore stadium deal, Art Modell stands to make as much as $75 million from personal seat licenses — payment for the option to purchase tickets — and more money on top of that from parking and concessions. All told, Modell could net more than $30 million annually out of Baltimore's publicly funded generosity.

The Washington state legislature recently voted to build a new $320 million, baseball-only stadium for the Seattle Mariners, with state and local governments picking up most of the tab. Nashville is preparing a stadium package worth $300 million. Twenty years after New York City paid $76.5 million to renovate hallowed Yankee Stadium, estimates for another round of renovations range as high

as $600 million. A proposal for a new stadium for the team on Manhattan's West Side begins at about $300 million and ranges to upwards of $1 billion.

For that kind of money, it seems absurd not to at least explore the economics of buying a franchise. If private owners are going to be that expensive, maybe they are a luxury that a smart community can afford to dispense with. "I think it's possible," says Ken Silliman, who handles development issues for Mayor White in Cleveland. "It's an option that should not be neglected by a city like ours, though it's an extreme challenge."

Daniel Alesch, a professor at the University of Wisconsin-Green Bay, thinks new publicly owned NFL teams would not be a far-fetched idea at all if there were a way around the one-owner rule. "It's perfectly plausible," says Alesch, who recently studied the Green Bay Packer enterprise for the Wisconsin Policy Research Institute. "You'd have to come up with an upfront investment, but it's very likely to become profitable. You can contract out to real football people to run the team, and the thing can become self-sustaining."

Not everyone is so sure. If a city did purchase a big-league team with the intention of running it as a nonprofit entity, through a stadium authority or some other quasi-public agency, even taxpaying sports diehards might find themselves queasy with the high-finance aspects of ownership. "You're putting the government entity in a high-risk position," says David Petersen, managing director of the Price Waterhouse sports consulting group. "Another risk you have is that you buy the team and then you don't have enough corporate support to buy the luxury boxes."

For many cities, filling the premium seats would not be a problem. Operating both a team and a stadium at a profit, on the other hand, would be. The New Orleans Superdome bathed in a $70 million sea of red ink in its first 12 years of operation. Ever-changing state and municipal administrations and their accompanying ideologies present yet another challenge. "In theory, this may be sound," says Michael Thiessen of Stein & Co., a sports franchise consultant that works with cities. "But I think I'd have some concerns from the political side, though not necessarily from the public policy side. There would be so many political problems involved, beginning with who the coach is all the way to the sponsors. Is it a Pepsi town or a Coke town? Does the mayor lose his job if the team is playing crappy?"

Instead, Thiessen suggests perhaps a minority interest in a team, enough to avoid complete fiduciary responsibility while retaining a voice in a relocation decision. But a minority ownership interest is still no guarantee. The only real assurance is a 51 percent stake.

And the Green Bay experience does not suggest any serious problems with the choice of a soft drink or a coach. Green Bay's operations run as well as those of any privately owned NFL team, and better than many.

If anything, the vitality of a community-owned franchise may be just what professional sports needs at a time when fan cynicism is compounding daily. Or so the elected officials in Green Bay argue. And they seem to have the courage of their convictions. Some time ago, when her own wedding day conflicted with a Packers game, county executive Nusbaum discovered that the groom's father and the minister were both insistent on rescheduling the service. Nusbaum conceded. For one thing, she wasn't going to change anyone's mind. Besides, for all she knew, most of the wedding guests were shareholders.

CHAPTER 19

Houston and Other Cities Design Their Sports Stadiums for Comfort

Chuck Ross

Fans visiting more than one of this season's four new professional football stadiums are more likely to feel, rather than see, something in common among the structures. Designs range from traditional to contemporary, and roofs range from domed to retractable to nonexistent, but all feature amenities unheard-of in the last generation of NFL venues.

Stadiums are seeing their opening plays this fall in Houston, Seattle, Detroit and Foxborough, Mass. Houston's Reliant Stadium, home of the new Houston Texans, incorporates a translucent, retractable Teflon-fabric roof. The roof of Seattle's new Seahawks Stadium, home to the team of the same name, is cut away, so that the field is open to the elements while 70 percent of the seating remains sheltered. The Detroit Lions will play under domed protection in Ford Field, while the New England Patriots — and their fans — will brave the elements in open-air Gillette Stadium.

Pats Fans Sit in Lap of Luxury

Regardless of how dry fans' heads stay, however, their seats are sure to be more comfortable than ever. Take, for example, $325 million Gillette Stadium. Patriots faithful at the team's old Foxboro Stadium were used to aluminum bleacher seats and portable toilets in the concourses. Attendees now have 19-in.-wide seats in the general stands, 60 restrooms throughout the stadium, more than 350 points of sale and open concourses with sight lines to the field, keeping attendees in touch with the action even during beer runs.

"Patriots fans are an exceptionally loyal bunch," says Carrie Plummer, spokesperson for stadium architect HOK Sport + Venue + Event (HOK-SVE), Kansas City, Mo. The Kraft family, owner of both the stadium and the Super Bowl champion team, wanted to reward visitors with comfortable surroundings that reflected New England's maritime and industrial heritage. Though family patriarch

Originally published as "Comfort, Diversity Hallmarks of New NFL Stadiums," *Building Design and Construction*, September 2002, by Associated Construction Publications/Reed Construction Data, Oak Brook, IL. Reprinted with permission of the publisher.

Robert Kraft initially saw Baltimore's Ravens Stadium as the ideal model, HOK-SVE designer Jonathan Knight convinced the family that what it needed was a "custom-fit shoe," according to Plummer.

Constructed by the design-build joint venture of Boston-based Beacon Skanska and Southfield, Mich.–based Barton Malow Co., with structural consulting by Bliss & Nyitray, Miami, the resulting open-air design reflects Kraft's desire for a "front door," framed by abstracted versions of a classic New England lighthouse and iron arch bridge. Red masonry blocks that form the base of the design harken to the brick factories and warehouses constructed along area rivers in the mid- to late 19th century. More modern-day amenities include 1,000 television monitors throughout the facility, two 120,000-sq.-ft. club lounges that seat a total of 6,000, and 80 luxury suites that accommodate 16 to 36 high-paying fans each.

Detroit's Down-Home Dome

This blend of old and new also can be seen in Detroit's new $500 million Ford Field. Like Baltimore's Oriole Park at Camden Yards, Ford Field weaves an existing structure — a series of seven warehouses originally constructed for Hudson's department store — into the fabric of a new design. Sited in a downtown location opposite the newly constructed home for the Detroit Tigers baseball team, Ford Field helps complete the new Stadium District, intended to contribute to the city's revitalization. And, as with the Patriots' new stadium, the owner — in this case Ford Motor Co. CEO William Clay Ford Jr. — played a decisive role in the design program.

"Mr. Ford's vision was that he wanted everyone to know that they were in Detroit — and he didn't want it to stick out like a sore

thumb," says Michael McGunn, project manager and vice president with locally based SmithGroup, the project's architect and engineer of record. To limit the stadium's prominence in the city's skyline, designers sank the playing field about 45 feet below street grade. Curtain wall along one side of the base and translucent panels around the roof line are intended to keep patrons of the domed stadium from feeling claustrophobic.

Additional design team members included Rossetti Associates Architects, Birmingham, Mich., which designed the stadium itself, and Kaplan McLaughlin Diaz, San Francisco, which designed the warehouse renovation. In addition to providing a gateway into the stadium, the warehouse also includes approximately 350,000 sq. ft. of leaseable space. Hunt Jenkins, White/Olson LLC, Indianapolis, is the general contractor, and Thornton-Tomasetti, New York, is the structural engineer on the project.

Seahawks Digs Reflects Tech

In the Pacific Northwest, a more futuristic design is the new home of the Seattle Seahawks. Like Ford Field, $430 million Seahawks Stadium is situated within the city. While a masonry base provides a nod to surrounding turn-of-the-century architecture, field-spanning trusses and prominent video screens make an even bigger statement about the high-tech origins of team owner and stadium developer Paul G. Allen.

"With Paul Allen, you know there's going to be some kind of technological expression, and it's there," says Kelly Kerns, senior project manager and project leader for sports and stadiums with Ellerbe Becket, Minneapolis, the stadium's architect, in association with locally based LMN Architects. The U-shaped plan faces the city at its open end. Two 720-

ft.-long steel rainbow trusses support the roof, which covers 70 percent of the seating area and leaves the field open to the elements. Video screens at both ends of the field provide differing views — one in a landscape orientation, the other in a portrait orientation — of game action.

The design team benefited from its previous experience working together on another prominent project for Allen. The building team, which also included general contractor Turner Construction Co., New York, designed and constructed the Rose Garden, home of Allen's Portland Trail Blazers basketball team.

Houston's Ninth Wonder

Architects for Houston's new $417 million Reliant Stadium faced a unique challenge in their plans for a home for the city's new Texans team. Designers for the other three stadiums had to consider important regional and site-specific references, but sports consultant HOK-SVE along with its design teammates, had to contend with a legend.

Though now woefully outdated, the Houston Astrodome was internationally recognized as a landmark achievement when it opened in 1965. Surpassing the innovations presented in the world's first domed stadium was one of the goals set forth by the new facility's owner, the Harris County Sports & Convention Corp.

"The Houston Astrodome was called the 'Eighth Wonder of the World,'" says HOK-SVE's Plummer. "In a way, they wanted to construct the 'Ninth Wonder of the World.'"

Designers met the challenge with their own unique roof design — a retractable version, unique among NFL stadiums, constructed of a translucent fiberglass fabric. The roof can open or close in 10 minutes, gliding along 1,000-ft. supertrusses that span the length of the field. The space-age roof is intended to glow from within when closed for evening events, including RodeoHouston, the city's yearly livestock show and rodeo. Attracting approximately 2 million attendees annually, the rodeo is the venue's second major tenant.

Houston Stadium Consultants, a joint venture of locally based LAN/Daly and Hermes Architects, was the architect of record. The general contracting team consisted of locally based Manhattan and Atlanta-based Beers Skanska. Walter P. Moore was the structural engineer.

The NFL construction boom isn't stopping with these four stadiums. Three more new or renovated projects are scheduled to open next year, with major renovations at Chicago's Soldier Field and Green Bay, Wis. Lambeau Field, and a new stadium in Philadelphia.

CHAPTER 20

Kansas City and Other Towns Use Stadiums and Arenas for Inner-City Renewal

Parke M. Chapman

When the 18,000-seat Sprint Center opens in Kansas City next year, local officials hope that the arena will give downtown an economic jolt. After all, other large cities have used arena-led redevelopment campaigns to revive blighted districts.

What Kansas City officials are hoping for is an instant replay of what happened when Denver plopped a new major league ballpark in the middle of a rundown industrial area. It became the centerpiece of a $2 billion redevelopment that has produced a vibrant new neighborhood.

Kansas City has all of the pieces of the puzzle — the $276 million arena is part of more than $2 billion in subsidized redevelopment activity — except one: The city has yet to land an NHL or NBA franchise.

A speculative stadium or arena project is indeed a high-stakes proposition. In San Antonio, where the $186 million Alamodome was built 13 years ago, the city is still trying to lure an NFL franchise. To get the Tampa Bay Devil Rays to commit to playing in the $110 million

Sun Coast Dome in 1998, the City of St. Petersburg had to pony up $67 million for renovations to the eight-year-old facility.

But filling the stadium is only the first step in the ambitious redevelopment projects that Kansas City and other cities have planned around sports facilities. It's not enough to bring fans to the neighborhood 80 nights a year: The new urban arenas like Sprint Center are expected to justify their massive public subsidies by generating permanent improvements to the surrounding neighborhoods.

"The Sprint Center has already made a vital contribution to the redevelopment of downtown Kansas City," says Kevin Grey, president of the non-profit Kansas City Sports Commission. "The arena has already created some strong momentum among local businesses that want to be near it."

Commercial space within a few blocks of the Sprint Center is slowly filling up with tenants. But one local leasing broker says that much work remains to be done before the

Originally published as "Arena-Led Urban Revivals," *National Real Estate Investor*, November 2006, by Penton Media, Inc., Skokie, IL. Reprinted with permission of the publisher.

CBD can be called vibrant. Phillip James, senior vice president at Grubb & Ellis/The Winbury Group, believes that momentum is gradually building downtown. "I'm hoping that our growing residential base will help fill restaurants and office buildings downtown," he says.

Mile High Miracle

When a downtown sports attraction clicks, the results can be impressive. One example is Denver's Coors Field. Back in the early 1990s, local officials decided to build the 50,250-seat, $380 million stadium in a rundown district along the northern edge of the Denver CBD.

One Denver City Council member described this strip of dilapidated 1930s warehouses and industrial buildings as "double ugly." Instead of facing the usual not-in-my-backyard objections, Denver's big worry was if suburban sports fans would venture to this seedy part of town.

"People were really skeptical, but Coors Field was a home run in just about every way," says Sherman Miller, executive managing director of Cushman & Wakefield's western region.

Since Coors Field opened in 1995, the surrounding Lower Downtown area has been reborn as "LoDo," a hip residential district known for its restaurants and art galleries. Fans who throng to the team's 81 home games routinely circulate through the district where they shop and eat.

More than 90 restaurants, thousands of residential units and dozens of art galleries are located in the 25-square-block district. Retail and residential property values have tripled over the past decade, says Miller. Lofts in the area are among the city's priciest apartments.

Even the LoDo office market is thriving. Unlike Denver's metro market, which was 14.9 percent vacant at the end of September, the LoDo submarket had a 6 percent vacancy rate, according to Cushman & Wakefield data. The district is still growing, too.

In September, local developers won the bidding to create a mixed-use project on a 19.5-acre Union Station site located only a quarter-mile away from Coors Field. "The stadium is really what got LoDo started," says Miller, who adds that critics nearly foiled plans to build Coors Field on that site.

Foul Ball

The success of Denver and other cities such as Pittsburgh has encouraged planners and developers to believe that the introduction of a sports facility can act as a catalyst for neighborhood upgrades.

Steve Weathers, president and CEO of the Regional Growth Partnership in Toledo, Ohio, says that successful downtown arenas all share certain traits. Most tend to be near bus and subway stations, which reduces the hassle of stadium parking. It's also ideal if a critical mass of residents and office workers live and work within walking distance. Many will spend money along the way, he says. Another ingredient is keeping the facility active with concerts and other events when the team's away. "You need to draw people to the arena all year round," he says

Despite the enthusiasm for in-town stadium developments — more than a dozen have been built around the country since 1990, according to the Urban Land Institute — experts continue to debate the overall economic benefits.

Andrew Zimbalist, an economics professor at Smith College in Northampton, Mass., has studied the economics of arena development for decades. He says that arenas absorb dollars that could have been spent more effectively for economic development elsewhere in the city while imposing new costs, including security for patrons and residents.

According to Zimbalist's analysis, rental fees and revenue-sharing deals with sports teams rarely cover the direct and indirect costs of a new arena. He says that when the construction costs borne by the city and/or state are factored in, even the most successful stadiums rarely break even. Zimbalist says that building a speculative arena development such as Kansas City's Sprint Center is "irresponsible."

Central Access

Whether or not arenas and stadiums can jump-start economic revival in urban neighborhoods, it's clear that when such projects are built on sites away from business and residential centers, it's hard to discern any community-wide payoff.

One example is Atlanta's Turner Field. Built in 1996 as an Olympic stadium and future home of the Atlanta Braves, the $235 million project is hemmed in by highways and surface parking — two miles outside of downtown Atlanta. And it's not conveniently connected to the MARTA rail system, so fans must either utilize a shuttle bus or find their own form of transportation. After a decade, few restaurants or retail businesses have sprung up near Turner Field.

"The city didn't want to take any risks by developing a stadium in downtown Atlanta, so it built Turner Field on the edge of the city in the middle of highways," says Janet Marie Smith, former vice president of planning and development for the Atlanta Braves. In her career, Smith has worked on Turner Field, Camden Yards and Fenway Park.

"Baltimore's Camden Yards was really the first urban ballpark whereby officials actually

made the arena part of the city," says Smith, adding that in 1988, Baltimore officials viewed the stadium as a way to grow the downtown economic base. The stadium is an easy walk from Baltimore's popular Inner Harbor seaport district, making it a tourist draw, and has attracted restaurants, museums and shops. "It has ended up being the model that many other cities have tried to copy," she says.

Steel City Success Story

Pittsburgh is another example of how a sports project in just the right spot can spur development. The 65,050-seat Heinz Field opened five years ago near the site of the old Three Rivers Stadium on the northern edge of downtown. On another side, the Steelers' new home adjoins the $216 million PNC Park, which was built in 1999 for the Pirates.

"The idea was to create a mixed-use district between the two stadiums on what was formerly a bunch of parking lots," says Bernard McShea, senior vice president of business investment at Pittsburgh economic development group Allegheny Conference.

The new development also played off the northward expansion of the business district, which includes the $67 million Alcoa headquarters that opened in 2002 just 100 yards away from PNC Park. McShea says that Alcoa's decision to occupy space across the Allegheny River was viewed as a bold step at the time.

"Once they moved into the area, we started seeing some restaurant owners lease space. It definitely helps that the office is only a short walk across the Roberto Clemente Bridge from downtown Pittsburgh, too," says McShea. There are now roughly 1,000 new housing units in what has become known as the North Shore district.

"When we began redeveloping the Three Rivers site in 2003, the city made it clear that this would become a mixed-use area," explains Barry Ford, president of Continental Real Estate, which helped redevelop the 12-acre Three Rivers stadium site. "The stadiums were a way for them to create added opportunities for this area. They also demanded that an esplanade and park be developed on the riverfront."

Earlier this year, Continental built a $30 million, two-building headquarters for Del Monte Foods. And in May, Continental announced plans to develop its fourth office building in the North Shore district. Ford says that this 190,000 sq. ft. property, between the football and baseball stadiums, is already half-leased.

Tough Sell in the Heartland

For Kansas City, igniting that kind of new urbanist spark may be more difficult. The city, with a population of just 460,000, sits at the edge of an 18-county metro area of 2 million that spreads out north and west across a landmass roughly six times as large as the city of Pittsburgh.

Many upper- and middle-class white residents left Kansas City during the 1980s and early 1990s for booming suburban areas. That trend began to reverse itself in the mid–1990s and Kansas City has its share of loft conversions and downtown condo projects now. But it is still a struggle to lure upscale consumers downtown. In late October, the city announced a plan to raze four problem buildings in downtown Kansas City (one is an old Greyhound Bus Terminal).

A major focus of redevelopment is the so-called Power & Light District project. This $850 million mixed-use project, which is being developed near the Sprint Center by Baltimore-based Cordish Development, is one of the largest mixed-use projects in the Midwest.

Anchored by H&R Block's recently completed 1.3 million sq. ft. headquarters, the Power & Light District will also feature shops and galleries styled after Manhattan's hip SoHo district. The project's title harkens to the early 20th century when the district had a coal-fired power plant, which was demolished in 1930.

"It's hard to go downtown and miss all of the redevelopment activity," says Thomas Willard, CEO of Kansas City–based Tower Properties. Willard owns a 5 million sq. ft. portfolio of mostly office properties in the Kansas City metro area.

"There are two or three different catalysts driving the growth downtown, and the Sprint Center is clearly one of them. Buildings near the center are in greater demand, too," says Willard, adding that Class-A office vacancy rates in the metro region have been slowly declining in recent years.

Still, by any measure, downtown Kansas City is a troubled market: Grubb & Ellis data show that the CBD office vacancy was hovering at 21.5 percent at the end of September, up from 20 percent at the end of 2005.

New office supply doesn't appear to be an issue: There was only 550,000 sq. ft. of new office construction underway at midyear, which is a small fraction of the 12.8 million sq. ft. CBD office inventory.

"We see the Sprint Center as one very important piece of the puzzle here because the entire CBD is economically depressed," says developer Willard. "We're now just waiting to see what happens."

CHAPTER 21

Landover and Other Cities Are Forced to Find New Uses for Old Stadiums

Charles Mahtesian

When the dazzling new Staples Center arena opened in Los Angeles last October, basketball and hockey fans marveled at the $400 million building's amenities. The design, more *Architectural Digest* than *Sports Illustrated*, features massive glass atriums, terrazzo floors, a state-of-the-art scoreboard, restaurants, retail stores and a swank private club. Some hailed it as the most spectacular arena ever built. And yet, on opening night, the *Los Angeles Times* greeted the occasion with this yawning headline: "When Will It Become Obsolete?"

It's a fair question to ask. Staples Center represents the cutting-edge for the time being, but if the nation's stadium- and arena-building boom continues, even gaudy Staples may find itself reaching obsolescence not too far in the future. In that case, it will join a growing herd of white elephants that now clutters the urban and suburban landscape.

The remarkable thing about America's discarded sports facilities is that, for the most part, they are not ancient or dilapidated. Most of them were built within the past 30 years.

They have become casualties of the throwaway stadium syndrome that is afflicting professional sports all over the country.

A few miles outside the nation's capital, in Landover, Maryland, the USAirways Arena sits empty. Considered a state-of-the-art building when it opened in 1973, it has been stripped of its professional basketball and hockey teams. Once the Wizards and Capitals departed for a newly constructed facility in downtown Washington, D.C., the arena was reduced to scrambling for the occasional horse show, concert or rally to fill a few of its 19,000 seats.

Dozens of cities are currently stuck with empty, obsolete or underutilized arenas. According to Fitch ICBA, a bond rating agency, 41 major league sports teams are playing in facilities built since 1990. Another 49 are either seeking new facilities or have them under construction. Approximately $6 billion is projected to be spent on new ones that will open over the next several years. You don't have to be a municipal finance expert or even a sports fan to figure out that for almost every new

Originally published as "Throwaway Stadium," *Governing*, Vol. 13, No. 1, January 2000, by Congressional Quarterly Inc., Washington, D.C. Reprinted with permission of the publisher.

major league palace that opens, another one loses its reason for existence.

Some of the lifeless arenas and stadiums — or at least the properties — do eventually find a productive role to play. Baltimore recently approved a proposal from a nonprofit, church-based group that would turn the site of Memorial Stadium, abandoned home of the Orioles, into a YMCA and housing for low- and moderate-income senior citizens. More often, though, the ultimate fate is simply conversion to asphalt. The site of what used to be Atlanta's Fulton County Stadium is now a parking lot for Turner Field. In Denver, some of the 28 acres occupied by the soon-to-be-razed McNichols Arena will provide parking for a new football stadium.

Like USAirways Arena, some facilities survive by accepting second-banana status, hosting tractor pulls, school graduations and minor league sports. In some instances, that model works well. Philadelphia's Spectrum, the city's premier arena for nearly three decades, now serves to complement the First Union Center, its newer rival, as part of the First Union Complex. The two stadiums engage in joint marketing campaigns, share staffs and are positioned for different event markets. The hockey Flyers and basketball 76ers take advantage of the 126 luxury suites in the new building, while the Spectrum hosts more modestly priced minor league hockey and soccer games, as well as events too small to occasion the newer building.

But arenas in most cities don't have that sort of option. And since many of them are either publicly owned, publicly financed or otherwise integral to a community's development and planning scheme, an ever-increasing number of localities are being forced to come to grips with the harsh economic realities of the throwaway era.

Five years from now, says Bill Dorsey of the Association of Luxury Suite Directors, "just about everyone will have a new field. These things have been romanticized by writers, but these are just buildings. They're a business and they have a price."

The dawn of the throwaway era can be traced back to 1988, when both the Miami Arena and the Palace of Auburn Hills, in Michigan, opened their doors. Both buildings looked glitzy and modern, but the glitz concealed a fundamental difference. The Miami Arena, although built at a cost of $52 million, had 16 luxury suites for well-heeled and free-spending clientele. The Palace boasted 180 suites. Within a matter of months, the fate of both arenas was sealed. The Palace was going to be a success; the Miami Arena was not.

Within a few years, the NBA Miami Heat were looking to flee to a new home more hospitable to the heavy wallets. This year, they got it: the brand-new $185 million AmericanAirlines Arena, with six $500,000-a-year "star boxes," 20 suites, 54 loges and 304 courtside luxury seats. The cheapest premium package sells for $10,000 a year. The Miami Arena, meanwhile, lost not only the Heat but also the National Hockey League Panthers, who received their own new facility in neighboring Broward County.

Today, the 11-year-old, 20,000-seat Miami Arena is used for minor league hockey and a few other not-ready-for-prime-time events. The Detroit Pistons, meanwhile, remain happily ensconced in their Auburn Hills home. "Premium seating is the financial underpinning of the modern arena," says Dorsey. "It is largely responsible for this. Once that started happening, other teams had to do it in order to compete."

Pro sports haven't been so kind to all the suburban arenas. Back in the 1970s and '80s, the trend was for teams to follow the out-migration from the central cities. Now, the trend has been reversed — teams are moving back downtown. Unlike shuttered downtown facilities, the suburban arenas have limited options for reuse.

When an arena is located downtown, it sometimes can be used to complement a convention center trade. That doesn't work for places such as the USAirways Arena, 15 miles beyond the city limits. The suburban white elephant arenas aren't much use for office space, either, so frequently the only choice is to go for commercial development — provided someone can be found who is interested in the property.

As quite a few communities have learned, those customers aren't easy to find. In 1996, when the NFL Detroit Lions announced their move out of the Silverdome in suburban Pontiac, and back to the big city, Pontiac officials hastily convened a task force on the field's 50-yard line to explore alternative uses for the domed stadium. They disbanded just as quickly.

The one consolation for Pontiac has been the Lions' lease on the city-owned Silverdome, which runs until 2004. Since the team plans to break ground on the new stadium sometime this year, they will likely have to pay Pontiac to escape. Meanwhile, Pontiac officials continue to mull over options for future use of the land. The Silverdome is located at the intersection of two major freeways along the I-75 corridor, so an industrial park is one possibility; there is also talk of an Indian gambling casino, with visions of new gold in property-tax payments and thousands of new jobs for local residents. But those dreams are still a long way from fulfillment, or even ground-breaking.

No matter what Pontiac decides, it is unlikely to replicate the solution found by Ohio's rural Richfield Township. Built in the middle of farmland halfway between Akron and Cleveland, the Richfield Coliseum became home in the 1970s to the NBA Cleveland Cavaliers. The Cavaliers' owner gambled that commercial development would surely follow the franchise. He was wrong. The Coliseum bathed in red ink for years, and when the city of Cleveland came calling with a sweetheart arena deal to move the Cavaliers back downtown in 1994, the team jumped at the offer. The owners of the Coliseum, a building whose heating costs alone ran as high as $250,000 per month, decided it made more sense to keep the place dark than to operate it.

Meanwhile, the owners entertained a variety of proposals that included turning the arena into a televangelist's headquarters, a private jail, a movie-production facility, a retirement village, an Olympic training center, or an outlet shopping mall. In the end, though, the Coliseum found a use that no one predicted. In January of last year, the 327-acre property was purchased by the Trust for Public Land, which then transferred it to the National Park Service to become part of the Cuyahoga Valley National Recreation Area. "It doesn't have unique attributes as such, but it does have some wetlands," says Christopher Knopf of the Trust for Public Land. "It was really a preventative action to keep traffic from going through the national park."

For environmentalists and many local residents, the deal represented a major victory in a battle over development that had been going on since the early 1970s. But not everyone was thrilled. When the owners mothballed the Coliseum, local schools took a hard hit from the loss of tax revenues. Now, there will be no chance to recoup those losses, or for any further development at the site.

"The county probably should have stepped up to the plate, bought the facility and the 250 acres and land banked it for long-term economic development," says Summit County Councilman John Bolek, whose district includes the Coliseum site. "It does look nice now, but was it really in our best interests to add 250 acres to the eight or nine thousand acres already in the park?"

CHAPTER 22

Los Angeles and Other Cities Use Community Benefits Agreements to Develop Sports Facilities

Madeline Janis-Aparicio *and* Roxana Tynan

In December 2004, Los Angeles Mayor Jim Hahn held a press conference to celebrate city council approval of a massive plan to modernize L.A. International Airport. A centerpiece of the press conference was a $500 million community benefits agreement (CBA) that would dramatically improve quality of life for low-income communities near LAX.

Aside from the size of the agreement, most striking was the breadth of its support. Labor unions, environmental groups, business leaders, community-based organizations, elected officials — all offered words of praise for this legally binding contract that covered everything from reduction of air and sound pollution to job training to enhanced opportunities for women- and minority-owned businesses.

Months and months of arduous negotiations paved the way for this consensus. In the end, nearly every sector recognized the value of the CBA, both as a means for addressing economic and environmental concerns as well as

a way to transcend the customary acrimony that accompanies large-scale development projects.

The LAX CBA was a groundbreaking achievement for a number of reasons. It was by far the largest such agreement ever negotiated and also the first with a governmental entity rather than a private developer. But perhaps the most significant dimension of the agreement, and the process that led to it, was the broad-based alliance that made it possible. Thus the agreement highlights not only the promise of CBAs as a policy and organizing tool, but also the power of coalition building to advance social justice campaigns.

Coalition Building and the Promise of Community Benefits

Community benefits agreements — project-specific contracts between developers or cities and community organizations — are safeguards to ensure that local community resi-

Originally published as "Power in Numbers: Community Benefits Agreements and the Power of Coalition Building," *Shelterforce*, Issue No. 144, November/December 2005, by the National Housing Institute, Maplewood, NJ. Reprinted with permission of the publisher.

dents share in the benefits of major developments. They allow community groups to have a voice in shaping a project, to press for community benefits that are tailored to their particular needs and to enforce developers' promises.

The CBA process begins with interested members of the community, who identify how a proposed development project can benefit residents and workers. Once a list of potential benefits is determined, community members meet with the developer and/or city representatives to negotiate an agreement. Each CBA is unique, reflecting the needs of a particular community.

The CBA concept was pioneered by the Los Angeles Alliance for a New Economy (LAANE), which in 1998 worked with then City Councilmember Jackie Goldberg to incorporate community benefits provisions into the development agreement for Hollywood and Highland, a large entertainment and retail project in the heart of Hollywood. The first full-fledged CBA came in 2001, when a large coalition of community groups negotiated a far-reaching agreement with the developer of Los Angeles Sports and Entertainment District. This was followed by four more CBAs on projects across Los Angeles. A dozen additional projects in Los Angeles have community benefits provisions incorporated into their respective development agreements.

Many communities across the country are now using the community benefits model. Groups in New York, Milwaukee and San Diego have recently won far-reaching CBAs, while in San Jose two projects have incorporated community benefits provisions into development agreements. Groups in numerous other cities, including Denver, Seattle, Miami and New Haven are actively pursuing community benefits agreements.

At the heart of the community benefits strategy is coalition building. The logic is simple: if enough stakeholders come together with a common vision for economic development, savvy developers are likely to want to negotiate an agreement. The CBA process offers developers an attractive alternative to litigation and polarizing public debates, which can delay or doom a project.

CBAs are critical because of the current "back to the city" movement. For the first time in decades, many large U.S. cities are experiencing population growth. Sports stadiums, entertainment arenas, hotels, office parks, "big box" retail outlets, upscale residential projects and other such developments are occurring much more often in already-inhabited areas. These projects offer tremendous opportunities for low- and moderate-income neighborhood residents, but hold tremendous risks as well.

While many of these projects are bringing sorely needed jobs and tax revenues back to areas that have been disinvested, there is usually no guarantee that the "ripple effects" of the projects will benefit those residents who need them most. CBAs give community residents a role in the process and help ensure that the people who remained loyal to the cities during the darkest years share in the benefits as urban areas are rediscovered.

Developers of these large projects have a particular social responsibility, not only because they are moving into existing communities, but also because taxpayer dollars subsidize their projects. Large redevelopment projects almost always benefit from subsidies such as land parceling through eminent domain, new streets and other infrastructure, property tax reductions or abatements, tax increment financing and industrial revenue bonds or other loans.

The process of negotiating a CBA encourages new alliances among community groups that may care about different issues or have different constituencies. This is critical because developers often use a "divide and conquer" strategy when dealing with community groups, making just enough accommodation to gain the support of one group, while ignoring the concerns of others. (Sometimes this accommodation is seen as little more than a monetary payoff to a single group.) The developer can then claim that there is some community support for the project and obtain necessary government approvals, even though most community issues have not been addressed.

Similarly, a developer may agree to build a project with union construction labor, while ignoring the concerns of those unions whose members will fill the project's permanent jobs, and then claim the project has "labor's support." By addressing many issues and encouraging broad coalitions, the CBA process helps counter these "divide and conquer" ploys.

If neighborhood groups are poorly organized and, therefore, have little leverage over developers and governmental agencies, seeking a CBA will not help and could result in a poor precedent being set for future projects. CBA negotiations cannot be effective without a certain amount of working political capital. Of course, if the CBA negotiation process becomes routine, then community groups' capital should generally increase. In addition, the coalition-building aspect of the CBA negotiation process should increase a community's bargaining position.

One of the advantages of CBAs is their flexibility: community advocates can negotiate for whatever benefits their particular community needs the most. In fact, when community groups come together over a proposed development, it is an excellent occasion to assess the community's needs. This assessment — and the coalition building that can accompany it — can spark organizing and advocacy well beyond any single fight.

A New Model for Social Justice

In order for progressives to build power, they must create broad and permanent coalitions. The price of fragmentation is all too evident in the setbacks of the past three decades. Likewise, the promise of strong, diverse alliances has been demonstrated by numerous victories over the past several years.

In Los Angeles, for example, the success of such high-profile battles as the Justice for Janitors and living wage campaigns was made possible by the emergence of a formidable labor-community coalition that has grown steadily over the last decade and now wields considerable power. This coalition is broad-based and continues to expand its reach to include new constituencies. One critical partner has been the religious community, which has largely been organized by the trailblazing Clergy and Laity United for Economic Justice (CLUE). CLUE has succeeded in mobilizing a large swath of the region's congregations using an interfaith approach that has brought Catholic, Episcopal, Lutheran, Methodist, Unitarian, Jewish, Muslim, Buddhist and other denominations into the battle for social justice. Community-based organizations have also played a central role in coalition building. Some of these are pre-existing issue-based groups, such as housing and environmental organizations, while others have formed around the principle of economic justice. Elected officials have joined the movement as well, as have teachers and academics.

The emergence of the labor/community/clergy model reflects a hard-won realization by each that a progressive agenda simply cannot be advanced without a stable and diverse power base. Equally important is a sophisticated analysis of how to leverage this power. In Los Angeles and a number of other cities, this analysis has given birth to organizations capable of waging a "comprehensive campaign."

The comprehensive campaign model recognizes that a multi-pronged strategy is needed to translate political power into concrete progressive change. Policy, research, organizing, communications, litigation — all must be part of a progressive organization's tactical arsenal. Groups that engage in organizing without a research capacity, for instance, often find themselves stymied because they lack a strategic understanding of the opposition forces arrayed against them. Other groups may have a strong research capacity but are limited without the base provided by an organizing program.

Progressive organizations that have adopted the comprehensive campaign model are winning impressive victories. In 2004, Wal-Mart suffered a crushing electoral defeat in Inglewood at the hands of a labor/community/clergy coalition that also included many elected officials and small business leaders. All the elements of a comprehensive campaign — research, organizing, political advocacy, litigation, communications — were employed to stop Wal-Mart's attempt to build a Supercenter without any public review or planning process. In the end, despite a $1.5 million war chest, Wal-Mart was outflanked by a progressive alliance that drew upon years of power building and strategic savvy to win over public opinion.

The living wage victory in Los Angeles and its aftermath similarly highlight the enormous potential of a model built around a vision of economic fairness and security, supported by power building and a comprehensive strategy. Progressives chose a clear injustice — poverty wages subsidized by tax dollars — and forged a broad-based coalition to address it. Based on credible research, a policy solution was proposed and then advanced through a dynamic organizing and lobbying campaign, while a values-based communications strategy conveyed a powerful message to the public and to policymakers.

In the end, not only did the living wage law pass over the strenuous objection of a popular mayor, but the political culture of the region was transformed. The idea of a living wage is now embedded in the public mind, and it exerts substantial influence on policy debates at the city, county and even state level.

In cities across the country, labor unions and community-based organizations are joining forces. These labor/community partnerships form the cornerstone of powerful coalitions capable of advancing a progressive agenda.

The Future of Community Benefits

Over the past several years, community benefits work has evolved into a bona fide movement, with an increasing number of organizations across the country using the CBA model as an integral part of their advocacy. The growth of the CBA model is inextricably linked to the creation of new broad-based coalitions willing to embrace partnerships with both traditional and nontraditional allies.

As progressives seek to reverse the gains of the right and advance an agenda of social and economic justice, they would do well to study the community benefits movement, which has offered a way to transcend the differences that too often have splintered progressive forces. Indeed, community benefits provide a potent example of coalition building that extends beyond progressive groups to a wide array of stakeholders. Such alliances point the way toward a promising future in which the common aspirations of the majority are harnessed for social progress.

CHAPTER 23

Memphis Uses Minor League Team's Stadium to Revitalize Their Downtown

Desiree French

When Dean Jernigan and his wife, Kristi, moved back home to Tennessee in the early 1990s, downtown Memphis — once a thriving metropolis on the east bank of the Mississippi River — was still recovering from the riots of 1968 and urban flight. Several blocks languished in disrepair. Abandoned buildings, boarded-up storefronts, empty lots, and run-down pornographic shops littered the landscape, robbing the city of its vibrancy.

A few bright spots kept the pulse of downtown Memphis beating — the swanky Peabody Hotel, renovated just a decade earlier, and a rejuvenated Beale Street, the home of the Blues. Both projects, while critical to downtown's revitalization, would be no match for what was to come.

Dean, the founder, former president, and chief executive officer of Storage USA in Memphis, embarked on a journey that would take the city to new heights.

It began with a single phone call. Jernigan was told the local Double-A minor league baseball team was leaving Memphis for Jacksonville. He responded by purchasing a new Triple-A franchise, the Memphis Redbirds,

the farm team for the St. Louis Cardinals. Despite the skeptics, he also built a $72 million baseball stadium in downtown Memphis just blocks from the Mississippi River. Autozone Park, with more than 14,000 seats, would become the highest-priced baseball complex built in minor league baseball. The Memphis Redbirds Baseball Foundation, which Dean and Kristi founded in 1998, would be the first 501(c)(3) nonprofit in professional sports to own a stadium and a team.

The decision to locate the ballpark downtown was greeted by some with scorn and disbelief. There were those who thought it should be in the eastern suburbs, near the game's fan base. But Kristi was adamant. "The downtown," she explains, "is our living room." She argued that it is where visitors are taken to get a firsthand glimpse of the city, to absorb its culture, and to be entertained.

Kristi insisted the ballpark could help fill a huge void downtown and have an impact that would transcend baseball. She was right. The eight-block baseball project also included the preservation of historic buildings; the construction of new commercial, residential, and

Originally published as "Community Builders Profile," *Urban Land*, Vol. 63, No. 4, February 2004, by the Urban Land Institute, Washington, D.C. Reprinted with permission of the publisher.

educational facilities; and the transformation of vacant lots and run-down buildings into viable space.

According to Jeff Sanford, president of the Center City Commission, a government entity that coordinates public/private partnerships to redevelop the downtown, "Dean and Kristi's vision has been instrumental in the turnaround of downtown Memphis. Their decision to locate the Triple-A ballpark downtown proved not only to be the right one but a catalytic one." Little by little, restaurants sprung up, shops opened, and additional development plans surfaced.

Not so impressed was the couple's first banker, who pulled out of the project, leaving the Jernigans to fend for themselves. They began construction on the stadium in 1999, using their own money. The city and county kicked in $8.5 million, and $72 million worth of tax-exempt bonds were eventually sold to finance the project. As the Jernigans searched for a new lender, however, the construction site sat idle. Before long, it became the butt of local jokes and was dubbed the "Big Hole."

No one's laughing now. Today, the Memphis Ballpark District, a 20-acre site, includes the Autozone — which opened in 2000 — renovated office space, a 315-unit apartment building, a parking garage, and a public elementary school. Sanford estimates development worth $75 million to $100 million is now taking place in the Ballpark District, which was the recipient of a ULI Award for Excellence in 2002.

What is perhaps most remarkable about the Jernigans is their selflessness. From the beginning, they ceded ownership of the team and the stadium to the Memphis Redbirds Baseball Foundation. The foundation, made up of local civic and business leaders, funds two inner-city youth programs — Returning Baseball to the Inner City (RBI) and Sports Teams Returning in the Public Education System (STRIPES). Since 1998, more than 3,000 children have gone through RBI's summer program, and another 6,500 have participated in STRIPES through neighborhood schools.

Proceeds from the stadium — ticket sales, concessions, naming rights — are filtered back to the community, which pleases the Jernigans no end.

Dean says the motivation behind funding these charities is to challenge inner-city kids to learn life skills. "Baseball teaches kids how to be a team member, how to compete, and how to lose and win. It also teaches them a skill that can be used to get athletic scholarships," he says. Adds Kristi, "It keeps them engaged."

"To say Dean and Kristi had an impact on Memphis would probably be an understatement," says R. Marc Jordan, president of the Memphis Regional Chamber of Commerce. "The stadium has received the most acclaim. But there have been other things that they have done. It didn't stop or start with that. They do a lot behind the scenes."

A few years ago, Dean assisted with negotiations that brought to town the Memphis Grizzlies professional basketball team. With support from others, he organized two local groups — MPACT Memphis and Memphis Tomorrow.

Memphis Tomorrow is a small group of CEOs of major companies. They meet regularly to work on significant breakthrough initiatives that focus on such topics as early childhood development, crime, and redeveloping the city's music industry. MPACT's members are emerging leaders aged 40 and under who are being groomed to participate in the community, serve on local boards, and become active in the political process.

Kristi, an investment manager and senior vice president at Green Square Capital Management in Memphis, has a key role in the city's future development as chairperson of the Riverfront Development Corporation, a nonprofit that contracts with the city to operate and manage development along the Memphis riverfront.

Like her husband, Kristi is also the impetus behind a few initiatives, including the Urban Arts Commission and Light It Up. The latter is a downtown illumination project that supports highlighting and promoting the city's buildings, structures, and bridges with lights that enhance their appeal.

Kristi admits to having the civic bug. "I would drive around downtown after the park was built and say, 'We can do that, and we do that.' You just see so much that can be done."

What's next for this couple? Only time will tell. But for now, says Dean, "I'm very proud of what we've been able to do in Memphis.... I think it's community building at its best."

CHAPTER 24

Miami Grapples with Use of Public Funding to Finance New Sports Stadium

David Wilkening

The once popular practice of spending public money to finance sports stadiums has recently been striking out. That's no surprise when you consider the books economists and journalists are writing these days: "Loot, loot, loot for the home team," is a chapter in a 2005 book called *The Great American Jobs Scam* by Greg LeRoy, founder of the Washington, D.C.–based nonprofit development watchdog group Good Jobs First. The 1999 book *Field of Schemes* offers a similar take. Its author, journalist Neil DeMause, sums up the situation as follows: "In almost eight years of reporting on stadium deals, I've spoken to every economist I can find about the impact of sports stadiums. And I've yet to find a single independent economist (by which I mean one not actually working for a sports team or league) who thinks that stadiums are any use as an economic engine."

LeRoy explains in his book that the whole system of public financing is usually traced to the 1950s. Until then, team owners paid for their own stadiums — with few excep-

tions. The trend started in 1953 with the first team relocation in half a century, the Boston Braves' move to Milwaukee. They were lured there with a new stadium built with public money. Since then, politicians everywhere have been "taken in by the assumption that the presence of a professional sports team is a leading contributor to the vitality of cities," LeRoy writes. "That notion has so captivated politicians that they are willing to give sport team owners subsidies that are far beyond what other private-sector businesses can hope for."

Earlier this year, city and county officials in Miami stepped up to the plate with a $490 million plan to finance a new stadium for professional baseball's Florida Marlins. The Marlins, a relatively young team, have only been in the major leagues for a decade, but have won two World Series in that time. "The Fish," as they are affectionately known, have for years wanted a stadium of their own (they currently share space with the NFL's Miami Dolphins in Dolphin Stadium). Since 2000, a pro-stadium contingent for the Marlins has appealed to the

Originally published as "Footing the Bill for a Ballpark," *The Next American City*, No. 15, Summer 2007, by the Next American City Inc., Philadelphia, PA. Reprinted with permission of the publisher.

Florida state legislature six times to help fill the whopping hole in their financing plans. This year, the city of Miami, Miami-Dade County, and the Marlins teamed up to appeal to the state for $60 million.

Though the funding bill has failed before, an aura of excitement surrounded this year's plan, which would generate stadium money largely from Miami-area tourists and not Miami residents. Miami-Dade County would pitch in $145 million in hotel and sports facilities taxes. The city of Miami would contribute $108 million in tourist development and hotel taxes, and the Marlins would contribute $207 million — $45 million up front and $162 million in future rent payments to the county. The Marlins would also cover potential cost overruns. The new Florida governor, Charlie Crist, a Republican who took office in January, is a baseball fan whose first job after law school was as an attorney for minor league baseball. Miami Mayor Manny Diaz came out strongly in favor of the latest plan, as did Cuban-born Miami-Dade County Commissioner Pepe Diaz. Even though, according to the Baseball Almanac website, estimated attendance at Marlins games has slipped from 37,893 people per game in 1993 to 14,384 per game last year, Pepe Diaz says his constituents in District 12 are firmly behind the new ballpark. "I think [the plan] benefits us in many ways. Whether or not there are economic benefits, I don't know, but I'm sure it helps out with jobs," he said in an interview.

In early May, however, the Florida state Senate failed to approve the $60 million funding bill before the end of the legislative session, even though the Florida House had already approved it. In other words, Miami and the Marlins will have to wait until next year. "I have a warm spot in my heart for baseball, so I think we ought to keep trying," Governor Crist told the Associated Press. Mayor Diaz said he was disappointed but would not give

up trying to keep the team in South Florida. He said the city might look to local resources to fund the project without a state contribution.

The question is: should Miami bother? Nationwide, there is growing opposition to funding sports programs with taxpayer monies. In a 1997 Rasmussen poll on the subject, 64 percent of respondents answered "no" to the question of whether taxpayer dollars should be used to build a professional sports facility. Still, Adam M. Zaretsky, an economist at the Federal Reserve Bank of St. Louis, wrote in a 2001 policy paper on the subject, "Should cities pay for sports facilities?" that between 1987 and 1999, 55 stadiums and arenas were refurbished or built in the U.S. with more than $8.7 billion. Fifty-seven percent of that, or roughly $5 billion, was financed by taxpayers.

Clearly, the debate about whether stadiums are good for cities extends far beyond Miami. The NFL's San Diego Chargers spent five years trying to secure funds and a location to replace the outmoded, 40-year-old Qualcomm Stadium. San Diego residents also want a new stadium: in a January 2006 poll conducted by the *San Diego Union-Tribune*, 68.6 percent of 27,575 residents polled said the city should donate land to build a new football stadium. An overwhelming 95.6 percent said they would support a new stadium if the Chargers paid for it, along with the requisite infrastructure improvements.

According to the proposal the Chargers made to the city in October 2005, the new football stadium, completely funded by the Chargers and their development partner, would be built on 60 of the 166 acres of current Qualcomm Stadium land in Mission Valley. The remaining acreage would be used for parks, streets, parking garages, and commercial development. But as the Chargers' general counsel, Mark Fabiani, explains, the plan didn't pan out because the city of San Diego, teetering on the brink of bankruptcy, decided to set aside the question of stadium funding for other priorities.

The Chargers consequently could not find a suitable development partner, according to Fabiani, "not because the project wouldn't have worked out, but because no one wanted to get mired in the city of San Diego's chaos." Not surprisingly, last year the city amended the terms of its lease with the Chargers so that they could begin to look elsewhere for a home. And plenty of new cities are lining up to court them, including nearby Chula Vista, National City, and Oceanside, California. Even Las Vegas, Nevada, showed interest, though the Chargers' contract restricts relocation talks to cities within San Diego County. "Private funding for a stadium is very difficult to pull off," Fabiani says. "In California, people are just not eager to subsidize these stadiums."

Stadiums have fared better in other cities. In Minneapolis, for example, after ten years of struggling with the issue, the Minnesota Twins last year reached an agreement on a new $522 million stadium that will be partially funded by a sales tax of 15 cents for every $100 in sales in Hennepin County, where the team plays ball.

But there seems to be a growing heap of evidence that stadiums don't make such good long-term investments for cities. Robert Baade, an economics professor at Lake Forest College in Lake Forest, Illinois, studied baseball stadiums specifically. He looked at the per capita income in 30 cities that have built new sports stadiums over the past 30 years and found that in 27 of the cities, there was no observable economic impact.

"In the other three cities, income looked to have gone down as a result of the stadium," Baade says. Stadiums do offer some clear benefits to cities. "Bars next to stadiums see an increase in customers on game days," Baade says. But even that has a down side, however, because the bars only do well when a team is winning. "When a team is losing, who wants to go out and celebrate another loss?"

Baade found that, "In only a small fraction of the cases examined does manufacturing activity ... correlate significantly with the presence of a new or renovated stadium. We conclude that measurable economic benefits to area residents are not large enough to justify stadium subsidies and that the debate must turn to immeasurable intangible benefits like fan identification and civic pride."

Stadium boosters in Miami are vowing to try again next year, especially if it means keeping the Marlins from pulling up stakes and heading to a new city. One man watching the Marlins' quest with special interest is Jack McKeon, the former Marlins manager who led the team to their World Series victory in 2003. Now 76 and semi-retired in Elon, North Carolina, the cigar-smoking, tough-talking McKeon (nicknamed Trader Jack) still works as a part-time consultant for the Marlins, mainly as a talent scout. "It would be a shame if they don't have baseball in Miami," he says. The sentiment is certainly shared by South Florida Marlin fans, whatever their numbers.

CHAPTER 25

Montgomery Receives Income from Stadium Operations to Offset Public Expenses

Jim Noles

In the quirky world of minor league baseball, the moniker of the Montgomery, Alabama, Biscuits is in a league of its own. But while the name may be unique, the city's decision to give the team a downtown stadium home is not. The idea of coupling downtown minor league ballparks with urban redevelopment efforts is one that smaller cities employ with increasing frequency. But can such stadiums actually serve as catalysts for urban revitalization?

In Montgomery, where there was no shortage of naysayers, a cadre of believers kept the faith, recalling the glory days of minor league baseball in Montgomery—1972 to 1977—when the Montgomery Rebels won the Southern League title five times in six seasons. These believers included Mayor Bobby Bright and the Montgomery Riverfront Development Foundation (MRDF), a collection of civic and business leaders united in a mission of revitalizing the city's downtown commercial district and sharing the mayor's belief in the role baseball could play in fulfilling that mission.

"Even back in the 1990s, studies had shown that another minor league baseball team would be viable in Montgomery," says MRDF chair Gordon Martin. "The main questions were where the team would play and, if necessary, how to finance the construction of the stadium. With regard to location, the choice was either downtown or in the eastern suburbs."

As far as MRDF and Bright were concerned, downtown was the answer. "Downtown sports venues are almost always a positive for a community," asserts Sharon Gaber, associate dean of Auburn University's College of Architecture, Design, and Construction and chair of the university's community planning program. "New stadiums generate a series of backward-and-forward linkages in the surrounding neighborhoods. Businesses such as merchandise shops, bars, restaurants, and gas stations — these are places that people patronize before and after the game."

Speaking as one who has long studied the potential economic impact of downtown

Originally published as "The Minor Leagues," *Urban Land*, Vol. 64, No. 7, July 2005, by the Urban Land Institute, Washington, D.C. Reprinted with permission of the publisher.

stadiums, Tim Chapin, assistant professor of urban planning at Florida State University, agrees with Gaber, but with an important caveat. "Downtown stadiums like we've seen in places such as Toledo and Durham have to be part of a larger package," he asserts. "They have to be part of a larger development plan. Absent any other efforts at downtown redevelopment, a really nice, shiny new stadium downtown will remain just that — a really nice, shiny new stadium downtown. But if a community uses it to send a signal that it is willing to invest in its downtown and then follows through on that promise, downtown stadiums can be a magic part of the formula."

Convincing the majority of Montgomery's residents to buy into the stadium's $26 million price tag presented a challenge. When Bright floated the idea of financing the stadium's construction with a two-cent increase in the city's lodging tax, nearly half of the people polled opposed the idea. Nevertheless, the Montgomery city council, relying on pro forma earnings projections for the stadium's operations, voted 7–1 to build what would become known as Riverwalk Stadium.

Two months later, the stadium's ownership group, Professional Sports Marketing, announced that it had acquired the Orlando Rays and was moving the Class Double-A farm club of the Tampa Bay Devil Rays to Montgomery. A name-the-team contest soon followed, garnering some 2,800 entries and producing the team's new identity — the Montgomery Biscuits.

Mindful of the challenges it would face, Montgomery selected a distinctive location for its new stadium, tucked in a warehouse district south of the Alabama River and just down the railroad tracks from the Union Station railway terminal. During the Civil War, the Confederacy housed 700 Union prisoners of war at the site in "a foul, vermin-abounding cotton depot," according to the nearby historical marker. In later years, a pair of freight depot warehouses belonging to the Western Railway of Alabama replaced the cotton depot and were still standing a century later when Montgomery decided to build its new stadium there.

Although one depot building had to be demolished, architects HOK Sports incorporated the second building as the front of the new stadium, serving as a ready reminder for Biscuits fans of the heyday of Montgomery's railroads. The Biscuits took to the field for their first home game in April 2004 against the Huntsville Stars in front of an overflow crowd of 7,378.

For Montgomery, however, the 7,000-seat stadium came with a hefty price tag — $26 million. To help finance construction, the city signed Professional Sports Marketing to a 20-year lease. The company guaranteed a minimum of $200,000 in annual rent, provided to the city through a 10 percent cut of ticket, food, beverage, souvenir, and advertising sales. Montgomery also collects 33 percent of the rental income from the stadium's 20 luxury suites, and if stadium naming rights are ever sold, Montgomery will collect a share of that money, also.

From a financial standpoint, the Biscuits' first season at their stadium lived up to Montgomery's best expectations. The team drew 322,946 fans, trailing only the Jacksonville Suns in attendance in the Southern League. According to figures published by the local *Montgomery Advertiser* newspaper, the Biscuits' inaugural season produced almost $700,000 in rent and another $175,000 in sales tax for the city.

Similar hope can be found in the streets surrounding the new stadium. The city has embarked on a $29 million renovation and expansion of downtown's existing civic center, coupled with the construction of an adjacent four-star, $53 million hotel. Nearby, over-looking the Alabama River, a new amphitheater offers a venue for outdoor concerts. Martin also enumerates other benefits. "One, by developing the area to the east of the stadium for parking, it gave us the focus to clean up a rather dilapidated part of town," he says. "Two, just across the street from the stadium, the Montgomery Brew Pub and Restaurant has reported a 20 percent increase in business; it is undergoing an expansion right now. Third, across from the brew pub, local devel-opers are turning three buildings into loft apartments and condominiums."

Other improvements include a recent $8 million renovation of the once-empty Winter-Loeb Building, which is located across the street from the stadium and now boasts a 100 percent occupancy rate. Nearby, the former Schloss & Kahn grocery warehouse is also being renovated, and plans are afoot for the construction of what will be called Grocer's Alley, a New Orleans–style promenade of restaurants and stores.

CHAPTER 26

New York Sets Example for Partnership with Community Groups for Affordable Housing at Arena Project Site

John Atlas

In June 2004, inside Brooklyn's Borough Hall, a stage was packed with New York's most important political, labor, community and religious leaders. One of them, Bertha Lewis, executive director of New York ACORN, leaned forward, stretched her arms into a "V" and bellowed to the audience of 1,300, "What do we want?"

"Jobs! Housing! Hoops!" the crowd answered. It was an often-repeated mantra at this rally announcing ACORN's (Association of Community Organizations for Reform Now) support for New York–based Forest City Ratner Companies' (FCRC) Atlantic Yards sports arena and urban development plan.

Bruce Ratner, FCRC chief executive officer and chairman, planned to move his professional basketball team, the New Jersey Nets, to Brooklyn into a new, 19,000-seat arena, the crown jewel of a $2.5 billion development that would include 60-story skyscrapers totaling over 2.4 million square feet of office and retail space, and some housing. The Atlantic Yards development, designed by celebrity architect Frank Gehry, would be situated in an already congested downtown area, affecting at least four neighborhoods of low-rise brownstones, inhabited by an army of 1970s-era urban homesteaders, "old lefties," ex-hippies and young activists.

Outside Borough Hall, protestors—mostly middle-class activists—accused Ratner of "Manhattanizing" Brooklyn and questioned ACORN's backing. Why wasn't ACORN—the leftist, poor people's organization known for organizing campaigns against corporate abuse and political corruption—outside on the picket lines protesting against political cronyism and developer greed?

ACORN was being accused of "selling out" by supporting a deal that would funnel huge government concessions to a private development that will increase population, burden traffic, alter the Brooklyn skyline and bulldoze many residents through eminent domain condemnations.

Still, Lewis confidently led ACORN into supporting one of the largest and most con-

Originally published as "The Battle in Brooklyn," *Shelterforce*, No. 144, November/December 2005, by the National Housing Institute, Maplewood, NJ. Reprinted with permission of the publisher.

troversial building projects proposed in New York City in decades.

Let's Make a Deal

Since the 1960s, numerous attempts have been made to bring a major league sports facility to New York City. Owners of the Mets, the Jets and even the Yankees couldn't do it. Former Mayor Rudy Giuliani tried and failed. There were too many obstacles to overcome, especially community opposition. The massive arena development would require the condemnation of hundreds of housing units, tax breaks by the city, the purchase of Metropolitan Transportation Authority rail yards and lots of government subsidies. Ratner would also need community support to help him secure the backing of city and state officials.

When Lewis and other ACORN staff heard about this project, their first thought was to oppose it, to stop the rampant gentrification occurring in downtown Brooklyn, especially the displacement of black and brown, low- and moderate-income folks. ACORN's members were leery of the Nets arena project, but their overwhelming concern was the lack of affordable housing. Their initial opposition turned to irresistible support after ACORN leaders came up with a plan that members couldn't refuse.

In January 2004, Lewis led about 30 activists into Forest City's boardroom to propose a partnership that would preserve profits for FCRC and provide major benefits for disadvantaged Brooklynites. ACORN would help sell the Atlantic Yards project to government agencies, community groups and the media. In exchange, ACORN wanted an unprecedented 50 percent of the proposed 4,500 rental units set aside as below-market, affordable apartments — an unusually large share of subsidized housing for a private development.

"If we can pull this off," says Lewis, "it would represent a breakthrough ... a model for big city development projects."

Partnering with ACORN was not a stretch for Ratner; he understood the benefits. Before becoming a developer, he served as New York City's commissioner of consumer affairs from 1978 to 1982, during Mayor Ed Koch's administration. And he was director of the Model Cities Program under Mayor John Lindsay's administration. (His brother Michael heads the Center for Constitutional Rights, the public interest law firm founded by the late radical lawyer, William Kunstler.) At the unveiling of the Atlantic Yards plan, Ratner stated, "Great urban planning incorporates many different uses into a cohesive neighborhood — and truly great urban planning invites the public to participate in the space, whether they work there or live there or they're drawn there to visit." But critics charge that this project is far from great urban planning.

In an effort to carve out a place for low-income families in this mammoth development project, ACORN, along with several allies, spent more than a year negotiating a community benefits agreement with FCRC. The agreement was to provide poor and working-class people with more affordable housing, more cultural activities and more jobs. And if ACORN succeeded, it would have triumphed over community opposition and reaffirmed itself as a serious political force in the city. At a press conference on May 19, 2005, ACORN, New York City Mayor Michael Bloomberg and Ratner announced that an agreement had been reached.

A Community Victory

The centerpiece of the community benefits agreement was the 50 percent set-aside for affordable housing in one of the world's most expensive cities. The CBA would also provide job opportunities and other services for low-income residents — from hiring to contracting to day care services. Twenty percent of the rental units was earmarked for low-income households and 30 percent for middle-income households. Rent payments would be subsidized by the New York City Housing Development Corporation, a state public-benefit corporation which plans to use a combination of bonds and reserves from investments to finance the subsidies.

The plan, developed by ACORN's housing expert, Ismene Speliotis, sets rents at 30 percent of the household's income. Speliotis even insisted that ACORN be given the responsibility of marketing the units. (Another point of contention for critics.) "Nobody is going to care as much as ACORN that the appropriate people are marketed to, reached and housed," says Speliotis.

To keep the displacement rate low, the agreement stipulates that displaced property owners will be fairly compensated and that displaced tenants will be given a new, comparable apartment at their existing rent in the new complex. Minority-owned and women-owned construction firms will receive 20 percent and 10 percent (respectively) of the construction contracts, and public housing residents and low-income people from the immediate area would have priority for any jobs.

The seven other signatories of the agreement were Downtown Brooklyn Neighborhood Alliance, Brooklyn United for Innovative Local Development, the All-Faith Council of Brooklyn, First Atlantic Terminal Housing Committee, Downtown Brooklyn Education Consortium, Public Housing Communities and the New York State Association of Minority Contractors.

ACORN believes this deal will have a domino effect, that the agreement can be used as a model to show other developers that the interests and needs of the local community can be served.

Despite the unprecedented agreement, some wondered whether they had compromised too much. Was this the best agreement ACORN could have gotten? Lewis and other ACORN leaders decided that building affordable housing was worth it. Lewis, speaking to a New York City reporter, said "...that when you take all of it together, this is a net gain for Brooklyn especially, and for New York City."

Controlling Gentrification

To Lewis the battle is really about who will benefit from accelerated gentrification in Brooklyn. She believes that some degree of gentrification is inevitable, given the housing pressures facing Manhattan and with more professionals putting down roots in the other boroughs.

Moreover, Lewis believes ACORN's plan will result in a mix of upscale, middle-income and poor people. Neighborhoods that only have the very poor — or what sociologists call "high poverty" areas — have the worst schools and public services, as well as the highest crime rates. The question is whether a neighborhood can be "improved" without its long-term low-income residents being pushed out.

ACORN is betting that by expanding the overall number of both market-rate and subsidized housing units in the area it will help end the tug-of-war between the poor and professional class for the existing housing stock. And by creating 15,000 new jobs that will provide low-income residents with living wages, Atlantic Yards will ultimately help improve the lives of Brooklyn's poor and working-class residents.

While Brooklyn has become the place of choice for many upscale households, more than 20 percent of its two and half million residents live below the poverty line. In a place where the working poor and middle class are already being driven out by rent gouging and gentrification, arguments from the gentrifying class about its right to preserve its neighborhood are not very compelling.

Pragmatism vs. Radicalism

For 35 years ACORN has tried to mix political pragmatism and radical ideas. Unlike ideologues on both ends of the political spectrum, ACORN knows that the perfect is often the enemy of the good. It understands the art of compromise, but only after pushing the limits by mobilizing its grassroots base through confrontation and protest. "Rather than wait until something happens to us," says Lewis, "we go out and help shape the results."

If ACORN had joined the opposition, it was unlikely the Atlantic Yards deal would prevail. Instead, ACORN (the activist, poor people's organization) and Ratner (the rich developer) found a way to work together for the common good. "We've been in that community for 22 years," Lewis says. It's ACORN's mission to protect it.

At the end of 2005, the Atlantic Yards development is a long way from fruition. There's still the state environmental review, the Public Authorities Control Board approval and, of course, more community opposition. And if Atlantic Yards gets built, ACORN will need all of its muscle to ensure that promises are fulfilled and the poor are protected.

CHAPTER 27

Newark's Proposed Arena Sparks Political Debate About City's Future

Jason Stevenson

Three Newark city council members made all the usual arrangements to organize a March 2 press conference to announce their opposition to the city's downtown arena proposal: They reserved the council chambers, stacked the audience with supporters, invited local TV and newspaper reporters and crafted a highly critical press release. They did not, however, invite Mayor Sharpe James and the city's business administrator, Richard Monteilh, the two most vocal supporters of a Newark arena.

But as Augusto Amador, the East Ward councilman and leader of the council's anti-arena faction, was about to finish his opening statement, an angry-looking Mayor James and Monteilh [pronounced MonTAY] burst into the room. Dressed in black warm-ups, James, a former track coach, swaggered in poised for a fight. Monteilh wore a business suit, but mirrored the mayor's belligerence as they sat down loudly in the front. Amador paused, visibly unnerved by the appearance of rivals, and then continued his statement. But from that point on, the press conference was over. A skirmish had begun.

A combustible mixture of rivalry and intimidation has long fueled Newark politics, and for many of those present the meeting's chaotic turn was not a surprise. Amador and his colleagues blasted away at the mayor — accusing him of pursuing a fiscally unsound arena to satisfy his ego. They objected to using public dollars to finance two-thirds of the arena's $300 million cost and argued that the city's chief problem was the rise in property taxes caused by its first revaluation in four decades.

Unwilling simply to listen, Mayor James jumped up to respond. He parried their attacks by stating that the city council determines taxes, not the mayor, and he accused Amador of lying about his record. Setting out his case for the arena, James bellowed, "This project is about creating thousands of jobs for Newark residents!" As the invective increased on both sides, an exasperated Amador shut down the press conference.

For all their expended energy, rarely do Newark's political representatives get it right. Stripped of the hyperbole and finger pointing, the arena involves a simple economic ques-

Originally published as "Arena Politics in Newark," *Shelterforce*, No. 135, May/June 2004, by the National Housing Institute, Maplewood, NJ. Reprinted with permission of the publisher.

tion: Is the project's initial public and private investment likely to encourage additional development that will raise tax revenue and create jobs for residents? This question, and its complicated answer, are missing from the debate. Neither side offers convincing arguments for or against the arena. And woven into their disagreement are a dozen past feuds that hobble any rational discussion.

It is becoming increasingly clear that the real problem is *not* a dissembling city government or a disjointed community, but rather the absence of commonly accepted economic development priorities, and no discernible effort by the key players to develop them. The arena fight is merely the latest outburst of Newark's decades long shouting-match over what kind of city it should be.

The Downtown Core

Two-dozen acres of abandoned buildings and parking lots, situated less than a thousand feet from Newark City Hall, are targeted for the 18,000-seat arena. Ranks of parked cars outnumber people in this neighborhood that was once a hub for small-scale manufacturing, but now hardly stirs. The site is adjacent to the noisiest and busiest blocks of the city: Newark's transportation hub of Penn Station, the Gateway office towers containing thousands of commuters and the city's retail epicenter at the crossroads of Broad and Market streets. "This is the perfect location for the arena, the best place in New Jersey," says Monteilh.

The arena is slated as the home ice for the New Jersey Devils hockey team and represents the latest manifestation of the city's effort to host a professional franchise. The city also announced in May that an expansion team of the Major Indoor Soccer League would join the Devils in the new arena, drawing fans from the Portuguese, Brazilian and other Latino communities that continue to grow in the city's East and North wards.

Since 1998 the city has sought to place a sports facility in downtown Newark, coming close several times. But the current arena is not a stand-alone project. It is part of Newark's "Downtown Core Redevelopment District," an ambitious plan announced by Mayor James in February. Surrounding the arena will be a municipal building for the Newark Board of Education, a 300-room hotel, a 3,500-car parking garage and significant office and retail space. It is an enormous undertaking for a city that often dreams big.

The conference table in Monteilh's City Hall office displays a model of the Downtown Core District. He describes the arena as an engine able to transform dozens of city blocks. Indeed, the model's white cardboard boxes represent planned construction to be scattered thickly throughout the downtown, and even into residential neighborhoods. "The arena is critical to the success of the Core," Monteilh says. "It is the catalyst. Without the arena, we would probably not pursue the other buildings."

High-priced sports stadiums built at public expense are generally unpopular with taxpayers, and opposition to these projects has gained currency since the 1998 book *Field of Schemes* rebuked them as welfare for wealthy team owners. To counter these attacks, Mayor James claimed in a Newark *Star-Ledger* op-ed that the arena is secondary to the Downtown Core's primary goal of "building and revitalizing a city," for once playing down his famous passion for the arena. Meanwhile, City Hall has cranked out numerous press releases predicting the core project will create 13,500 permanent jobs and generate $1.15 billion in new construction and $28 million in new taxes for Newark. But no detailed financial figures or market studies have been offered to support these projections. The state's decision to renovate the nearby Continental Arena, the Devils' current home, could hurt a Newark arena's ability to attract non-sporting events. Moreover, the Devils lose $10 million a year, according to a 2003 review of the National Hockey League, and the Major Indoor Soccer League has had an unstable history. When pressed, city officials respond that it is too early for details, and point out that the mayor has appointed a "blue ribbon" panel to advise him on all financial issues. The panel announced in late April that it was still gathering information and will issue an opinion this summer.

But that hasn't stopped the city from deciding to spend its money. In early May the state's Local Finance Board and the Newark City Council approved the city's financing plan, in which the Newark Housing Authority will sell bonds to raise about $220 million. According to the *Star-Ledger*, the city plans to spend $210 million from that sale on the arena — about 30 percent of the city's annual budget. (The Devils will pay the balance of $100 million.) The remaining $10 million from the bond sale would be spent on neighborhood and capital improvement projects. The city will pay off the bonds with the annual lease payments of $12.5 million received from the Port Authority of New York and New Jersey (PA) for the right to operate Newark's marine terminal.

Newark has been involved in a long-running lawsuit against the port authority for allegedly cheating the city out of almost $2 billion under the previous lease. In 2002 Monteilh concluded an agreement with the authority to settle the lawsuit and provide Newark with a payment of several hundred million dollars to fund a "capital project" — a thinly veiled reference to a downtown arena. Some Newark residents say the money could be put to better use elsewhere, and have filed a lawsuit to block the city's plan. Thus, the

$200 million PA windfall both enables the administration to finance an arena, and exposes the city to legal challenges by those who oppose it. But while the lawsuit slowly meanders through the courts, conditions in Newark have inhibited a wider public debate about the project.

An Elusive Renaissance

Newark today lives with two conflicting myths. Newark is not, as some suburban residents still imagine, a bombed out wasteland of public housing towers and stolen cars. But neither is the city undergoing the full-throttle "renaissance" that Mayor James touts.

Mayor James is Newark's biggest booster and arguably the most powerful politician in New Jersey. During his 18 years as mayor the city has achieved some impressive gains, including the 1997 opening of the New Jersey Performing Arts Center (NJPAC). The $180 million, 2,700-seat concert hall has drawn visitors from the city and the suburbs, despite skeptics who scoffed at a concert hall located just a dozen miles from New York's Lincoln Center — *and* in downtown Newark. Nonetheless, the city's expectations for NJPAC as a catalyst for further development have yet to be fulfilled.

In 1999 the city joined with Essex County to build Riverfront Stadium for the Newark Bears, a storied minor league baseball team that played in Newark until 1949, and whose Web site now proclaims the team to be "Leading Off the Renaissance." The stadium was one of the most expensive minor league parks ever built, with Newark fronting half of its $36 million price tag. The stadium, plagued by cost overruns, poor attendance and few sponsors, costs Essex County taxpayers a million and a half dollars a year in debt service. And like the current arena project, the minor league stadium received tremendous support from Mayor James. Many Newark residents recall the fantastic promises about NJPAC and Riverfront Stadium — and are approaching the Downtown Core District with considerable skepticism.

Ray Codey, head of economic development at New Community Corporation (NCC) in the city's Central Ward, calls Newark's neighborhoods "the heartbeat of a city" that have nonetheless been neglected in favor of downtown development. Codey says that most of the neighborhood development that has occurred has been small-scale retail or housing, principally financed and completed by community groups and state agencies.

Alfred Faiella, Newark's former deputy mayor for economic development, defends the city's downtown preference by stressing that core projects produce "long-term commercial viability" not found in neighborhoods. Faiella, who ran the city's development office for three decades, has seen his legacy continue under Monteilh. Monteilh believes the downtown arena would best "leverage" the PA funds to create opportunities for more revenue. "Anything else would be pissing that money away," he says.

But one group of Newark residents disagrees with that assessment. In November 2002, the organization SCORE (School, Community, Opportunities, Revaluation and Emergencies) filed a lawsuit on behalf of six Newark residents to challenge the city's use of the port authority lease. "My clients don't want public money to support this arena," says SCORE attorney Ira Karasick. "They believe the city's financial policy is not only unsound, but illegal." Plaintiff William Stewart, a resident of Newark since 1947, says the arena was not a major motivation for the original lawsuit, "This case is about Newark's senior citizens having problems with higher property taxes."

SCORE's lawsuit accuses the administration of several illegalities. But the heart of the case involves a link between the PA settlement and a 1999 state law requiring that the city put aside certain revenues for property tax relief. According to Karasick, the administration violated laws governing how cities raise and spend public money to convert the PA lease into cash for the arena. As he sees it, the city should devote the $200 million settlement to address Newark's social concerns, including property tax relief. The city council's recent approval of the arena financing will not halt the SCORE lawsuit. "Our challenges to the financial arrangement are still completely valid, and we are amending our complaint to address the changes the city made to the arena financing deal," says Karasick.

By taking the city to court, SCORE is copying the strategy used successfully by a group of East Ward residents to delay the city's condemnation of their property for a 1999 arena proposal. In that case, architectural project manager Hal Laessig and his wife, artist Yoland Skeet, received notices informing them that their neighborhood was "in need of redevelopment." When defensive officials at city hall stonewalled their requests for more information, they learned from local newspapers that the city intended to demolish their houses to construct an arena. Before their property could be condemned, Laessig, Skeet and their neighbors sued the city for flouting public meeting rules and other procedures. Karasick served as their lawyer. A year later, in January 2000, a state judge ruled the city violated the law and the administration halted its condemnation process. "I really can't believe we won," recalls Laessig. "We got a judge who didn't care who he would upset." Using the court decision to negotiate higher property values, Laessig and his neighbors sold their houses to the city. However, financing squabbles derailed that proposal, and the neighborhood was abandoned with neither residents nor an arena.

SCORE's strategy of focusing on rising property taxes is not likely to become a city-wide movement, says Richard Roper, president of the Roper Group, a consulting firm. "Higher property taxes impact homeowners, but they are largely invisible to renters," he explains. Since around three-quarters of Newark residents are renters, Roper believes rising property taxes will only mobilize homeowners concentrated in the East and North Wards, and will not rally the entire city. Without a unifying complaint, the city's scattered arena opponents must rely on lawsuits. The courts enable precision attacks on Newark's economic development agenda, but their confrontational style inhibits any compromise or swaying of opinions. Karasick admits that his efforts generate more litigation than discussion, but he blames the administration's unresponsive nature to comment or criticism. "Unfortunately, the lawsuits have proved a strong and necessary tool — they spawn action," he says. Action is important to NCC, a long-time opponent of Mayor James, and a supporter of the SCORE lawsuit. "They have given aid and assistance," Karasick says of the prominent CDC. In a city without a tradition of effective dialogue on development priorities, the lawsuit has become the community's loudest, though most limiting, voice for change.

The *Star-Ledger*, New Jersey's largest newspaper, at first supported a downtown arena for Newark. In 2002, when team owners were shouldering a substantial portion of the cost, and when it was assumed that two major teams, the Nets basketball team and the Devils, would be tenants, the *Star-Ledger* welcomed the project. But when Mayor James unveiled the latest arena concept in February, with the city contributing two-thirds of the $300 million price tag, a *Star-Ledger* editorial rebuked the mayor, saying, "There are questions that must be answered before any time, money or land is consumed by this project." The administration's response is that public spending on catalytic projects is Newark's only method to attract outside developers. "We don't have the resources to do development ourselves," Monteilh says.

But the real resources Newark lacks are those devoted to strategic planning and community dialogue. Newark is a city in which economic development is completely detached from realistic goals and financial accountability. The planning staff within City Hall is small, and most are lawyers more comfortable with contracts than blueprints. The city's master plan process has sputtered off and on for five years, and Newark's major CDCs have been struggling to make their voices heard. Meanwhile, the arena appropriation includes $25 million in pre-development funding for hiring planners, engineers and consultants — a vast amount for a city that usually ignores this type of work.

At press time several opponents of the arena are circulating a petition to place the arena's financing plan on the ballot as a public referendum, representing another challenge to this project. If the SCORE lawsuit or referendum drive is successful, it could postpone or perhaps defeat the arena. But no lawsuit or vote can bring the administration and the community together to discuss a common vision for what the city can be, and should be. If Sharpe James loses this arena, a new project, perhaps even another sports venue, will soon raise the same intractable issues, no doubt accompanied by more lawsuits. For a city still seeking to fulfill its promise of true revitalization, the real conversation has yet to begin.

References

Field of Schemes: How the Great Stadium Swindle Turns Public Money Into Private Profit, by Joanna Cagan and Neil deMause. Common Courage Press, 1998.

"Referendum Sought on Proposed Newark Arena," by Jeffrey C. Mays and Matthew Futterman, Newark *Star-Ledger,* May 21, 2004.

"Newark Council Approves Financing for Arena Proposal," by Jeffrey C. Mays, Newark *Star-Ledger,* May 6, 2004.

"Indoor Soccer Added to Newark Arena Plans," by Ronald Smothers, *The New York Times,* May 5, 2004.

"Arena Panel a Work in Progress," by Jeffery C. Mays, Newark *Star-Ledger,* April 28, 2004.

"Fog Shrouds Newark Arena," Editorial, Newark *Star-Ledger,* March 1, 2004.

"Devils Will Win, Newark Will Win, Jersey Will Win," by Sharpe James, Newark *Star-Ledger,* February 29, 2004.

"If You Build It, They Will Come?" by Terry Golway, *The New York Times,* July 13, 2003.

"Newark's Tax Abatement Program Hobbled by City Failure to Escrow: More than $120 million collected but nothing set aside for tax relief," by Tim O'Brien, *New Jersey Law Journal,* January 13, 2003.

CHAPTER 28

Olympia and Other Cities Ask Their States to Fund Sports Facilities

Jim Brunner

Sonics owner Clay Bennett will find plenty of company when he heads to Olympia next month to ask the Legislature for help building a new basketball arena.

Across the state, sports promoters and cities are angling for taxpayer money to construct new arenas or patch up old ballparks.

A Florida racetrack developer wants $166 million in state sales taxes for a NASCAR track in Kitsap County. Kent wants the state to pitch in at least $10 million toward a $50 million arena to lure the Seattle Thunderbirds hockey team. In Centralia, boosters hope taxpayers will cover two-thirds of an $80 million rodeo arena. The state's five minor-league baseball parks want $18 million in renovations, including $1.3 million for a new grandstand roof at Tacoma's Cheney Stadium.

The wish list tops $240 million — not including whatever the Sonics ask for.

"Wow. Form a line to the right," said House Majority Leader Lynn Kessler, D-Hoquiam.

Although lawmakers anticipate a budget surplus, Kessler said building new sports arenas isn't a top priority, especially for profitable businesses like the NBA and NASCAR.

"The public is getting worn out, especially by large franchises asking the taxpayers to pick up so much," Kessler said. "I think the proposals we'll look at more seriously are those where the team makes a more substantial investment and doesn't make the state taxpayers pony up all the money."

The smaller proposals may stand a better chance.

Gov. Christine Gregoire released a proposed construction budget last week that includes $3 million for the proposed Kent arena and $6 million for the minor-league parks.

The larger requests were not mentioned in the governor's budget and could prove more controversial, since they would require new legislation to extend or redirect taxes.

Sonics and NASCAR

The biggest proposals are expected to come from Sonics owners and NASCAR promoters, whose previous bids for state aid flopped.

The Sonics' proposal is the biggest mys-

Originally published as "Get in Line, Sonics: Legislature Getting Plenty of Arena Requests," *The Seattle Times*, December 28, 2006, by The Seattle Times Company, Seattle, WA. Reprinted with permission of the publisher.

tery at the moment. Bennett is planning a large suburban arena suitable for professional basketball, concerts and major-league hockey. He has said that arena will require a significant public contribution, but has not released details.

A glut of new arenas could create problems for existing ones. A Seattle task-force report last year warned that KeyArena could become a financial drag on Seattle Center if it faces competition from a new state-subsidized Sonics arena in the suburbs. And Seattle Mayor Greg Nickels said he'll ask that Seattle be compensated by the state if that happens.

The other big-ticket proposal is for a new NASCAR racetrack in Kitsap County.

Despite finding little support for the idea last year, NASCAR promoters plan to return to Olympia next month with essentially the same proposal for a $345 million, 80,000-seat track.

Track developers want to divert $166 million in state sales tax to pay for construction, matched by $166 million in private money. Another $13 million would come from a ticket tax at the track, which would be owned by a public-development authority, much like Qwest and Safeco fields.

Grant Lynch, vice president of Florida-based racetrack developer International Speedway Corp., said he has met with more than 50 state legislators since the summer trying to convince them of the project's merits.

"If you take the time out of session to sit down with legislators and you can get a couple quality hours of their time, they begin to understand what sets this project apart," Lynch said.

Backers are selling the NASCAR track as a potentially huge tourism draw, capable of bringing hundreds of thousands of free-spending tourists to the state and boosting tax collections.

But those financial projections have been criticized by State Treasurer Mike Murphy as unrealistic.

Critics point out taxpayers would be left holding much of the construction bill if NASCAR failed to meet attendance expectations and generate the extra tax revenue claimed by promoters.

"It's you and I that will be paying it if the track does not make it," said Ray McGovern, an organizer of the Coalition for Healthy Economic Choices in Kitsap, a group opposing the NASCAR proposal.

Rodeo Arena

In Lewis County, backers of a proposed indoor rodeo arena say it would help the Centralia area recover from the 550 jobs lost when the state's last coal mine closed last month.

Planning for the proposed Regional Equestrian Center, or "REQ Center," started before the mine closure, but backers hope the economic-recovery argument will prove compelling for state lawmakers.

The domed arena would cost between $50 million and $80 million, according to early estimates. Sketches call for 7,500 permanent seats, a concrete floor with removable dirt for rodeo events, 20 luxury boxes and an attached exhibition hall. While designed largely for rodeos and livestock shows, the arena could also hold concerts, dirt-bike races and other events.

Centralia businessman Larry Hewitt, who is leading the REQ Center effort, said backers may be able to build the project with private money, but they're seeking possible taxpayer assistance as an option. "It's a relatively small amount of money, all things considered," Hewitt said.

Rep. Gary Alexander, the ranking Republican on the House budget committee, whose district includes Centralia, said he plans to introduce legislation that would allow Lewis County to create a public-facilities district to fund the arena.

Similar to the NASCAR proposal, that would allow some sales taxes to be diverted to the rodeo arena project instead of being deposited in the state general fund.

Hockey in Kent

In Kent, city officials are moving rapidly on a plan to build a 6,500-seat arena to lure the Seattle Thunderbirds hockey team from Key-Arena.

Like the Sonics, the Thunderbirds want out of KeyArena, complaining it is inadequate. The team's lease expires in 2008, and Kent leaders hope their new arena can be completed by then. The arena would be constructed across from the Kent Commons, on what are now large school playfields.

City officials say they need at least $10 million in state aid for the $50 million project. Gregoire included $3 million in her recent budget proposal. If Kent can get enough state aid, the city plans to sell bonds to pay for construction, to be paid back primarily from rent and concession agreements.

"I'm feeling very confident we've got a winner here," said Ben Wolters, Kent's economic development director.

The arena's anchor tenant would be the Thunderbirds, the junior-league hockey team with 40 home games a year. But it also could host ice shows, concerts and monster-truck rallies, Wolters said.

Minor-League Baseball

By comparison, the requests from the state's five minor-league ballparks are small. The teams, which all play in publicly owned ballparks, got together last year to ask for a total of $25 million. The Legislature agreed to give them $7 million. The teams are lobbying to get the remaining $18 million.

That would pay for a new grandstand roof at Tacoma's Cheney Stadium, a new concessions building and risers at Spokane's Avista Stadium, and locker-room upgrades and left-field seats for Everett Memorial Stadium. Dust Devils Stadium in the Tri-Cities would get a new scoreboard and Yakima County Stadium would get a grandstand roof to shield fans from the sun.

Randy Lewis, Tacoma's lobbyist, said one argument for the minor-league ballparks is their fan-friendly price tag.

A family of four can catch a Tacoma Rainiers game at Cheney Stadium for $20. "That is still going to be the case," Lewis said.

CHAPTER 29

Pasadena Asks Citizens to Vote on Sports Team and New Facilities

Rebecca Kuzins

New Year's Day has always been a special time at the Rose Bowl. On that day, a capacity crowd attends the Rose Bowl Game, the grandfather of all college football games, which has been held at the stadium since 1923. All eyes are on Pasadena, California, as people across the country watch the Rose Parade and the Rose Bowl Game on television.

But "America's Stadium," as Rose Bowl officials like to call it, fares less well on many other days of the year. The Rose Bowl, which is owned by the city of Pasadena, operates at a deficit and must borrow money from a municipal golf course to fill the gap. In the fiscal year ending June 30, 2006, the income from the golf courses accounted for nearly $1.8 million, or about 28 percent of the bowl's almost $6.4 million total revenue.

The Rose Bowl has a long-term lease with the University of California at Los Angeles (UCLA) football team, which generated over $1.5 million in income last year. The stadium also hosts a monthly flea market and, in the past, held rock concerts. But these days,

there are far fewer concerts for any stadium and the Rose Bowl's sound system is inferior to that offered in newer venues in the Los Angeles area. Now, Rose Bowl officials are scrambling to attract other activities that will make the stadium more profitable.

However, the most serious problem faced by the Rose Bowl — as well as the city-owned Cotton Bowl in Dallas and the Orange Bowl in Miami — is their inability to compete with the more modern sports arenas in metropolitan areas across the country.

"They're aging facilities," says Dan Barrett, principal of Barrett Sports Group, a consulting firm based in Manhattan Beach, California, that developed a strategic market plan for the Rose Bowl. "They don't have state-of-the-art amenities, like premium seating and video scoreboards. The older scoreboards don't allow [for] the same advertising opportunities. It's a challenge for both owners and tenants," he adds.

Recent events at the Cotton Bowl illustrate how tough that challenge can be. The

Originally published as "The Case of Three Bowls," *Urban Land*, Vol. 66, No. 7, July 2007, by the Urban Land Institute, Washington, D.C. Reprinted with permission of the publisher.

facility was built in 1930, and since 1937 has been the site of the annual Cotton Bowl football game, now called the AT&T Cotton Bowl Classic. However, this past February, the Cotton Bowl Athletic Association voted to move the game to the new Dallas Cowboys stadium, beginning in 2010. The Cowboys' facility, currently under construction in nearby Arlington, Texas, will cost $1 billion, the most ambitious stadium in the history of the National Football League (NFL).

Officials of the State Fair of Texas, who operate the Cotton Bowl, downplayed the move, saying that it was not a factor in their planned renovation of the facility. "It's never been about them. The Cotton Bowl guys have not been in the loop on the planning of all this from the get-go," State Fair president Errol McKoy told the *Dallas Morning News* in February.

Two months later, the Cotton Bowl's fortunes took a turn for the better after it renewed contracts for the annual Red River Rivalry football game between the University of Texas and the University of Oklahoma. These teams' contracts were set to expire in 2010 and there was speculation that they would move their games to the new Cowboys stadium or to other arenas. However, in April, the teams announced they will continue to play at the Cotton Bowl through 2015 — in exchange for hundreds of thousands of dollars in new city-funded incentives. (Grambling State and Prairie View A & M universities, which also play an annual football game at the Cotton Bowl, also extended their contract another five years to 2015.)

State Fair officials are soliciting other colleges to play at the Cotton Bowl and said that Oklahoma State, Louisiana State, Baylor, and Notre Dame universities are considering holding annual or periodic games there. However, other universities in the area may not be interested in the Cotton Bowl because their teams play in larger, more modern football arenas.

"We are competing within the two- or three-state-area university stadiums that have been renovated and enlarged," says Cotton Bowl manager Roland Rainey. "We used to be larger than the universities and could make more money. The University of Texas, University of Oklahoma, Texas A & M, and University of Arkansas all have larger seating capacities, and some have added suites. When you sell that kind of luxury package, it's difficult to move those suiteholders into other stadiums. We're not as attractive as we've been in the past, now that they have all these other big stadiums."

The proposed renovation of the Cotton Bowl began this past January. The initial phase of the project included installing a Jumbotron video scoreboard and removing the old chair-back seats, which will be replaced with bench-style seating. During the second phase, scheduled to begin next January, the number of seats will be expanded from 72,000 to 92,100 and the restrooms, concessions stands, press facilities, and stadium's facade will be overhauled.

The city of Dallas appropriated $20 million for the initial improvements. Last November, Dallas voters approved $30 million worth of bonds to finance the second round. However, some council members, as well as some candidates running for mayor in the May elections, questioned the allocation and speculated about whether the $30 million could be put to better use.

Other Dallas residents are asking the same question. In a *Dallas Morning News* poll conducted in March, 48 percent of the respondents said the city should not fund the renovation, arguing it no longer made sense since the AT&T Cotton Bowl announced it was leaving the stadium. Another 40 percent were in favor of the remodeling, while the remaining 12 percent were undecided or had no opinion.

Like the Cotton Bowl, Miami's Orange Bowl also lost a major annual game in 1996, when the Orange Bowl Classic football game moved to Dolphin Stadium, home of the city's NFL team. The Orange Bowl Classic had been played at the Orange Bowl since the facility opened in 1937, the same year the University of Miami football team started playing its games there.

The university's lease will expire in 2009 and the city of Miami is negotiating with university officials for a lease extension. However, the University of Miami is seriously considering leaving the Orange Bowl in favor of Dolphin Stadium. A spokesperson for the university's football team said the university expects to reach a decision on a venue by this summer. [As of late June, the university had not decided whether it would remain at the Orange Bowl, and a spokesman for the football team said the university was still negotiating with the Orange Bowl and Dolphin Stadium. In the meantime, the team will play its next football season at the Orange Bowl, which will commence on September 1].

The Orange Bowl also is undergoing an extensive renovation. Work began last August, with the installation of new light towers and fixtures. In May of last year, the city hired Jones Lang LaSalle (JLL), the real estate services and money management firm that renovated Madison Square Garden in New York and Soldier's Field in Chicago, to provide leadership and management services for the remodeling. Last September, two architecture firms, HNTB and Bermello Ajamil & Partners, were selected to provide architectural and engineering services.

After lease negotiations with the University of Miami are completed, the city and university will be asked to approve the next phase of the renovation plan, says John Paccionne, senior vice president of JLL. Although the details have not been hammered out, the plan will include expansion and remodeling of concession areas and restrooms, upgrades to con-

course and seating areas, the addition of premium seating options, and installation of an up-to-date video scoreboard.

These "programmatic items," Paccionne explains, "will have a positive impact on revenues. By returning the Orange Bowl to its [previous] level of prominence, it will become more attractive to other events and tenants. This will have a positive effect on the revenues for the Orange Bowl."

Miami has made $84 million available to fund these renovations. However, city officials have estimated the total cost of renovation at about $175 million, so additional money will be needed. JLL is studying the amount of money that will be raised through increased revenue at the remodeled Orange Bowl to determine how much of this money could be used to finance the renovation.

The situation at the Rose Bowl differs in some ways from the problems facing the Cotton and Orange bowls. Los Angeles, unlike Dallas or Miami, has neither an NFL team nor a state-of-the-art NFL arena to compete with. In addition, the building is a revered landmark in southern California. Designed by noted architect Myron Hunt and constructed in 1922, the Rose Bowl is listed on the National Register of Historic Places, and that status, combined with Pasadena's powerful contingent of architectural preservation activists, helps ensure its survival.

Nonetheless, the Rose Bowl is in need of some resuscitation. General manager Darryl Dunn has been working to revive the facility since he took over in 1999, including improving the facility's relationship with UCLA's football team. UCLA recently agreed to extend its lease until 2023, but demanded that the Rose Bowl expand its underground locker rooms. Ground breaking was held in May of last year, and the locker room improvements are scheduled to be completed before the start of this year's football season. The city of

Pasadena has allocated $16.3 million to finance the project.

"It stabilized a difficult relationship," says Dunn, referring to the UCLA lease extension. "We're so fragile. If UCLA left, or any of our tenants left, it could be devastating for the Rose Bowl."

Dunn was less successful in attracting an NFL team to the Rose Bowl. He had met with NFL commissioner Paul Tagliabue and other league officials to persuade them to use the Rose Bowl for NFL games when, and if, the league brings a team to the Los Angeles area. The NFL expressed interest, proposing a $500 million renovation of the Rose Bowl.

But many Pasadenans adamantly denounced the proposal. The area near the Rose Bowl is the site of a children's museum, a municipal swimming pool, and a golf course, and also is a favorite site for joggers and walkers. Pasadena residents argued that bringing an NFL team to the Rose Bowl would increase traffic congestion and make it difficult, if not impossible, for residents to make use of the other facilities near the stadium. Architectural preservationists also maintained that the NFL renovation proposal would destroy the architectural integrity of the facility.

In June 2005, Pasadena's city council rejected the NFL's proposal. In response, some city council members and citizens placed a referendum on the November 2006 ballot, asking voters if they wanted to renovate the Rose Bowl for professional football use and lease the facility to the NFL. That measure was resoundingly defeated, with 72 percent of the voters rejecting it.

That left Rose Bowl officials to consider what they call "Plan B" — or how to generate more income, tenants, and events to the facility without a professional football team. Dunn says the Rose Bowl now hosts a number of "minor events," such as a children's fitness walk and an alumni club meeting. He is meeting

with officials of the San Francisco Giants, who generate $5 million a year by holding minor events at AT&T Park, to see how the Rose Bowl could schedule similar activities. Dunn is also considering other uses for the facility, such as blocking off a portion of the stadium for concerts or plays.

Of greater importance, Rose Bowl officials are considering a $250 million to $300 million renovation that would provide more comfortable seating, expanded restrooms and concourse areas, and easier access into and out of the facility. HOK Sport, an international architecture practice, has drafted a master plan for the renovation that ultimately must be approved by Pasadena's city council. Some of these improvements could be financed by offering ticket buyers a range of preferred-seating options.

Barrett Sports Group conducted a public survey in 2006, in which UCLA season ticket holders and other respondents expressed interest in purchasing private suites, loge boxes, and club seats. Based on these responses, the group recommended installing 40 private suites at prices ranging from $55,000 to $75,000 a year for each, 50 loge seats at $25,000 each, and 2,500 club seats at around $2,000 each. Barrett estimates these seats would generate about $5.5 million a year in additional revenue.

The Rose Bowl also is considering selling naming rights to the field, press box, locker rooms, and gates; charging ticket and parking surcharges; and pursuing grant opportunities as other ways of raising funds. It also plans to organize a philanthropic campaign aimed at attracting private funding. Renovation is scheduled to begin in 2009 and be completed in two years.

"The Rose Bowl is a very special stadium," says Dunn. "It's the icon for Pasadena. It's still in good condition, but it's old. It deserves the opportunity to get younger."

CHAPTER 30

Richmond and Other Cities Entice Minor League Sports Teams to Stimulate Their Economy

Charles Gerena *and* Betty Joyce Nash

A mom shepherds a dozen 12-year-olds to seats in the Freezer for a birthday party. A dad totes a toddler to rink-side during a break in the game so he can hurl a puck onto center ice. And throughout the game, families of varying sizes and ages come and go at will.

No doubt about it, a Richmond Renegades ice hockey game is major family fun.

Minor league sports teams like the Renegades are popping up in small and mid-sized cities throughout the Fifth District. These increasingly popular enterprises can put big points on a community's economic scoreboard by satisfying a growing appetite for affordable family entertainment, by boosting civic pride, or by renewing a city's sagging downtown.

Since sports compete with concerts, shows, and other leisure events, minor league teams don't always make a big splash. However, they do catch dollars that might otherwise leak from the local economy, says economist John Connaughton of the University of North Carolina at Charlotte.

"Minor league sports is a way to spend your entertainment dollars where most of the money stays in the community," explains Connaughton. "When you go to a movie, a lot of money gets on the bus and heads out of town. If you go to a concert, about 80 percent of the ticket sales and merchandise expenditures leave the community."

The Minor Miracle

The minor league sports boom began in the late 1980s when baseball team owners learned how to market their teams as a form of low-cost entertainment, explains Arthur Johnson, author of the book *Minor League Baseball and Local Economic Development*.

"[Today,] there's a new breed of owner who knows how to market the product and knows how to run the organization as a business. It is the success of baseball that drove [other sports]," says Johnson.

As major league baseball expanded, so did the minors, where most players gain pro-

Originally published as "Playing to Win: Minor League Sports Score," *Region Focus*, Spring 2000, by the Federal Reserve Bank, Richmond, VA.

fessional experience. In 1989, 23 million fans nationwide watched 164 minor league teams play ball. Ten years later, the number of fans reached 35 million, and the minors added a dozen teams.

The Fifth District experienced similar growth in attendance. In 1989, 29 minor league teams drew 3.2 million spectators. Though the number of teams grew by two in the past decade, the number of fans rose to 5.9 million.

Minor league baseball has been a fixture in some southern communities for over a century, but fan interest has varied with time. It peaked in 1949 when attendance reached nearly 40 million nationwide, then fell in the 1950s when television brought major league games into people's living rooms.

Two important events set the stage for the current renaissance. In 1990, Major League Baseball (MLB) established standards involving seating capacity and other features of minor league ballparks. Teams were asked to either upgrade or replace their ballparks in order to retain MLB affiliation and lucrative player development contracts.

At the same time, communities were being enticed by the allure of minor league baseball. They were willing to pitch in for the cost of new stadiums, which averaged about $9 million between 1985 and 1995.

With multimillion-dollar facilities attracting fans and the major leagues covering some of the expenses of affiliated teams, the investment potential of a minor league ball club gathered a momentum all its own. Franchise values soared over the outfield wall.

Whereas a minor league baseball team could be bought for a few thousand dollars in the 1970s, it now costs $500,000 to purchase a team at the Rookie level, the lowest professional level in the minors. A team at the Class-AAA level — the highest in the minors — can cost as much as $10 million. Investors now

band together to purchase teams, says Miles Wolff, commissioner of the independent baseball league — the Northern League — and former owner of the Durham Bulls.

Wolff got in the game early. He paid $24,000 for the Bulls in 1980, then sold the team for between $3 million and $4 million in 1990. He followed the course of other profit seekers at the time — buy a minor league baseball franchise cheap, make it popular, and sell it to a group of businessmen for a big payoff.

As the cost of the franchises grew, though, so did the expectations for financial returns. "A team has become an investment, not a hobby," says Wolff.

This transformation is evident in the 200 percent rise in gross revenues for minor league baseball from 1991 to 1998. Owners tap into more revenue sources than ever before — corporate sales, luxury suite rentals, advertising on fence signs, and merchandise sales.

"Our clubs have done an outstanding job of maximizing their revenue," notes Pat O'Conner, vice president of administration and chief operating officer of the National Association of Professional Baseball Leagues, an umbrella group of minor league baseball organizations.

At the same time, O'Conner says that expenses have doubled. If a team has a player development contract with Major League Baseball, operating costs such as player salaries and benefits are subsidized. However, in 1997, MLB stopped paying for other items like uniforms and equipment used in home games.

In addition, owners are challenged to provide some of the amenities found in major league ballparks. For instance, the Salem Avalanche spent $10 million to build a snazzy stadium in 1995. The Salem, Va., ballpark includes luxury suites and a breathtaking view of the Blue Ridge Mountains.

Such amenities, say stadium operators, can pump up ticket sales and dispel the old image of players running around a dirt field while people watch from metal bleachers.

"We are not trying to compete with the major leagues," says Joe Preseren, general manager of the Avalanche. "On the other hand, we want to present a first-class product. We don't want the old run-down vision."

The Puck Drops Here

Just as the minor league baseball owners wound up their marketing arms to pitch a valuable business, so did the owners of minor league hockey teams.

Fresh from his sale of the Durham Bulls, Miles Wolff bought a minor league hockey franchise. He paid $50,000 for the Raleigh Ice Caps in 1991, then sold it for $2 million just four years later.

Wolff managed his hockey investment the way he manages his baseball investments. "It's selling and marketing," he says. "It's a business."

Tapping into a fervor created by hockey great Wayne Gretzky, minor league hockey gained momentum in the late 1980s. As the National Hockey League expanded, it needed fresh talent.

Enter the East Coast Hockey League (ECHL), a minor league franchise system that hit the ice in 1988 with five teams. The market for hockey teams looked solid in the Southeast where indoor arenas sat empty during certain times of the year, according to Jason Rothwell, director of communications with the ECHL.

Today, the Fifth District is home to nine of the ECHL's 28 teams. These teams play 35 games at their home arena every year, attracting 2,400 to 8,000 fans per game. Attendance at ECHL games in the Fifth District grew from about 400,000 in the 1989–1990 season to about 1.7 million in 1998–1999.

The ECHL covets its role in developing athletes for the major leagues, but it also knows the value of providing affordable entertainment for families. "We consider ourselves an entertainment industry," says Rothwell. "We look at our competition; we look at movies, the things a family is going to do on a Friday or Saturday night."

To maintain low ticket prices, the league enforces a strict salary cap for players and encourages teams to travel by bus. By keeping expenses down, ECHL teams continue to be an attractive investment. Demand for franchises has driven purchase costs from $25,000 in 1988 to a current $2 million, Rothwell says.

Such dizzying franchise values can compel owners to sell. Not so for Art Donaldson, a Greensboro, N.C., lawyer and one of four investors who launched the Greensboro Generals in 1999. (The team name was resurrected from a 1950s-era hockey team.) A transplanted New Yorker and longtime hockey fan, he wasn't happy when the NHL Carolina Hurricanes briefly replaced the minor league team in Greensboro.

"I wasn't a season ticket holder," he says. "Basically I wasn't going to pay the price. Their average ticket price was about $45; ours is about $10."

As an added bonus, fans can get chummy with players in the minors. "Win or lose, people come down and get autographs," says Donaldson, who also owns an arenafootball2 (af2) team called the Prowlers.

Touchdown

The Prowlers is one of 15 af2 teams that kicked off in April. Af2 is an offshoot of the 14-year-old Arena Football League and is played indoors on turf that measures 50 yards from post to post — about half the size of an outdoor football field.

By adding af2 franchises to their portfolios, investors can increase their potential for profit, says Donaldson. "What they [investors] are trying to do is cut down their costs," he says. "With the staff, and so forth, you can't just let these people go at the end of the season."

Not all team owners come to af2 with a hockey connection. Bobby Pearce, a lawyer from Charleston, S.C., says he wanted an ECHL franchise ever since he helped launch the Charleston Stingrays hockey team in 1992. When a deal failed to materialize, he put together an investment team and bought an af2 franchise — the Swamp Foxes.

Pearce estimates start-up expenses for the Swamp Foxes at about $1.2 million. He is optimistic that the team can generate about $1 million in annual sales and break even by filling 4,500 seats each game. Furthermore, he believes his initial investment of $175,000 in franchise fees already has appreciated. Franchise values are expected to hit $500,000 within three years, according to af2 officials.

"If hockey can do so super here, indoor football should do as well, if not better," says Pearce.

Invisible Impact

Like the excitement in the air at a game, some effects of having a home team just aren't visible. Instead, a baseball or hockey franchise can be viewed as a resource, says economist Tom Regan, chairman of the Department of Sport Administration at the University of South Carolina.

"It adds intangibles," notes Regan. Sports teams can be an important part of a community's economic development strategy and its civic image.

Take, for example, the now-legendary attempt to move the Durham Bulls baseball team in Durham, N.C., to a regional stadium.

"Although I was going to move the team ... about six miles from where it was, you would have thought I was taking them to Indianapolis or something," says Bull's owner Jim Goodmon, president of Capitol Broadcasting Co. Inc.

Durham, a city with a downtown in decline, put up a fuss at the thought of losing part of its identity, says Ted Abernathy, manager of the Office of Economic and Employment Development for the city of Durham. "The Bulls are part of our heritage, part of what makes us a city."

So the city gave the Bulls a new ballpark in the mid–1990s. In turn, Goodmon built one office park near the stadium and plans another. He also plans to invest $250 million to transform a downtown Durham landmark, the decrepit American Tobacco Co. complex, into office, retail, and hotel space.

Abernathy says officials are unable to estimate the overall economic value of keeping the Bulls in Durham. "What we do know is that we're talking about something in the neighborhood of $10 million a year in direct expenditures around the ballpark, 500,000 people a year at $10 a ticket, plus concessions and parking."

A minor league sports team also can elevate perceptions regarding the quality of life that a city or region offers. "It creates an image of your community as a family community, a good place to live," notes Abernathy.

Community demand for teams and escalating franchise values are driving today's minor league expansion phenomenon. However, saturation in some sports markets could be looming.

"In the next five years in the industry, I don't think you're going to see the same expansion rates you've seen in the previous five," says Rothwell about the ECHL.

Longevity in the world of sports hinges on building a loyal fan base as well as following the sound business practices that support any small business, experts say.

"The good franchises with cash flow and good debt equity will be fine [but] the others will perish," says USC's Tom Regan.

CHAPTER 31

Rock Hill Approves Innovative Financing Method to Construct Sports Facility

American City & County

Rock Hill, S.C., is financing an $11.2 million soccer complex with the help of certificates of participation (COP) and bond insurance to lower the total cost of the financing. When the complex is completed next February, it is expected to generate millions of dollars annually for the city.

With a population of more than 56,000, Rock Hill is situated just 25 miles from the Charlotte, N.C., metropolitan area and has grown at a moderate pace to become the fourth largest city in the state. For several years, the city has been focusing on diversifying its textile-based economy to include manufacturing, technology and health industries.

In the process, Rock Hill steadily has gained status as a destination for national softball tournaments. In fact, the 34-week softball season in 2003 generated approximately $7.5 million for the growing city. The visiting teams, along with their loyal fans, purchased a total of 15,000 nights in local hotel rooms. The 2003 National Softball Association Youth Girls World Series Tournament, which had approximately 430 teams participate, generated a sizeable $3.4 million in revenue for the city.

That success inspired city leaders to nurture the city's sports tourism industry. They decided to build a 65-acre soccer complex and regional park and drew up a plan to become a premier location for local, regional and national soccer events. The city was faced with the question of how to finance the $11.2 million project at a reasonable cost without overreaching. Based on Rock Hill's solid A-rated category general obligation bonds, city leaders decided to structure a COP issue. COPs are backed by annual appropriations from the general fund in contrast to a full faith and credit pledge of a general obligation bond.

Rock Hill's COP is based on anticipated revenues from hospitality fees that are levied on meals outside residents' homes. The city has seen a steadily rising stream of revenue over time from those fees, except for a brief period following Sept. 11, 2001. The top 10 restaurants (hospitality fee providers) in the

Originally published as "Kicking Off a New Venture," *American City & County*, Vol. 120, No. 4, April 2005, by Penton Media, Inc., Overland Park, KS. Reprinted wth permission of the publisher.

city account for approximately 23 percent of the total revenue generated. Based on the revenues collected in 2003, the hospitality fees will provide more than two-and-a-half times coverage of the COP debt service. In the unlikely event that hospitality fees are insufficient to pay debt service, the city will make annual payments from the general fund.

The revenue stream provides further protection to bondholders because additional bonds cannot be sold unless the revenues provide one-and-a-half-times coverage of annual debt service. In addition, a debt service reserve fund of no more than 10 percent of par also was funded at inception.

In return for those various bondholder protections, Armonk, N.Y.-based MBIA Insurance Corp. agreed to insure the bond issue. As a result of the insurance, Rock Hill's bond rating for the transaction rose from an A rating to an AAA rating, saving the city an estimated minimum of $140,000 in interest, after the cost of insurance.

The city is applying the net proceeds of the transaction to developing the soccer complex and park, which features active and passive recreation areas for residents and visiting players and fans. Two of the eight soccer fields to be constructed will be fully outfitted for tournament regulation play. The complex also will include a soccer pavilion and a pedestrian trail around a lake, as well as parking for 650 vehicles. Locally based Leitner Construction began building the complex in February 2005.

Residents, players, fans and hospitality providers all will have something to cheer about when the facility opens next year. Conservatively, city leaders estimate the complex will generate between $2.5 million and $3.5 million in new revenue for the city when the project is completed.

CHAPTER 32

St. Paul Serves as Focus for Statewide Study on New Sports Stadium

Stadium Task Force

The Stadium Task Force was created by the Governor and the Legislature to study and make recommendations regarding the asserted needs of the Minnesota Twins, the Minnesota Vikings, and the University of Minnesota football team, for new stadiums.

Although the issue of a new baseball stadium previously had been studied a number of times by the Legislature, the Metropolitan Sports Facilities Commission ("MSFC"), and private groups, the needs of baseball and football had not been considered together. In addition, despite the fact that the Vikings began raising the issue of a new stadium for football several years ago, there had not been a sustained legislative discussion of what to do, if anything, for professional football.

The Task Force had eighteen members: six appointed by the Governor, six by the House, and six by the Senate. Our membership included elected and appointed public officials and individuals from the private sector. Some of the members had extensive experience with previous stadium discussions, and some were newcomers.

During our hearings, we listened to representatives of the sports teams, the MSFC, local governments, architects, contractors, financiers, present and former players, other Minnesotans who wanted their voices heard, and from fans who have always shown their loyalties to teams and athletes with the word "Minnesota" on their uniforms. The members had the opportunity to learn from and build on the work of many others, such as the MSFC, New Ballpark, Inc., and Minnesotans for Major League Baseball.

Though our recommendations are not unanimous, we worked toward a consensus on the disputed issues and avoided relying on narrow majorities of task force members to reach conclusions.

Recommendations and Rationale

1. We recommend that the Governor and the Legislature should take action during the 2002 legislative session on proposals for a new stadium for professional baseball and a stadium to be shared by the Minnesota Vikings and the University of Minnesota Gophers football team.

Originally published as *Final Report of the Minnesota Stadiums Task Force*, January 25, 2002, addressed to the Governor and State Legislature, by the State of Minnesota, St. Paul, MN.

We recognize that the 2002 Legislature and the Governor have several critical responsibilities, including balancing the operating budget, passing a capital budget, and redistricting.

Nonetheless, the Task Force recommends that action in 2002 is important for the Twins and the future of professional baseball in Minnesota because there is a real possibility that the Twins could be eliminated through the contraction of the number of major league baseball teams. We note that the lease for the Minnesota Twins has expired and is currently on a one-year extension for the 2002 season.

Like Minnesotans generally, none of the Task Force members were pleased with the pressure tactics and crisis atmosphere caused by Major League Baseball. Regretfully, we have had to conclude realistically that the 2002 baseball season could be the last one for the Minnesota Twins unless Minnesota acts to facilitate the construction of a new stadium this year.

The situation for the Vikings and the Gophers is just as important, though to some it may appear less urgent. Some witnesses noted that the Vikings' lease at the Metrodome extends until 2011. Nonetheless, the Task Force recommends that Minnesota act this year on football too. The National Football League has a program for assisting in the financing of new stadiums and the program is scheduled to end this year. The Task Force sees a significant funding opportunity that may not be available in the future. The Vikings also assert that without a new stadium, they will need new revenue streams to remain competitive in Minnesota. We also learned about the revenue shortfalls being incurred by the Gopher athletic programs. A facility shared by the Gophers and the Vikings would produce revenue increases for both organizations.

Metrodome Renovation or A New Football Stadium

The MSFC has suggested that renovating the Metrodome would be more cost effective than building a new stadium. This approach has advantages. The MSFC described a plan for such a renovation which they estimated would cost substantially less than building a new stadium. In addition there is already an infrastructure supporting Metrodome operations.

On balance, the Task Force concluded that a new football stadium was a superior solution. There was doubt that a renovation could be completed without disrupting at least one football season. We do not have an alternative venue for football if renovation did conflict with a season. The Vikings also raised reasonable concerns that cost estimates for renovation were too low. A renovated Metrodome would still lack many of the fan amenities characteristic of newer stadiums. Perhaps most important to the Task Force was the fact that the Vikings are strongly opposed to renovating the Metrodome as an alternative to a new stadium. The MSFC could not finance its major renovation plan without substantial Vikings participation and a new, longer term lease. The Vikings made it clear they would not contribute to a renovation and would not extend their lease at the Metrodome. For these reasons, the Task Force concluded that renovation of the Metrodome was not feasible and that a new stadium shared by the Vikings and the Gophers football team was a superior solution.

2. The Governor and the Legislature should adopt legislation providing for state participation in financing, but not funding, new stadiums. This financing should occur only if financing from other sources, such as private investors and local governments, is inadequate.

As we discuss below, the Task Force prefers that financing for new stadiums come from team owners or other private investors or from local governments if private investment is insufficient. If these other sources of financing are inadequate, only then should the state participate in the financing, provided that there is a substantial contribution made by the team owners. We recognize that full private financing of stadiums is rare. In Minnesota, local governments have been essential participants in previous stadium financing arrangements. Only after an appropriate financial commitment from the team owners and other private sources, and from the local unit(s) of government, should there be any expectation of a possible financial commitment from the state. Furthermore, any participation by the state should be financed through user fees, taxes imposed on professional sports related activities and/or items, or through other sources that demonstrate a relationship between the source of state funding and those that economically benefit from, or participate in the operations of, professional sports teams in the state.

In recognition of how controversial the issue of government, particularly state government, involvement in stadium funding has been, we have these observations to support our recommendation:

a. Some of the economic benefits claimed for sports stadiums are hard to justify. We were persuaded that the income taxes the state receives from visiting players was one economic benefit that could be quantified. As player salaries have increased, the direct benefit to the state of having our own professional teams has increased. In addition, the revenue spent in Minnesota by teams who benefit from revenue sharing is derived in part from economic activity in other states such as media payments and, therefore, is likely a net economic benefit to Minnesota. The Task Force was impressed, too, by the benefits many of the teams' communities received from the charitable giving of the teams and the players.

b. The facilities run by the Amateur Sports Facilities Commission and financed with public funds have provided opportunities for Minnesota athletes to excel, and brought outstanding athletes here from all over the world.

c. The Mighty Ducks and Mighty Kicks programs have provided state funds to help build hockey rinks and soccer fields throughout Minnesota.

d. Over the years, Minnesotans have spent millions of dollars to provide facilities for collegiate athletics on the campuses of the University of Minnesota system and the Minnesota State Colleges and Universities(MnSCU) system.

e. Public financing helped build Metropolitan Stadium, the Met Sports Center, and the Metrodome for professional and amateur football, baseball, basketball, soccer, hockey and other events and activities.

f. Public financing from state and local sources was crucial to the continued viability of Target Center and the construction of the Xcel Energy Center. Portions of the public financing were premised on the use of the facilities by amateur sports teams.

Finally, there are intangible benefits to having professional teams in Minnesota that cannot be overlooked. The Task Force has found that professional and college sports are part of the identity of many Minnesotans. In addition, the Task Force has found that these teams add something that is impossible to accurately measure, but that is important to countless Minnesotans. The Task Force has found that, to a considerable degree, pro and college sports play a part in the cultural vitality of Minnesota for many, not only in the Twin Cities, but across the state and throughout the region.

The Task Force has determined that in teams such as the Minnesota Twins and Minnesota Vikings, and in the generations of Minnesotans to whom a love of and a loyalty to the home team has been handed down, the state has something worth saving.

3. The Task Force recommends that state participation in financing stadiums be drawn from limited revenue sources, not from the general fund.

The Task Force spent considerable time discussing revenue streams that may meet the parameters mentioned above, which could be widely considered as paid by those most directly benefiting from the use of the facility. The Task Force believes that the following revenue streams deserve closer examination by state policymakers and are potential revenue sources to finance state participation.

a. Sports Memorabilia. Imposing a statewide sports memorabilia tax applied to all professional sports, including clothing. This memorabilia tax would be in addition to the existing sales tax on memorabilia, and would include a new statewide tax on clothing items with sports insignia.

b. Player Income Tax. Estimate the ongoing revenues from income taxes paid by the visiting players of professional sports teams that use the facility and use those revenues to support the state's investment in the construction of a new facility or facilities.

c. Media Access Charge. Businesses and individuals who use the sports facilities to broadcast or report on games and events that take place within the facility should

be charged for access to the facility or facilities.

d. Sales Tax on Facility Food and Beverages. Impose an additional tax on the sale of food and beverages at the sports facility; this would be in addition to the state sales tax of 6.5 percent and any local option sales tax that may be in place.

e. Ticket Tax. Impose an admission tax on the tickets sold to attendees at all events at the facility, both game and non-game events. This is in addition to the state sales tax of 6.5 percent, and any local option sales tax, that may be in place.

f. Naming Rights. The Task Force believes that the value associated with naming rights of the facility should be considered as a potential source for public financing, but that the landlord may want to reserve the right to contract with the team to negotiate with interested parties on the state's behalf, recognizing that the value of the naming rights may be greater if negotiated as part of a more comprehensive sponsorship package. If naming rights are used for stadium construction, the franchise ownership and the landlord should negotiate an agreement on naming rights revenues.

g. Personal Seat Licensing. The sale of personal seat licenses (PSLs) have been used as a financing source in other facilities and result from the sale of the right to buy a season ticket. If PSL's are utilized, the amount directed to stadium construction should be negotiated between the franchise ownership and the landlord.

h. State Loans to Local Units of Government. The Task Force recommends consideration of low- or zero-interest loans to local units of government.

i. Gaming Revenues. The Task Force urges the Legislature and the Governor to consider gaming related revenue streams as an option to support public financing of new professional sports facility.

j. Metrodome Assets. Should the Metrodome be left with no principal tenants, it is expected that the facility would be sold or demolished and the land redeveloped. The revenue from the sale of the Metrodome land and other assets of the Metropolitan Sports Facility Commission could be considered for a state contribution to the costs of a new facility.

k. Sales Tax Exemption. The Task Force also recommends consideration of a sales tax exemption on any materials used in the construction of the new facility or facilities. While these proceeds would otherwise be deposited in the general fund, they are receipts that would not be available to the state but for the project. To the extent that public funds are used to finance some portion of the construction, imposing a sales tax could lead to the state paying more interest to finance the sales tax.

l. Car Rental Charge. The Task Force recommends that the state impose a charge on car rentals in the metropolitan area. We recognize this charge does not fit neatly into the user or beneficiary category. Nonetheless, it has been used to finance stadiums in others states and is a reasonable option.

4. The Task Force's recommendations include several other financial considerations that should be addressed by the legislature and the Governor.

The state should consider granting a local unit(s) of government the authority to establish a local options sales tax to finance the local government contribution. To the extent a community already has local tax authority, the State should consider expanding the existing authority to allow proceeds to be used for facility financing.

The Task Force also recognizes there is a state interest in using these sports facilities for either collegiate or amateur athletics. The Task Force recommends consideration of some state funding should the lease for any facility include provisions for collegiate or amateur athletic use.

The Task Force also recommends that any state financing be done in the least costly way possible, without sacrificing the goal limiting the impact to the direct beneficiaries of the facilities. For example, if the state intends to issue debt to finance its share of the project cost, the state should explore strategies to ensure that as much of the state participation as possible can be done through the issuance of tax-exempt bonds.

However, the Task Force also recognizes that several of the revenue streams identified will be problematic as the primary source of revenues for debt service payments, primarily because there will not be a history of collections prior to issuing the debt. This may result in a reduced amount of debt that can be issued using these revenue sources as the payment for the debt service, given the requirement to have sufficient coverage on the debt, or a "cushion" of having expected revenues exceed debt service payments by some margin. The Task Force recommends that these limitations not be "fixed" by issuing general obligation bonds that could pose risk to the general taxpayers of the state.

The Task Force also recognizes the efforts of the state on the Streamlined Sales Tax Project, which is aimed at addressing sellers' concerns about the multiplicity of tax laws and the burden created in trying to comply with tax laws across states that are not uniform. Recognizing that increasing uniformity may ultimately allow the state to capture tax revenues lost on Internet sales, currently estimated at hundreds of millions of dollars annually, the Task Force urges careful consideration of the recommendation put forward in this report. It may be advisable to impose a gross receipts tax on the facility revenues, for example, rather than relying on specific extensions of the sales tax. The Task Force recommends that the Minnesota Department of Revenue be asked to comment more specifically on the revenue options identified in this report and recommend strategies for implementation to minimize any adverse impact on the Streamlined Sales Tax Project.

The Task Force also supports the further consideration of citizen ownership of the professional baseball franchise through the issuance of equity stock. While accomplishing a slightly different goal, the Task Force also believes the sense of public support accomplished through the issuance of commemorative stock, not defined as ownership under Minnesota law or the Securities and Exchange Commission Rules, would justify some consideration for a limited portion of the financing for either or both of the baseball or football facilities.

The Task Force also expressed concern that the state not be considered as a party responsible for financing any cost overruns in the project budget. The Task Force recommends that the responsibility for cost overruns and construction management be clearly delineated in the lease between the franchise and the facility landlord, but under no circumstances should the state be considered as a financing source for cost overruns. A construction management team should be in place prior to letting of any bids for the facilities.

5. The Task Force does not recommend a particular site for either a baseball or football stadium.

The Task Force recommendations are site neutral. The Task Force anticipates that the state will identify parameters for determining state participation and the location of the facility or facilities will be determined through a negotiated agreement between the franchisee (tenant) and the local unit(s) of government (landlord).

6. The Task Force recommends that any state financing not be released until the team has negotiated a lease with a landlord, which may be a local unit of government. State financing, if any, would be released only if the lease between the team and the landlord includes:

a. A listing of all revenue streams generated from use of the building with a specification of what revenues are available to cover team operations, which accrue to the building landlord and which are available to the state (such as naming rights),

b. Clarification of the operations and management responsibilities between the team and the landlord,

c. Delineation of the responsibility for repair and replacement in the facility, including an annual inspection by the landlord and a representative of the state,

d. Provisions within the lease that some portion of the tickets for professional sports games are accessible and affordable,

e. Protection of the public interest in the event of a default by the team or a disruption in the season due to a player strike,

f. A lease term that is at least as long as the term of any public financing that may be in place at the state or local level, not to exceed 30 years,

g. Terms specifying responsibilities for construction management and cost overruns between the landlord and the team,

h. Statement of public ownership of the facility, and clarification of ownership of the furnishing and equipment within the facility,

i. Terms which outline the security offered by the team on the lease;

j. Binding commitments of financing sufficient, when taken in conjunction with the state financing, to ensure that the project is fully funded prior to the release of the state funds,

k. Documentation on the final design and construction specifications, and

l. In the event of state financing, terms that outline the use of the facility for amateur and collegiate athletics.

7. The Task Force recognizes that Major League Baseball's business structure needs to be reformed.

Many studies have shown that Major League Baseball teams in markets with relatively little revenue from local media will continue to struggle financially. The Twins will continue to have few resources for building a competitive team even with a new stadium unless Major League Baseball implements significant reforms. The major necessary reforms are more equal revenue sharing, particularly from local media revenue, and some form of payroll equalization formula to reduce the disparity between high payroll and low payroll teams. The National Football League's salary cap and revenue sharing have helped to create teams whose success does not depend on the size of the local media market or the owner's bankroll.

The Task Force supports the further consideration of a shared appreciation agreement between the owners of the professional baseball franchises and the public entity owning the facility. Upon the sale of the professional baseball franchise, or its relocation out of the State of Minnesota, during the term of the lease agreement, the franchisee would pay a percentage of the appreciated value of the franchise to the public entity.

8. The Task Force recommends that public participation in financing facilities for professional sports be designed to ensure that professional sports events are accessible to, and beneficial for, a broad community of Minnesotans.

Any professional sports facilities with public financing should include specific provisions for maintaining the accessibility and affordability of some portion of tickets to professional sports events held in the facilities. The potential for use of the facilities by high school and other amateur sports teams should also be protected. In addition, facilities that benefit from public financing participation should be designed to be integrated into the host city and its neighborhood. An architecturally significant design could become an attraction in itself, as well as enhancing the physical environment of a community and economic development opportunities.

The members of the Minnesota Stadiums Task Force submitted their final report to the State's Governor and Legislature on January 25, 2002. The Task Force's deliberations were very comprehensive in nature, and included public hearings with representatives of sports teams, the state legislature, local government officials, architects, contractors, financiers, sports fans, and everyday taxpayers and citizens. Notwithstanding the inclusive preparation process used for collecting the information upon which to base their final report, their report is advisory in nature to the State's elected officials.

CHAPTER 33

Salem and Other Cities Compete to Host Sporting Events at Their Stadiums and Arenas

Nancye Tuttle

Officials in small American cities have discovered they do not have to be a Detroit, site of the 2006 Super Bowl, or a Salt Lake City, scene of the 2002 Winter Olympics, to attract sporting events. With well-run venues, and support from local businesses and residents, small-to-mid-size cities can attract thousands of visitors and pump millions of dollars into the local economy.

This month, Lowell, Mass., a former mill city with 125,000 residents, will welcome the World Men's Curling Championships, a week-long competition, attracting visitors from Europe, Japan, Canada and the United States. Visitors will pack restaurants and hotels, shop local stores and visit museums, spending an estimated $5.1 million.

In mid–March, Salem, Va., a city of 20,000 residents, was the scene of board-pounding college basketball, when the NCAA Division III Men's Basketball Championships attracted 3,400 fans to the Salem Civic Center, part of an expansive sports complex with a 7,500-seat football stadium and a 6,300-seat baseball park designed to host Division III national football, softball, baseball and volleyball championships.

In mid–July, the En-Joie Golf Course in Endicott, N.Y., a village that is part of 200,000-resident Binghamton, will host the BC Open, a part of the Professional Golfers' Association of America Tour, a tradition since 1971. With a purse of $3.5 million, it is a smaller stop on the tour. Yet, by all accounts, it is also one of the friendliest, giving more than $8 million to local charities over the years.

A well-run venue is crucial, officials say. In its nine-year history, Lowell's Tsongas Arena, which is owned by the city and managed by Philadelphia-based SMG, has gained a reputation for successfully staging sporting events, hosting national synchronized skating championships and world cup tennis. The arena is home to semi-professional and college hockey teams. "We have a wonderful venue, and one of our goals is to bring major events here," says Deborah Belanger, director

Originally published as "Cities Compete to Host Sporting Events," *American City & County*, Vol. 121, No. 4, April 2006, by Penton Media, Inc., Overland Park, KS. Reprinted with permission of the publisher.

of Lowell-based Merrimack Valley Convention and Visitors Bureau.

In NCAA sports, the Salem Civic Center is well-known. "It started with the Stagg Bowl, the national championship for Division III football," says Carey Harveycutter, director of the city-owned center since 1968. "It was a rousing success and led to an agreement with the NCAA to host Division III softball, [which] led to basketball, baseball and volleyball. Word got around that we knew how to run these events, and it just sort of snowballed."

Attracting sporting events involves cooperation and teamwork, and months or years of planning. In Lowell, pursuit of the curling championships began six years ago with talks between city officials and curling organizers, Belanger says.

The partnership plunged full-speed ahead in 2002, when the World Curling Federation awarded Lowell the 2006 championships. Today, the city is ready for the influx of visitors who will purchase 45,000 seats during the competitions, boosting the economy. "It will be fabulous," says City Manager John Cox. "Here we are, the city of Lowell hosting a real world event, an Olympic sporting event at Tsongas Arena. It's been an unbelievable journey, but well worth it."

Officials say resident participation, either through volunteering or attending the events, helps ensure success. "It's important to create a strong local base, even for events for which the community has no direct connection," Harveycutter says. "For football and basketball, we sell 1,500 to 2,000 seats locally. The competition is good, and local people enjoy it."

Hosting spectator sporting events can be economically profitable for smaller cities, and Salem experienced a big economic boost in March, Harveycutter says. "The championships bring in $4 [million] to $6 million a year in tourism dollars for the local economy," he says. "And it's clean money. They come in, spend it, leave, and you don't have to educate their kids."

The same is true for Endicott, says Alex De Persis, president of the Greater Binghamton Chamber of Commerce. "There are 75,000 to 80,000 [people] at the golf course, and we estimate they add $4 [million] to $5 million to the economy each July," he says. Those numbers make city officials and residents feel good about playing host to smaller, yet no less impressive, sporting events.

CHAPTER 34

San Francisco and Other Cities Use Sports Facilities as Anchor Tenants to Stimulate Inner-City Living

Philip Langdon

A July 27 *New York Times* article has stimulated debate about whether the trend toward "retro" sports stadiums has begun to wane and, if so, whether this will be good or bad news for cities.

"For more than a decade, what's new in sport design has been what's old — or at least old-fashioned," Christopher Hawthorne, a contributing editor at *Metropolis* magazine, wrote in the *Times*. Since 1992, when the Orioles opened their ballpark at Camden Yards, near the western edge of downtown Baltimore, major league baseball stadiums have, according to Hawthorne, favored "nostalgic touches" such as brick facades, old-fashioned signs, grass rather than artificial turf, and "nooks, crannies and other imposed eccentricities in the outfield."

From an urbanistic perspective, retro ballparks have generally been a big improvement over the multipurpose stadiums that sprouted in the 1960s and 1970s. Some of the baseball facilities built in the past several years, such as Coors Field in Denver and Pacific Bell Park in

San Francisco, front on city streets and are situated within an easy walk of apartments, restaurants, public transportation, and other amenities.

Minor-league teams, which have orchestrated a giant spurt of stadium construction in the past 15 years, have enthusiastically embraced the trend toward old-fashioned traits and downtown locations. One of the best Triple-A baseball stadiums is the Memphis Redbirds' home, 14,320-seat AutoZone Park, which won a CNU Award in June in recognition of its success in injecting life into downtown Memphis.

Like professional baseball players, the idea of building new stadiums with old-fashioned characteristics came up from the minor leagues. The concept materialized in 1988 when Pilot Field opened in downtown Buffalo. The new home of Buffalo's Bisons featured design flourishes that were an immense relief after the previous generation of emotionless football-baseball facilities, such as Pittsburgh's cold concrete colossus, Three Rivers Stadium.

Originally published as "Old-Style Ballparks, Fronting on Urban Streets, Spur In-City Living," *New Urban News*, Vol. 8, No. 6, September 2003, published by New Urban News Publications, Ithaca, NY. Reprinted with permission of the publisher.

Kansas City-based HOK Sport, one of the tiny number of firms that together dominate sports architecture, had at first wanted to give the Bisons' park an austere form that, according to Buffalo architect Peter Nowak, resembled "a concrete bomb shelter." Nowak and another architect, Ed Kowalewski, went to Mayor James D. Griffin and argued that this would be a mistake — the stadium for the Triple-A team should be designed more like the old ballparks that fans loved. Not long afterward, HOK Sport returned to Buffalo with a far different design — a stadium still built of precast concrete, but with steel-framed arches along the exterior and with a green metal roof, reminiscent of historic ballparks.

Pilot Field has done little to stimulate development in downtown Buffalo, probably because it was built in a relatively desolate area east of Main Street and because the Buffalo area's economy has been too weak to support an urban renaissance. The 21,050-seat ballpark itself earned plaudits, however. And the Kansas City firm, now known as HOK Sport + Venue + Event (HOK SVE), won enormous acclaim when it produced the first retro ballpark in the major leagues — 48,188-seat Camden Yards. The Baltimore Orioles park used a massive old brick warehouse on its perimeter as an appealing backdrop for the action on the field. The idea of fitting ballparks into the urban fabric and adorning them with materials and motifs derived from nearby buildings became the talk of the sports world.

Economic Stimulators

In metropolitan areas that have the taste and money to pursue urban pleasures, ballparks of this sort have helped generate vibrant mixed-use districts. Coors Field, a ballpark by HOK SVE that opened in Denver in 1995, has — in concert with other public and private improvements — stimulated extensive housing construction in lower downtown, or "LoDo." Within six years of the Colorado Rockies' first game at Coors, 600 lofts, apartments, and condominium units were developed in a warehouse area next to the stadium. Restaurants and sports bars proliferated.

The 50,249-seat stadium enticed many metro Denver residents to visit LoDo for the first time, and they found it to be an interesting, walkable, surprisingly safe place. The primary inhabitants of the area near the park, one third of whom own their residences, are single men and married couples without children. Despite being, on average, 50 years old, the residents for the most part tolerate the noise from young men spilling into LoDo's streets when the sports bars close at 2 in the morning. Some condos and lofts have sold in the $1 million range.

HOK SVE avoids describing its ballparks as "retro." The firm prefers to call the designs "context-based" or "context-driven" because in cities like Denver, Baltimore, and Cleveland, they take their cues from the materials and styles of structures nearby. Although many resemble buildings from the early 20th century, Earl Santee, head of the Major Baseball Group at HOK SVE, says context-based ballparks are not uniformly "traditional" in style. Jacobs Field, the 43,368 home of the Cleveland Indians, is "relatively Modern," he avers. Though limestone is used at its base, the nine-year-old park also prominently employs glass and steel and seems to harmonize with Cleveland's powerful steel bridges.

"Architecturally, the buildings have to be a fit for the neighborhood," Santee says. "They have to be the right scale, the right massing." Though he argues that "if you were in a modern city, you would do a modern building," many fans prefer the warmth and texture of traditional ballparks, so that's the direction in which ballpark has headed in the past decade.

Hawthorne argued in the *Times* that in recent projects such as HOK SVE's Great American Ball Park in Cincinnati, "the retro trend has grown stale." He further insisted that sports architecture is beginning to move from traditional styling toward something more "bold." Hawthorne's evidence was weak, however, consisting mainly of a pair of football stadiums — the 68,532-seat Lincoln Financial Field in Philadelphia and New York architect Peter Eisenman's design for the 63,000-seat Arizona Cardinals stadium, to built in Glendale, near Phoenix.

Rarely do football stadiums look or function like baseball parks. Football does not have a tradition and history as deep as baseball's. Football stadiums are bigger, they generate more automobile traffic on game days, and the team plays there only a few days a year (whereas major-league baseball teams play at least 81 homes games a year). Since football stadiums sit empty most of the time and generally have mammoth parking requirements, they don't make promising urban building blocks.

Anti-Urban Behemoth

Eisenman's design for the Arizona Cardinals, though praised in the *Times*, is downright anti-urban — surrounded by parking lots. Such big, isolated structures naturally tend to be designed as "object buildings" or "icons" rather than as contributors to lively, mixed-use urban districts. Photographers conspire with the architects, the team owners, and whatever companies bought the stadium naming rights to show how dramatic these venues look like from the air, as opposed to documenting how they look from the poor pedestrian's perspective. "They're designed for the blimp shot," Sandy Sorlien, a Philadelphia photographer, complained on the Tradarch e-

mail discussion list affiliated with the Institute for Traditional Architecture. Not uncommonly, architectural writers glorify such stadiums if they look novel and striking, even though their design and siting are unneighborly.

Some ballparks with retro styling are equally guilty of standing apart from the mix of urban life. Sorlien notes that the Phillies' 43,000-seat Citizens Bank Park, scheduled to open next spring, sits in a distant part of South Philadelphia in a "stadium ghetto," surrounded by a sea of parking lots and other sports facilities. The fact that the new ballpark's designers — Ewing Cole Cherry Brott of Philadelphia and HOK SVE — have incorporated arcades, patterned brick, and other traditional features only makes it seem "a cartoon of a real urban ballpark," Sorlien contends.

The Right Way at Wrigley Field

Chicago architect Philip Bess, one of the best new urbanist authorities on ballparks, sees Wrigley Field, which dates to 1914, as a model that's still worth emulating. "It generates street life, a kind of party atmosphere," Bess says. The Cubs games enliven the neighborhood, and the neighborhood adds to the character of the 39,214-seat park. The penchant of spectators for watching the games from nearby rooftops has become institutionalized, for better or worse, as clubs occupy some of the buildings.

Denver's Coors Field spurred conversion of nearby warehouses into living quarters, as had been anticipated. Now, says Santee at HOK SVE, "the biggest trend is new housing, which is a shocker." Surface parking lots are being redeveloped with high-density buildings that contain food-related businesses or other commercial uses on the ground floor and that have housing above.

Despite Americans' predominant desire for quiet in their living quarters, a number of individuals will pay extra to live within sight or earshot of a ballpark. Apartments with views into AutoZone Park command premium rents, says Frank Ricks of Looney Ricks Kiss, which designed the Memphis ballpark. (HOK SVE consulted on it.) San Diego and St. Louis both expect residential development to accompany ballparks that are under way or planned. The trend is for residential and commercial development to go hand in hand with ballpark development.

The biggest limitation on the trend is that many major-league baseball teams already have relatively new ballparks and that, according to Bess, "more than 100 minor-league stadiums have been built in the last 15 years." Slowing demand for new ballparks may put a crimp on mixed-use urban development for a while. But when ballparks are needed, the mixed-use model is the one to follow. Looney Ricks Kiss has been asked to work on proposals in Nashville; Bowling Green, Kentucky; Lancaster, Pennsylvania, and elsewhere. The concept of the multipurpose ballpark district is running strong. "They want baseball," Ricks says of the cities he hears from, "but they want other things around it.

CHAPTER 35

Seattle Designs Its Stadium to Fit Both the Neighborhood and the Community

Renée Young

The best seat in the house at the new Seahawks Stadium in Seattle isn't on the 50-yard line. It's in the southeast corner, at the very top of the upper bowl. "From there you have a corner-to-corner view of the field and an inspiring grasp of the surrounding city," says Kelly Kerns, project leader with architect/engineer Ellerbe Becket, Kansas City, Mo. "You feel like you're part of something amazing."

That's just what the Building Team for Seahawks Stadium and Exhibition Center hoped for. Set against a backdrop of snow-capped mountains and the shimmering waters of Puget Sound, the new complex offers links to historic Pioneer Square, the city's International District, and downtown, melding it all into a unique Seattle experience.

The new football/soccer stadium, 325,000-sq.-ft. exhibition center, and 2,000-car parking garage are the product of First & Goal, Inc., an entity formed by Paul Allen, the multibillionaire co-founder of Microsoft and owner of the Portland Trailblazers of the National Basketball Association. In 1996, Allen took a 14-month option on the Seahawks

when then-owner Ken Behring tried unsuccessfully to move the team to Los Angeles.

The deal required Allen to tear down the Kingdome and build a new stadium, at a time when Washington State taxpayers were soured by the $100 million in overruns that plagued construction of the $517 million Mariners baseball stadium. Allen put up $9 million to push through a referendum that, in June 1997, created the Washington State Public Stadium Authority and capped the public's obligation at $300 million. Allen guaranteed $130 million out of pocket, plus the cost of any overruns.

Reflecting the Culture

At 8:31 A.M. on March 26, 2000, the 25-year-old Kingdome was imploded by Aman Environmental (at a cost of $9.2 million), and the Building Team of Ellerbe Becket and Turner Construction's Seattle office, headed by senior vice president Thomas Gerlach, Jr., set to work creating a structure for the Seahawks, a possible future Major League Soccer

Originally published as "Nurturing the Community," *Building Design and Construction*, May 2003, by Associated Construction Publications/Reed Construction Data, Oak Brook, IL. Reprinted with permission of the publisher.

team, Seattle Flat Show Coalition and — most important — the community.

The building was designed to fit into an urban neighborhood, which includes the adjacent baseball dome, Safeco Field. "In the 1880s, the entire area was burnt to the ground," says Kerns. "As a result, all of the buildings there were built within the same 10- to 15-year timeframe — with the same construction elements, at the same height of about 85 feet."

To conform to the neighborhood's height limit, the stadium rests on an 85-ft.-high masonry base, from which rises the concrete seating and steel roof structure. Using a stained, colored concrete and concrete unit masonry, the masonry base echoes the historic structures found throughout Pioneer Square.

The U-shaped seating design and upper bowl, which sits a mere 50 feet from the sidelines, also creates a feeling of intimacy. "Paul Allen wanted to create the most intimate NFL stadium with unsurpassed sightlines — so we employed a 56-ft. cantilever, the largest in the NFL, of the upper bowl over the suite level, bringing the upper bowl seats closer to the field," said Kerns. With the open end of the "U" facing north toward downtown Seattle, spectators are connected to the surrounding communities, while those outside the stadium have views inside.

The new icon of the Seattle skyline is the stadium's 1.4 million pound roof, which spans 720 feet and features the largest post-tensioned arches in the U.S. The white-painted steel "rainbow span" connects the downtown high-rise structures with the Space Needle to the north.

This is no mean feat in a seismic zone of this nature. The structure was designed to withstand an earthquake of 7.0 strength; in fact, a lesser earthquake hit during construction in February 2001, causing only minor damage.

To decrease the lateral loads imparted from the trusses to the pylons during a seismic event, project structural engineer Magnusson Klemencic Associates of Seattle developed a creative application of industrial technology to solve the bearing condition at each end of the trusses. The plan uses base-isolating friction pendulum damper bearings that allow the roof to move 2 ft. differentially from the pylons.

The first application of this technology in the world on a large roof span, this solution reduced the amount of reinforcing in the cast-in-place concrete pylon walls and footings, which resulted in a $2.5 million savings and gave Seattle a monument to structural engineering.

Supported by 5,700 tons of steel, the roof itself is covered with UltraGard SR-50, a PVC membrane single-ply roofing system from Johns Manville. It covers 70 percent of the seats, but is open to the field.

From the project's beginning in early 1997, the team knew that this stadium, like the Kingdome before it, would be a significant feature of the Seattle skyline. For that reason, the project's schedule and budget needed to reflect the interests of the community as well. The complex is the only recent major public/ private project to come in on time and on budget in the Northwest.

Completed in June 2002 and opened for public view on July 20, the stadium hosted its first event — a soccer match between the Seattle Sounders and the Vancouver Whitecaps of the A League — last July 28, before 25,515 fans. The Seahawks lost their exhibition home opener 28–10 to the Indianapolis Colts on August 10 and their regular-season home opener to the Arizona Cardinals, 24–13, on September 15, 2002.

The $430 million facility features a cost per seat that is 7 percent less than the average of the last 13 new NFL stadiums. Change orders ran 10 percent below the average cost on comparable buildings. "The project team stayed very committed to being on time and under budget," says Tom Gerlach, SVP/GM of Turner's Seattle office. "The project is a model for public-private partnerships."

The five-level complex features 67,000 permanent seats (plus room for 5,000 more, qualifying the stadium to host a Super Bowl), 84 suites (one of which is reserved for season ticket holders, by lottery), 48 concession stands, 841 televisions (including 80 Philips high-definition TVs), and 63 restrooms — more than twice as many as at the Kingdome.

The playing surface uses an artificial turf by FieldTurf. (Grass will be installed in the event the stadium is ever host to a World Cup–caliber soccer match.) The facility is illuminated by 672 Musco sports lights and contains $1.75 million in public art. The end-zone pylon contains a $7.5 million video board, 84x24 ft., designed by Lighthouse Technologies, Hong Kong.

Seats are priced as low as $20. In the end zones are a dozen so-called "Red Zone" suites at field level — a unique feature among NFL stadiums.

To maximize the stadium's use on non-game days, the exhibition center can use 92,900 sq. ft. of flex space within the stadium. The result of the integrated approach of restaurant, exhibition, and sports venue is a urban leisure center for Seattle.

Demanding Diversity

The Building Team was dedicated to reaching Seattle's diverse population. Extraordinary steps were taken to meet the needs of fans with disabilities, says Kerns. Holding public forums and working with compliance consultant Kevin McGuire, himself a person with disabilities, they learned that disabled fans who have to travel long distances to attend games often can't sit through the whole event without rest, so they set up sleeping rooms for them in the First Aid areas.

Seven hundred seats were set aside for disabled fans, with another 700 for their companions, all in areas where fans with disabilities would not be obstructed by other cheering fans.

Town hall meetings were held to obtain input on community impact. As a result, $10 million was set aside for neighborhood improvements. Two of the groups the team specifically targeted to involve in the project were apprentices and minority and women business enterprises (M/WBE).

The Building Team voluntarily established a goal of hiring apprentices to fill 15 percent of all construction jobs, especially in the carpentry, electrical, masonry, painting, and plumbing trades. To encourage racial and ethnic diversity, Turner brought in a seasoned community affairs director, Ruby Jones, who spoke at numerous community meetings about career opportunities in construction.

The Building Team also set up liaisons with the trade unions and recruited apprentices from local union halls. The result: 19 percent apprentice participation, beating their goal by four percentage points.

"This is a good example of going beyond public policy," observed Building Team awards judge Philip Tobey, AIA, of the Washington, D.C., office of the SmithGroup. "The apprentice programs with Seattle Vocational are terrific."

To further diversity, the Building Team implemented an aggressive program to contract with M/WBE, even though a recent statewide initiative had done away with affirmative action requirements. "Projects you work on should reflect the community," says Jones.

"It's essential that you have this involvement if you're going to really reflect the community," says EB's Kerns. "We rely on local M/WBEs to help provide the local input that contributes to the success of the project."

Of the total $430 million budget, $81 million was awarded to some 116 M/WBE firms, including $69 million in construction contracts and $7 million in A/E work.

Locating M/WBE companies wasn't easy. The pool of certified minority and women workers had shrunk at an alarming rate after the passage of the state initiative. To find qualified businesses, Jones and her team conducted one-on-one interviews with prospective companies and worked to partner with them.

"For more than 30 years, M/WBE inclusion has been a part of the way Turner does business, so we needed to ensure that we had a viable group to work with not just for this project, but for other projects down the line," says Jones.

To ensure the appropriate work environment for minorities and women, the Building Team set a policy of zero tolerance with regard to on-site discrimination.

A key factor in the success of the program was the creation of the Turner School of Construction Management in Seattle. Conceived in 1969 by the firm's Cleveland office, the program has educated thousands of M/WBE contractors in basic and advanced construction techniques.

In Seattle, the program has been sponsored by the Associated General Contractors, the AGC Education Foundation, and the cities of Tacoma and Seattle. Since its creation in 2000, the Seattle school has graduated 52 M/WBE owners.

The stadium was designed to handle the community's needs well into the future. "The project includes spare infrastructure capacity, including the ability to expand the seating area," says Kerns. The parking garage structure is oversized to accommodate future additions.

According to competition judge Larry Griffis, of Walter Moore & Co., "For a huge, bulky stadium with massive scale, the design is good "

After maintenance and operating costs are met, any profits generated by the stadium and exhibition center will be split three ways — one part going to the Seahawks, another placed in reserve to cover any revenue shortfalls, and a third used to build youth playfields across the state.

First & Goal also funded a $6 million mitigation fund for three nearby neighborhoods. "The project stayed focused on the community goals from the very start — that was the key ingredient of success in the eyes of First & Goal and the Public Stadium Authority," says Turner's Gerlach.

CHAPTER 36

Sioux Falls and Other Cities Favor Neighborhood Sports Centers Over Large-Scale Facilities

Ronald A. Wirtz

It's easy to love shiny new buildings, and even easier when they are believed to be harbingers of local economic development. That's the pitch when it comes to stadiums, multiuse arenas and convention centers. But is it a strike?

Little attention is paid to the profitability of the superstructures themselves. Facilities rarely repay their construction costs, still many are fortunate to simply cash-flow in a given year. Rather, these facilities are designed to be spending magnets for the city — community loss leaders, if you will, similar to the way a grocery chain underprices soda to get people into the store. Once they've got you in the store for soda — or in this case, in the city for a ballgame or a trade show — you'll likely buy additional items to make up for the store's initial loss on soda.

As such, the main arguments in favor of publicly financed stadiums, arenas and convention centers stress the economic activity created outside, rather than inside, the walls of these facilities. While such benefits are real and legitimate, they are often inflated and oversold. "I think that's absolutely the case," said Mary Bujold, president of Maxfield Research, a Minneapolis firm. "Cities have blinders on to see whether the data [on local impact] is good."

Pick a Number

Current research indicates that stadiums and arenas have a particularly bad track record when it comes to delivering on promises of community economic windfalls. University researchers Mark Rosentraub and Mark Swindell found that three decades worth of studies "lead to the inescapable conclusion that the direct and indirect economic impacts of sports teams and the facilities are quite small" and do not create much in the way of new jobs or economic development.

There is little research on the economic impact of minor league teams and their playing venues. Queried via e-mail, Rosentraub

Originally published as "Stadiums and Convention Centers as Community Loss Leaders," *FedGazette*, March 2001, by the Federal Reserve Bank, Minneapolis, MN.

said, "Given the relatively small to nonexistent benefits from team sports at the higher levels, one should not expect anything or very, very little from minor league activities."

A Brookings Institution book on sports teams and stadiums noted the economic impact of a minor league baseball team is "equivalent to a large pet shop" in terms of revenue. A 1994 report investigated the impact of a $6 million stadium for a minor league baseball team in La Crosse, Wis. The report estimated total new annual spending at about $500,000, noting the impact was "substantially smaller" than claimed by stadium proponents. It suggested that public subsidies for such projects "should be carefully studied."

Convention centers tend to offer more bang for the public dollar. "[On] the convention side, you get a lot more economic impact," said John Kaatz of Convention, Sports & Leisure International of Minneapolis. "The sports side is less."

The reason for this is convention centers tend to attract more people from outside the region and state, which brings a larger amount of new spending to the community. But there is also a limit to that argument.

"As market size decreases, the strength of that [economic development] argument becomes shaky," Kaatz said, mainly because smaller markets often do not draw a significant number of visitors from outside the region. Nonetheless, smaller markets continue to use the argument, which Kaatz said "is a reflection of the fact that the whole [convention center] phenomenon has been generated from larger cities, and the argument has filtered down to smaller cities."

Analyzing the Analysis

Advocates of new venues often attempt to define a project's economic impact on the community in dollar terms. Although each type of facility has unique considerations, the economic impact of stadiums, multiuse arenas and convention centers involves many of the same factors, and their proponents are often guilty of the same mistakes.

Problem number one is that too many studies rely on "models and assumptions that are wrong," Kaatz said. "[The models] are simply unrealistic."

For example, most analysis includes average spending estimates for local and non-local event goers. These figures are usually provided by local or national associations — for example, the hotel lobby or convention and visitors bureaus — with an interest in these facilities. Using this data in his own work, Kaatz said it was not uncommon to revise these spending estimates downward.

Compounding any errors in average spending are estimates on the ratio of out-of-town attendees, who are assumed to spend significantly more on meals and lodging than local event goers. And the trifecta for some reports on economic impact is the inclusion of spending multipliers — the number of times a dollar will be spent or turned over once it is brought to a community. Kaatz said he's seen reports with multipliers as high as six; he believed a more reliable multiplier was about two on the high end.

These factors can lead to significantly different conclusions. Fargo, N.D., recently proposed building a new multiuse arena to host college hockey and other events. A study of the proposal by Maxfield Research estimated the direct economic impact of the facility at between $3.8 million to $4.4 million; a second analysis by a local university economist tagged the impact at $8.8 million to $15.3 million. Much of the gap stemmed from differing assumptions regarding out-of-town attendees and their spending habits. Voters apparently were unimpressed by the conclusions of either study, as a $48 million referendum on the facility last year "got thumped pretty bad," according Pat Zavoral, Fargo city administrator.

Game Substitutions

Impact reports typically ignore several other important factors. The most important are what economists call "substitution effects" — where spending for one activity merely replaces spending on other previous activities. While new entertainment options do likely bring in some new spending, advocates often mistake economic activity (all spending related to a sporting event or convention) with economic impact (new spending that otherwise would not have taken place).

Before basketball games and concerts came to town, for example, local event goers likely spent at least some of that money on other things, like bowling, or movies or fishing equipment. Such spending mobility represents a shift in spending rather than new spending. Tax dollars have also been used to encourage that shift. Geographic scope also has to be taken into account. Out-of-towners might simply be from a nearby town. While that might suit advocates just fine, it nonetheless offers little new spending in a regional sense, and scarce public resources have been used to redirect private spending.

Publicly financed venues can also end up competing with the private sector for event bookings. Missoula, Mont., studied the possibility of building a large convention center in 1996. A feasibility report noted that events with 1,000 to 2,500 attendees represented less than 1 percent of conference events in the region and "there is substantial competition among cities and towns for this limited number of large regional meetings." The study concluded that capturing a small number of big events would not justify the expense

of a large facility, and building a small conference center was "a duplication of services now being provided successfully by the private sector."

Even more overlooked is the substitution effect in public spending — other priorities that could have been funded, or taxes simply not collected. Dennis Coates and Brad Humphreys of the University of Maryland-Baltimore County have done extensive research on the economic impact of stadiums and arenas. They conclude in a recent paper that "impact studies typically do not address alternative uses of public funds. Indeed, politicians often seem to think that the means of financing the stadium generates free resources that have no alternative uses whatsoever.... [R]ules for sensible public investment should apply to stadium finance as much as they apply to public provision of highways, schools and airports."

Public spending on new venues also funnels most of the economic benefits — namely increased patronage — to lower-wage industries like lodging, eating and drinking establishments. Rosentraub's research on private sector employment and payroll in large counties found that these sectors make up about 8 percent of local jobs, but pay just 3 percent of all local wages. On the surface at least, public capital for other initiatives might produce better jobs and wages for local workers.

Measuring Public Good

One reason the math does not always add up regarding new venues is because advocates might be underselling the "public good" benefits that are hard to measure.

Bujold, of Maxfield Research, said weighing all the pros and cons — economically and otherwise — is much more complicated than cities typically undertake, and much of it cannot be easily boiled down to dollar terms. Bujold said that "a stadium is a kind of community gathering space. It's the idea that you get this nebulous effect to spur some community feeling," which she said was "hard to quantify" but nonetheless can spur a community's economy. "In small communities it becomes much more important. The dynamics there are entirely different."

Sports teams, for example, create a public good by virtue of the fact that they often engender community pride, interest and enjoyment outside of ticket-buying customers (what economists call externalities). "The magnitude of this benefit is unknown, and is not shared by everyone; nevertheless, it exists," wrote Roger Noll of the Brookings Institution.

How to measure the value of that benefit is an even bigger unknown. There have been few attempts to measure the "civic value" of sports teams and their venues, particularly outside of major metropolitan areas. In one recent case, researchers asked residents of Lexington, Ky., about their willingness to pay for a new arena for the popular University of Kentucky basketball team and a new stadium to attract a minor league baseball team.

By virtue of having an existing facility, the new college basketball arena represented an opportunity to improve a perceived public good (Wildcat basketball), while a new baseball stadium offered residents the choice of having a public good (a new baseball team) or not having a public good. Roughly two-thirds of Lexington residents said they were unwilling to pay higher taxes for either the basketball arena or baseball stadium. Of those willing to pay, almost half cited their desire to attend games, which the authors stressed was a private-good motivation rather than a public one.

Off-Ledger Contributions

Other intangible factors must also be considered in the final analysis of event facilities. Many sources, for example, pointed out that venues provide court and ice time for local teams or meeting space for community groups — a public good that doesn't show up in economic impact reports.

But by the same token, rarely do community groups lead with such arguments when stumping for a new facility, and in most cases local interests are served after private bookings. And a few sources also believed there are better ways to meet the public good portion of the equation.

The city of Sioux Falls investigated the possibility of building a 20,000-seat arena to compete with the likes of the Fargodome. A recent analysis has led the city to back off such a proposal, a move that pleased Dan Scott, president of the Sioux Falls Development Foundation.

"We think you'd be better off building neighborhood sports centers," which have comparatively lower overhead costs and much higher use, Scott said. The city has seen a rapid increase in demand for ice time at hockey rinks, and existing rinks are "in use from 5 in the morning to midnight," he said.

"I'm convinced that you have to use those dollars for facilities that have constant use," Scott said. "Meeting the need of the sporting community is a better use of the money.... I hope that's the direction we end up taking."

CHAPTER 37

Trenton Credits Waterfront Ballpark for Bringing People Back Downtown

Janet Ward

Twenty years ago, when Paul Mickle moved to Trenton, N.J., the city's waterfront was dominated by a defunct steelyard. U.S. Steel had abandoned the facility years before, taking with it some of the city's highest paying jobs and leaving behind mountains of slag and rusting metal.

For three decades, the steelyard was the unfortunate focal point of Trenton's downtown. "The city was bleak," says Mickle, now the city editor of *The Trentonian*, the local daily newspaper. "I've witnessed the renaissance."

If Trenton has undergone a renaissance, the role of Leonardo da Vinci was played by Clark, Caton, Hintz, the local architectural firm that created Waterfront Park. Home to the Trenton Thunder, the AA affiliate of the Boston Red Sox, Waterfront Park sits on the banks of the Delaware River on part of the 31-acre brownfield site that once housed the steelyard. Opened in 1994, it has spawned what most Trentonians consider nothing less than an economic miracle, turning a dilapidated

and unloved downtown into one of the hottest spots in Mercer County.

Mickle calls the ballpark "a real jewel," despite the fact that he has written critically about its cost overruns and other problems. "There are critics," he says. "I was one at one time. But it has changed the image and appearance of the city. It has become a desirable place that people want to come to."

People are coming for more than minor league baseball. The ballpark has become the hub of a downtown redevelopment process that now includes office buildings, shops and restaurants and a multi-purpose arena that is home to the Trenton Titans of the East Coast Hockey League. It also hosts college and high school basketball games, and concerts and shows. (This month, Marriott will open a hotel and conference center — the first hotel opened in downtown Trenton in 27 years — in a redevelopment triangle that includes the waterfront, the steelyard site and the capitol.)

"[The ballpark] has been the catalyst for hundreds of millions of dollars worth of devel-

Originally published as "If You Build It, They Will Come?" *American City & County*, Vol. 117, No. 4, April 2002, by Penton Media, Inc., Overland Park, KS. Reprinted with permission of the publisher.

opment," says Mayor Doug Palmer. "We set out to accomplish four goals: We wanted to bring people downtown after 5 p.m.; we wanted to keep people here after work; we wanted to change people's perception of the safety of the city; and we wanted to set the stage for private development. We have accomplished all four goals."

The Critics

The very idea that stadiums can serve as economic development sparkplugs makes economists apoplectic. Critics could paper a trail from San Francisco's PacBell Park to Boston's Fenway with reports and studies showing that, far from being catalysts for nearby development, stadiums actually are black holes where tax dollars go to die.

A sampling:

- "Our research suggests that professional sports may be a drain on local economies rather than an engine of economic growth," concluded University of Maryland, Baltimore County economics professors Dennis Coats and Brad Humphreys in their 1996 report, "The Stadium Gambit and Local Economic Development."
- "Public funding of sports, including funding of stadiums, is not a sound civic economic investment," wrote Robert Baade in "Stadiums, Professional Sports and Economic Development: Assessing the Reality." The 1994 report was published by the Heartland Institute, a Chicago-based think tank.
- "A new sports facility has an extremely small (perhaps even negative) effect on overall economic activity and employment," wrote Roger Noll and Andrew Zimbalist, economics professors for Stanford University in Stanford, Calif., and Northampton, Mass.–based Smith College,

respectively, in a 1997 article, "Are New Stadiums Worth the Cost?"

Pro-stadium forces argue that, theoretically, new stadiums offer a wealth of promises, both tangible (job creation and revenue from ticket, concession and memorabilia sales) and intangible (civic pride). However, the critics counter that, in reality, while new ballparks certainly serve as sources of pride, they fail to deliver on most of their other promises.

There are a number of reasons why that is true, but critics most often cite "public subsidy" as the crux of their arguments. In effect, they say, the vast amounts of tax money that go into the construction of new stadiums and arenas (and the associated infrastructure necessary to sustain them) negates any economic benefit to the community created by those facilities.

Before the explosion of interest in sports (sometime in the 1980s), it made sense for cities and counties to direct their tax revenues into sports facility construction because they generally kept the revenues generated by those facilities, as well as the rent paid by the teams that used them.

However, increasing interest in sports meant more leverage for team owners, who began demanding sweetheart deals from their host communities in exchange for not shopping their teams to other locations. For those charged with keeping an eye on local government finances, those sweetheart deals would be laughable if they were not so serious.

For example, Philadelphia is putting up some $600 million to build new stadiums for its NFL Eagles and MLB Phillies, both of which had threatened to leave. In return, the Eagles and Phillies will stay in Philadelphia. The teams also will get the revenue from ticket sales, stadium advertising, parking, salvage from the old stadium and stadium naming rights (a fairly recent and extremely lucrative phenomenon with some small potential for embarrassment, as with the Houston Astros' Enron Field).

It did not have to be that way. Had either team left the city's old multi-use stadium, it would have been in breach of contract, and no other cities were clamoring for either of them. "The city had all the leverage in the world," says Philadelphia Controller Jonathan Saidel. "But there were powerful political interests pushing for the deal, and the city capitulated."

It did so against Saidel's advice. "My position was: If it's too costly, and there's no good rate of return, we should use the resources for the betterment of the people of the city," he says. "If the owner of the Eagles can't make money on the Eagles, he needs to sell them to someone who can. He doesn't need to be holding up the city."

Saidel even authored an incisive and comprehensive report called "Stadium Overview: Myths and Realities," in which he concluded that "if the city's investment in new stadia will not be repaid by taxes associated with new economic activity or revenues generated by the stadia then the city is wise to use its scarce resources to address other concerns." At the bottom of each page in the report, Saidel invited "proponents of public funding for new stadia to present verifiable financial data to challenge any of the assumptions regarding new stadia and economic development in Philadelphia."

Because he is an elected official, Saidel's strong stance against the publicly funded stadiums could have put him in jeopardy in Philadelphia, where public sentiment ran strongly to the stadium deal. Still, he never wavered. "I was pretty damned out front with my opposition," he says. "But I still got 85 percent of the vote [when I ran] last year. It hasn't hurt me politically, but it hurts the city economically. We've got a school district and an infrastructure in crisis. Building two stadiums is not what we should be doing with our money."

That the Eagles and the Phillies would blackmail Philadelphia, a city with so many other priorities, provides ammunition for critics of public funding of sports facilities. And Philadelphia is not even the worst example.

Just across the state line, the Yankees and the Mets convinced outgoing New York Mayor Rudy Giuliani to guarantee them a total of $1.6 billion for the construction of new ballparks that would replace Yankee and Shea stadiums. Giuliani's promise was galling to New Yorkers because the city obviously has other immediate priorities — and because the Yankees and the Mets are two of baseball's wealthiest teams and could easily afford to build their own parks. (New Mayor Mike Bloomberg reneged on Giuliani's deal but did offer the two teams $5 million a year for the next five years to study plans for new stadiums.)

Philadelphia and New York are hardly the exceptions. In recent years, Nashville, Tenn.; Seattle; Pittsburgh; Cincinnati; Milwaukee; Detroit; and Charlotte, N.C., picked up most of the tab for the construction of new stadiums worth at least $200 million each. Of major cities, only San Francisco has bucked the trend. Of the $255 million paid to build PacBell Park in 1998–1999, the city contributed just $10 million in tax increment financing. The Giants and private investors ponied up the rest.

Since then, construction plans have faced tougher going. For example, in Fresno, Calif.; Miami; Minneapolis; and Boston, voters failed to approve stadium referenda; and in St. Louis, four Missouri legislators went on record to oppose public funding of the Cardinals' new park. "Let's face it, we are not going to revive this state's economy with the construction of a new baseball stadium," Sen. Sarah Steelman told the *St. Louis Post-Dispatch*.

Small Is Beautiful

So, is Trenton the anomaly? Not necessarily, says Bridgeport, Conn., Mayor Joe Ganim. Bridgeport's new ballpark, the Ballpark at Harbor Yard, has been "the jumping-off point for a lot of other major economic development projects downtown," Ganim says.

Like Trenton, Bridgeport is using its ballpark to anchor waterfront revitalization efforts. The city has invested about $17 million in construction of the Harbor Yard ballpark and a popular nearby arena that hosts Fairfield University's basketball team and the Sound Tigers minor league hockey team. "We were very businesslike in our transactions," Ganim says. "We made sure we got the best bang for our buck."

The ballpark was not without its critics in the beginning. "It was controversial," Ganim says. "A lot of people didn't want to spend the money. The city council was split. Now they're its biggest fans."

(Bridgeport and Trenton share another phenomenon; once their ballparks were built, they quickly became so popular that, when the cities decided to construct arenas, the decisions drew virtually no opposition.)

In Bridgeport and Trenton, ballparks do spur economic development. The reason is simple: "We came from nothing," says Mercer County Executive Bob Prunetti, who was instrumental in coordinating a consensus for the construction of Trenton's Waterfront Park. "State government was the city's whole industry. There was nothing else."

That is not true in many places, where museums, nightclubs, restaurants and theaters vie for consumer dollars. "To judge success [of economic development efforts], you have to measure where you've come from," Prunetti says. "Prior to building our ballpark, we had no hotel in our capital city. We had no theaters and no McDonald's. Now we have a hotel,

and we have a McDonald's. Two out of three's not bad."

The ballpark made all that possible in a way other kinds of facilities — museums or theaters, for instance — could not have, primarily because of the regional affection generated by sports teams.

"Some urban [sports] facilities built in blighted areas have had positive spinoff effects that no other type of development could have matched [because of] the regional support for professional sports," notes a 1998 report by the National Conference of State Legislatures. "Not only did the facilities stimulate development in the immediate area, but it happened with help from entire metropolitan areas. It is unlikely that suburban counties would ever subsidize core-city development in any other circumstance." (The report, "Playing the Stadium Game: Financing Professional Sports Facilities in the '90s," argues for caution in using public money to finance sports facilities.)

Regional support was critical in Trenton, where Prunetti managed to convince skeptical suburbanites that the ballpark belonged downtown. "I would only agree to build it in the city because I couldn't justify the economics of sending money to the suburbs," he says. "They're already doing well. We needed to use the money as a stimulus in a depressed area. That was our public policy purpose."

It also makes a difference that, in Trenton, Bridgeport and similar cities, ballparks are not designed as one-shot monuments; they are considered part of a larger development vision. "We didn't plan to build a ballpark," says Trenton's Palmer. "We planned to develop the waterfront. You need an overall vision, or you will fail."

"Stadium construction has a limited life in terms of an economic development impact," says Lisa Petraglia, director of economic research for Economic Development Research

Group, a Boston-based consulting firm that specializes in measuring economic development performance, impacts and opportunities. "When there's a vision that the stadium is part of a revitalization and not just an end point, then it can have an economic development aspect."

Petraglia says that "vision" is easier to achieve in smaller communities. A project like construction of a ballpark takes on more importance in a city that is not dotted with other entertainment opportunities, she says. That is why Bridgeport and its small-community cohorts in baseball's Atlantic League (the New Jersey cities of Newark, Camden, Atlantic City and Somerset, plus Nashua, N.H., and Central Islip, N.Y.) are "good case studies for using stadiums as economic development catalysts," she says.

Even so, the argument persists that a community's economic development is better served if public money is directed into real infrastructure (sewers, roads, water pipes) and education. Petraglia says that a valid argument against public funding of sports facilities can be made because non-fans should not be forced to support facilities that they will likely never use.

Palmer is not so sure. "People without kids pay school taxes," he says. "People pay taxes to build those concrete sound barriers even when they don't live near them."

Like schools and concrete sound barriers, sports teams go to a city's quality of life, Palmer says. "We used to be Trenton, the capital of New Jersey, and that's great," he says. "Now, we're Trenton, the capital of New Jersey and the home of the Thunder and the Titans. [Red Sox shortstop] Nomar Garciaparra played here. It may not sound like much, but it's a big deal to us."

CHAPTER 38

Washington, D.C., Think Tank
Encourages Public Officials
Not to Subsidize New Sports Stadium

Dennis Coates *and* Brad R. Humphreys

The September 28, 2004, press conference at the Washington City Museum was a lively affair. As the *Washington Post* described it: "The mood in the City Museum's Great Hall was near-giddy. John Fogerty's stadium anthem, 'Centerfield,' blared over loudspeakers. A crowd of kids, some wearing baseball uniforms and carrying balls, hunted for autographs from former Washington Senators."[1] The press conference was the culmination of years of haggling with Major League Baseball to bring the first baseball team to D.C. since the Washington Senators left in 1971.

More hard work is to be done, however. Williams now has to convince a majority of the D.C. Council to approve his plan to use tax money and the power of city government to build a new state-of-the-art ballpark for the team. To win support and council votes, he has touted the perceived economic benefits that will come from having baseball in D.C. again. Unfortunately for Mayor Williams, his claims do not withstand scrutiny.

The practice of professional sports teams

profiting at the expense of taxpayers is not new. The gambit routinely involves an individual franchise using its monopoly power to extract concessions from state and local governments. The Washington case differs because Major League Baseball, not the Expos, played the role of the monopolist pitting one potential suitor against another in search of the best deal. However, make no mistake: Major League Baseball's protracted decision-making process as it mulled over the relative merits of various locations — Washington; Northern Virginia; Portland, Oregon; Charlotte, North Carolina; San Juan, Puerto Rico; Monterrey, Mexico; and the other cities bidding for the franchise — was a classic exercise in concession extraction by a monopoly sports league.

Mayor Williams and others who wanted to lure the team to Washington and now want to build a new stadium claim that average D.C. taxpayers will not be burdened with the costs. Williams stated in his "Message from the Mayor" for October 1, 2004, that "the ballpark will be 100 percent financed by the team

Originally published as "Caught Stealing: Debunking the Economic Case for D.C. Baseball," *Briefing Paper*, No. 89, October 2004, by the Cato Institute, Washington, D.C. Reprinted with permission of the publisher.

owners, those who use the ballpark, and by DC's largest businesses ... our residents will not be asked to pay one dime of tax dollars toward this ballpark."[2]

According to Williams's proposed plan, the revenue to finance the construction of the baseball stadium will come from rent paid by the baseball team to use the new facility; taxes on tickets sales, concessions, parking, and merchandise sold within the stadium; and a "ballpark fee" (read: tax increase) on some of the District's largest corporations.

First, the team's share of financing the stadium is a 30-year lease committing the team to an initial rent of $3.5 million each year, increasing to $5 million by the fifth year, and then increasing by 2 percent minus $10,000 per year thereafter.[3] Of course, the conventional idea behind a lease is that a tenant pays rent for the use of a facility owned by somebody else. So the team will be renting the facility but will not be paying for its construction — despite the fact that the touted economic benefits that will follow in the wake of the team relocating to the District depend on the team being successful and profitable. Major league sports teams are certainly not mom-and-pop operations and can pay entirely for the construction of their own stadiums.

According to calculations of economist Scott Wallsten at the AEI-Brookings Joint Center for Regulatory Studies, the rent the baseball team will pay "is almost certain to decrease every year after 2009 when accounting for inflation. If inflation averages 3 percent over 30 years, the [team] will be paying about $3.3 million per year in today's dollars by 2035."[4] Thus, in just five years, D.C. taxpayers will be forced to provide another implicit concession — a de facto rent subsidy — to the baseball team.

Second, taxes will be collected on ticket sales, concessions, parking, and merchandise sold within the stadium. Concessions and merchandise are, in common parlance, food and beverages, T-shirts, hats, jerseys, and other souvenirs. It is likely that the D.C. residents who purchase food, beverages, and clothing while attending games would have chosen to eat and purchase clothes in D.C. — and pay taxes on those purchases — in the absence of the stadium and franchise. In other words, revenues generated inside the stadium may not be new revenues, even if they are dedicated specifically to paying for the new stadium.

Finally, a "ballpark fee" will be imposed on the largest corporations in D.C. Whether it is a surcharge or an increase in the corporate income tax rate, this so-called fee is a tax increase, pure and simple. Moreover, this tax will fall on D.C. residents if they happen to be owners or employees of the affected businesses, or if they purchase the goods or services produced by those businesses. Thus, claiming that D.C. residents will not feel the burden of this corporate tax increase is disingenuous. Corporations do not pay taxes, people do. Whether it is in the form of lower wages for workers, lower asset values for corporate owners, or higher prices for consumers of the goods and services those companies provide, this tax increase will touch D.C. residents in some way.

Do Professional Sports Produce Economic Benefits?

The proponents of new stadiums and franchises argue that there will be substantial economic benefits from proposed facilities and teams.[5] Indeed, a report from the District's Office of the Deputy Mayor for Planning and Economic Development claims that the team and ballpark will "create 360 jobs earning an annual total of $94 million."[6] That amounts to an astounding $261,111 per job. The wonder is that anyone finds such figures credible. Yet decade after decade, cities throughout the country have struggled to attract or keep professional sports teams, and the idea that a team brings with it large economic gains invariably arises. Part of this process is the commissioning of economic impact studies that purport to show just how much benefit the city or region will reap. As it turns out, claims of large tangible economic benefits do not withstand scrutiny. Careful analysis of past economic experience in cities that built new stadiums and attracted new teams does not bear out those claims.[7]

Impact studies rely on what economists call input-output models of local or regional economies into which the team and its new stadium are introduced to estimate the prospective economic impact. Those studies ask the question: what will happen if a new franchise and stadium enter this community? The results of those studies invariably reflect the desires of the people who commission them, and advocates of stadiums and franchises typically produce impact studies that find large economic benefits from building a stadium or enticing a team to relocate to the city.

All impact studies use multipliers to estimate the effect of each dollar spent directly on sports on the wider local economy. The multiplier effect implies that the dollars spent on sports entertainment will have ripple effects throughout the local economy. Critics argue that at best the multipliers used in prospective impact studies overstate the contribution that professional sports make to an area's economy because they fail to differentiate between net and gross spending.[8]

In computing the benefits of investment in a stadium, the appropriate focus is on net benefits, that is, benefits that would not have occurred in the absence of the stadium. Impact studies rarely consider what economists call the substitution effect. Indeed, not all the spending generated around and in the stadium

is new spending, and not all the taxes on that spending are net new tax revenues. As sport- and stadium-related activities increase, other spending declines because people substitute spending on sports for other spending. That is called the substitution effect. If the stadium simply displaces dollar-for-dollar spending that would have occurred otherwise, there are no net benefits generated. To classify all consumer spending on stadium- and sport-related activities as a benefit without taking into account the substitution effect greatly overstates the value of the investment.

Many fans attending the new team's games will come from the Maryland and Virginia suburbs. Those fans will bring their entertainment spending from the suburbs into the district — unless, of course, they would have frequented D.C. restaurants, bars, nightclubs, parking lots, and other businesses even without a baseball team in D.C. Put another way, suppose Joan Suburban has a season subscription to the National Symphony Orchestra. Every month or so, she leaves her Silver Spring condo, drives into the District for a few drinks and a meal in a Georgetown restaurant, and enjoys a concert. As she is also a baseball fan, Joan declines to renew her NSO subscription next year and instead buys a partial-season ticket plan for the new team. Every month or so, she leaves her Silver Spring condo, drives into the District for a few drinks and a meal in the revitalized area around the new ballpark, and enjoys a ball game. How much new economic benefit does the District gain? The mayor would have us believe that every dollar she spends should be counted as economic benefit attributable to the stadium. But what about the business lost by the Georgetown restaurant and parking lot?

The more suburban fans reduce their purchases at shops and eateries in other parts of D.C. and replace those purchases with ballgame spending, the lower the net impact of the stadium and franchise on the city's overall level of business development. It is anyone's guess how much of any new spending will flow into establishments outside the stadium and how much will be spent inside the stadium. Mayor Williams's case for building a stadium financed with tax revenue rests on the assumption that suburban residents of Maryland and Virginia who don't currently spend their entertainment dollars in the District will rush to do so once baseball season begins.

Previous studies have found this substitution effect in other cities. Economists Robert Baade and Alan Sanderson looked at the economic growth patterns of cities that hosted sports teams. On the basis of evidence from 10 metropolitan statistical areas over the period of 1958 to 1993, they found that leisure spending was realigned, not increased, and an insufficient number of fans were attracted from beyond the area to significantly contribute to the city's economy.[9]

Moreover, at least some of the redistribution in spending will be across neighborhoods within the district; a little less spending by D.C. residents in bars and restaurants in Georgetown or on Connecticut Avenue merely offset by a bit more spending in bars and restaurants that spring up around the ballpark is not obviously an improvement for the city of Washington.

In addition to the substitution effect, some economists have posited that there is a simultaneous effect at work. Dubbed by economists John Siegfried and Andrew Zimbalist as the "leakages and multipliers" effect, the theory suggests that — to the extent sport spending has a multiplier effect at all — spending on sports may have a much lower local multiplier than spending on other entertainment goods.[10] In other words, nonsports entertainment spending has a bigger ripple effect in the economy than sports-related entertainment

spending. Therefore, the economic gains from sports-related spending will never be large enough to fully offset the economic loss from a decline in nonsports entertainment spending. This reduction in earnings for nonsports industries would lead to a reduction in the earnings of workers in non-sports-related occupational groups. As our study of the economic effects of sports teams in other cities indicates, those two influences could have the likely effect of dragging down net incomes in D.C. on the arrival of the baseball team.

Sports Teams & Stadiums as a Drag on Economic Growth: An Analysis of the Data

In stark contrast to the benefits claimed by most economic impact studies commissioned by teams or stadium advocates, the academic research overwhelmingly concludes that the presence of professional sports teams has no measurable positive impact on economic growth as measured by the level of real income in cities over a 35-year period. Our own research suggests that professional sports may actually be a drain on local economies rather than an engine of economic growth.

The difference between the impact studies commissioned by teams or cities and the academic literature is more than simply a matter of prospective estimates versus retrospective facts. Academic studies consider a large number of metropolitan areas with major league professional sports over a long period of time and examine a variety of factors that are likely to predict either aggregate economic activity or the vitality of specific sectors of the local economy. In other words, those studies look specifically for the net effect of the sports environment on the economic health of metropolitan areas.

Our research examines all 37 U.S. cities that had one or more professional football, basketball, or baseball franchises between 1969 and 1996. The data set contains a wide variety of franchise movement and new stadium and arena construction.

We focus on identifying factors that affected either the level or the growth of income per person. Although attracting a new football team or building a new basketball arena might have had some effect on those variables, other factors certainly played an important role. Our approach is to quantify the sports environment by taking into account the presence of franchises, franchise entry and departure, stadium construction and renovation, the location of new stadiums and arenas, and the "novelty effect" of a new stadium or arena for professional football, basketball, or baseball.[11] We then estimate econometric models of the level or growth rate of income in metropolitan areas and include the variables reflecting the sports environment.

Taking advantage of the time-series cross-sectional nature of our data, we are able to control for city-specific factors that affect income per person, or wages per worker and employment in each of several sectors, including factors such as the decline of rust-belt cities and booms in sun-belt cities, and the effect of the business cycle. The use of city-specific effects, and the other variables, means that we are able to make sure that the estimated effects of the sports environment variables are not contaminated with other historical or location-specific influences on the economic vitality of the cities.

The results of our analysis indicate the following:

- The presence of pro sports teams in the 37 metropolitan areas in our sample had no measurable positive impact on the overall growth rate of real per capita income in those areas.

- The presence of pro sports teams had a statistically significant negative impact on the level of real per capita income in our sample of metropolitan areas.

- The presence of pro sports teams had a statistically significant negative impact on the retail and services sectors of the local economy. The average effect on employment in the services sector of a city's economy was a net loss of 1,924 jobs as a result of the presence of a professional sports team.

- The presence of pro sports teams tended to raise wages in the hotels and other lodgings sector by about $10 per year. But it tended to reduce wages per worker in eating and drinking establishments by about $162 per year.

- The presence of pro sports teams tended to raise the wages of workers in the amusements and recreation sector by $490 per year. However, this sector includes the professional athletes whose annual salaries certainly raise the average salary in this sector by an enormous amount. As it turns out, those workers most closely connected with the sports environment who were not professional athletes saw little improvement in their earnings as a result of the local professional sports environment.[12]

Our calculations also accounted for the effects of a variety of other local economic conditions on earnings and employment. On the basis of the estimated relationships, we computed the average effect of a professional baseball team and stadium on earnings, holding constant all other pertinent economic factors.

We found that, on average, professional baseball lowered the earnings of workers in eating and drinking establishments by about $144 per employee per year. Baseball also lowered the per employee annual earnings of workers in the hotel and lodging sector by about $38. Most striking of all, baseball lowered the annual earnings of workers in the amusements and recreation sector by $503. The last result is impressive in part because it includes the salaries of the baseball players themselves.

Those results suggest that there is a great deal of substitution of economic activity related to professional baseball for other amusement and recreation activities in cities that host teams. That substitution harms workers employed in alternative entertainment and recreation activities.

This evidence stands in stark contrast to the pie-in-the-sky forecasts used to justify subsidizing a professional baseball team.

The results we have just reported are based on the actual experience of U.S. cities with professional baseball over a period of nearly 30 years. The economic benefits touted by Mayor Williams are predictions about future economic impacts based on a flawed methodology.

Rather than use average values of stadium capacity, for example, we use the exact values of the variables for each of the 37 cities. In this way we are able to compute the effect of sports on earnings and employment in each of the cities.

The presence of professional sports in the Washington metropolitan area has, on average, sapped some strength from the service and retail sectors. Admittedly, the data do not include the completion of the MCI Center. Yet the effects of the center's presence in D.C. probably included a substitution effect similar to the ones we see elsewhere. Our results do, however, reflect the long presence of the Redskins, the arrival of the Bullets (Wizards) from Baltimore in 1973, and the departure of the Senators for Texas in 1971. These figures should give pause to even the staunchest believer in the claim that bringing professional

baseball to Washington will lead to significant positive economic benefits on net.

Because we developed a wide variety of measures of the sports environment in metropolitan areas, many of the individual elements have a positive impact in one sector that is offset by a negative impact in another sector. For example, on average, the arrival of a new basketball franchise in a metropolitan area increases real per capita income by about $67. But building a new arena for that basketball team reduces real per capita income by almost $73 in each of the 10 years following the construction of the arena, leading to a net loss of about $6 per person.

Similarly, in cities that have baseball franchises, the net effect of an existing baseball team playing in a 37,000-seat baseball-only stadium (the average capacity of the baseball stadiums in our data set) is a $10 reduction of real per capita income. This last point is particularly relevant for the D.C. situation. Although the proposed stadium undoubtedly will be larger than the average in our data set, the net effect will not likely be smaller than the $10 we estimated.

Note also that the waiters, waitresses, cooks, busboys, and other workers in the eating and drinking establishments that will arise will largely be D.C. residents. They are, presumably, precisely the people whom the stadium proponents argue will benefit from building the ballpark. But our estimates reveal that those people are harmed or experience, at best, only a very modest increase in incomes.

Conclusion

The policy implications of our results are no different from those of the previous studies that found no positive relationship between the presence of pro sports teams and growth in local economies. The evidence suggests that attracting a professional sports franchise to a city and building that franchise a new stadium or arena will have no effect on the growth rate of real per capita income and may actually reduce the level of real per capita income in that city. Moreover, specific sectors of the economy that are frequently predicted to be the big winners from stadium construction are likely to benefit very little or even be harmed by it. Yet government decision-makers and politicians continue to try to attract professional sports franchises to cities or to use public funds to construct elaborate new facilities to woo them. One thing is clear from the evidence: pro sports team owners are reaping substantial benefits for their teams by touting sports as an effective tool for economic development.

The impact study commissioned by Mayor Williams's office contains most of the flaws that have led economists to criticize such studies for decades. The pronouncements that no local tax dollars will go to stadium construction amount to economic hand waving.

If the actual economic impact of the proposed new baseball stadium in D.C. ends up resembling the economic impact of professional sports teams on other U.S. cities in the past, then at best this stadium will have no effect on the local economy. At worst, some sectors of the economy — businesses located near the new stadium and workers in closely related occupations — will benefit while others will lose, and the overall impact on the economy will be zero or negative.

A baseball team in D.C. might produce intangible benefits. Residents might have an enhanced sense of community pride and another opportunity to engage in a shared experience of civic expression. Perhaps some people will think that D.C.'s image as a "world-class city" will be further burnished.

Rooting for the team will provide satisfaction to many local baseball fans. Yet those intangible benefits largely accrue to people interested in being fans of the baseball team and showing their support by purchasing tickets to games and team paraphernalia. That is hardly a reason for the city government to subsidize construction of a ballpark, or for the baseball team to avoid paying the cost to build it. District policymakers should not be mesmerized by the faulty impact studies that claim a baseball team and new stadium can be an engine of economic growth.

Notes

1. Paul Schwartzman and Manny Fernandez, "After 33 Joyless Years, Fans Counting the Days," *Washington Post*, September 30, 2004, p. A1.

2. Executive Office of the Mayor, "In the News," October 1, 2004, http://dc.gov/mayor/newsletter/2004/oct/v3_issue20_1.shtm.

3. See Baseball Stadium Agreement Exhibits, Exhibit E, "Rent Schedule," http://www.dcwatch.com/govern/sports040929b.htm.

4. Scott Wallsten, "Paying for Baseball in D.C.," October 3, 2004, http://www.wallsten.net/papers/Wallsten_Paying_for_baseball_in_DC.pdf.

5. For examples of arguments used in favor of subsidizing major league sports in other cities and the subsequent experiences of those cities, see Raymond J. Keating, "Sports Pork: The Costly Relationship between Major League Sports and Government," Cato Institute Policy Analysis no. 339, April 5, 1999.

6. Office of the Deputy Mayor for Planning and Economic Development, "Mayor's Major League Baseball Briefing," October 2004, http://dcbiz.dc.gov/dmped/frames.asp?doc=/dmped/lib/dmped/100504 baseballbriefing.pdf.

7. See Robert A. Baade, "Professional Sports and Catalysts for Metropolitan Economic Development," *Journal of Urban Affairs* 18 (1996): 1–17; Robert A. Baade and Richard F. Dye, "The Impact of Stadiums and Professional Sports on Metropolitan Area Development," *Growth and Change* 12 (1990): 1–14; John L. Crompton, "Analysis of Sports Facilities and Events: Eleven Sources of Misapplication," *Journal of Sports Management* 9 (1995): 14–35; *Sports, Jobs, and Taxes: The Economic Impact of Professional Sports Teams and Stadiums*, ed. Roger G. Noll and Andrew Zimbalist (Washington: Brookings Institution, 1997); Mark S. Rosentraub et al., "Sports and Downtown Develop-

ment Strategy: If You Build It, Will Jobs Come?" *Journal of Urban Affairs* 16 (1994): 221–39.

8. Crompton; and *Sports, Jobs, and Taxes*.

9. Robert Baade and Allen Sanderson, "The Employment Effect of Teams and Sports Facilities," in *Sports, Jobs, and Taxes*, pp. 92–118.

10. John Siegfried and Andrew Zimbalist, "The Economics of Sports Facilities and their Communities," *Journal of Economic Perspectives* 14, no. 2 (2000): 115–34.

11. "Novelty effect" refers to the burst of interest in and attendance at professional sports events that accompanies the opening of a new stadium.

12. For further technical discussion of these results, see Dennis Coates and Brad R. Humphreys, "The Growth Effects of Sport Franchises, Stadia and Arenas," *Journal of Policy Analysis and Management* 18 (1999): 601–24; and Dennis Coates and Brad R. Humphreys, "The Effect of Professional Sports on Earnings and Employment in the Services and Retail Sectors in U.S. Cities," *Regional Science and Urban Economics* 33 (2003): 175–98.

III: The Future

CHAPTER 39

The "Real" Economic Impact of Publicly Financed Sports Facilities

Dennis Coates *and* Brad R. Humphreys

In recent years sports franchises have frequently used their monopoly power to extract rents from state and local governments. Typically, a franchise owner declares an existing facility unsuitable. Perhaps it is too old, or too small, or lacks enough luxury boxes or suites to raise the necessary revenues to field a competitive team. The owner reminds the local government and business community that many other cities would like to have a team, and those cities would also build a new stadium. Cities all over the country, desperate for a professional sports team, gear up to convince the owner to move. Often, the promise of a new stadium and a sweetheart lease convinces the owner to stay, but some franchises move. Regardless of whether the team stays or goes, taxpayers foot the bill for a new stadium, improvements to an existing stadium, or infrastructure needed to make the new stadium or arena as attractive as possible.

The practice of professional sports profiting at the expense of taxpayers is not new. Before the stadium gambit there was the tax shelter dodge in which the purchase and re-

organization of a team could generate up to five years of losses, which could be used to offset the new owner's income from other ventures. And there is the common practice of funding stadium construction using private purpose local bonds because their interest payments are exempt from federal income taxation and they therefore carry a lower interest rate. The net effect is that the federal government subsidizes construction of the stadiums and arenas built by state and local governments for professional sports franchises. Indeed, closing the loophole in the law that allowed this subsidy has simply been replaced by explicit state and local funding of stadiums that can be turned over rent free to franchises.

The recent spate of sweetheart stadium and arena deals is only the latest manifestation of owners of professional sports franchises getting richer at the public's expense. While not entirely new, this phenomenon has become front-page news across the country in recent years. Combined with the "build it and they will come" attitude of many city governments, the stadium gambit has led to

Originally published as "The Stadium Gambit and Local Economic Development," *Regulation*, Vol. 23, No. 2, Summer 2003, by the Cato Institute, Washington, D.C. Reprinted with permission of the publisher.

a marked increase in new stadium and arena construction, franchise relocations, and negotiations between teams and local governments.

Despite the beliefs of local officials and their hired consultants about the economic benefits of publicly subsidized stadium construction, the consensus of academic economists has been that such policies do not raise incomes. The results that we describe in this article are even more pessimistic. Subsidies of sports facilities may actually reduce the incomes of the alleged beneficiaries.

Trends in Stadium Ownership and Franchise Values

Public ownership of stadiums has increased over time. In 1950, the National Basketball Association (NBA) and the National Football League (NFL) had substantial public ownership of stadiums or arenas — 46 percent and 36 percent, respectively. Baseball's American League had 12 percent public ownership, whereas its National League and the National Hockey League had no publicly owned stadiums. By 1991, a minimum of 65 percent of facilities in any professional sports league were publicly owned. The high was 93 percent public ownership in the NFL. The median percentage of public ownership of stadiums and arenas was 75 percent.

During the time of increased public participation in stadium ownership, franchise values have also increased dramatically. In their book *Pay Dirt: The Business of Professional Team Sports*, James P. Quirk and Rodney D. Fort report that for teams sold in the 1970s and sold again during the 1980s franchise values rose at an annual rate of 12.5 percent in baseball, 12.3 percent in basketball, and 11.5 percent in football. For teams sold twice during the 1980s, the rates of increase were 23.5, 50.2, and 19.2 percent, respectively.

The increase in the value of franchises has shown no sign of slowing in the 1990s. For example, the franchise fees charged for expansion teams in the 1990s are large and rising rapidly. In 1992 the Colorado Rockies and Florida Marlins paid $95 million in expansion fees to join major league baseball. In 1997, the Arizona Diamondbacks and Tampa Bay Devil Rays paid $130 million. That is about a 37 percent increase in five years, or about 7.4 percent per year. To (re-)join the NFL, the Cleveland Browns paid an expansion fee of $530 million in 1998; the newly awarded franchise in Houston agreed to a $700 million fee, just a 32 percent increase in one year. But the most extreme case of expansion price inflation occurred in the NBA. The fee paid for expansion by the franchises in Minneapolis and Orlando in 1989 was $32.5 million; for Toronto and Vancouver, which joined the league in 1995, the fee was $125 million. That works out to about a 285 percent increase in just six years, or about 47 percent per year.

The owners of franchises in monopoly professional sports leagues have used the real or implied threat of moving to another city to persuade state and local decision-makers and politicians to provide them with lavish new stadiums and arenas at little or no cost. The owners appear to have profited handsomely from this stadium gambit, as suggested by the triple-digit increases in franchise values. In return, taxpayers receive non-pecuniary benefits in the form of increased civic pride and image, as well as other unmeasured consumption benefits associated with living in a city with professional sports teams. Taxpayers have also been told that new teams, stadiums, and arenas create jobs and raise tax revenues and income in their city.

Do Professional Sports Produce Economic Benefits?

What justification exists for the government subsidy of professional sports? The proponents of new stadiums and franchises are always quick to point out the economic benefits of the proposed facilities and teams. Cities throughout the country have struggled to attract or keep professional sports teams in recent years, and the idea that a team brings with it large economic gains invariably arises. Part of this process is the commissioning of economic impact studies that purport to show just how much benefit the city or region will reap.

More than 20 years ago, proponents of the half-billion-dollar Skydome in Toronto claimed that this facility would generate $450 million in Canadian dollars in the first year of operation and create 17,000 jobs in the Toronto area. Half a decade ago, prospective NFL team owners in Jacksonville, Florida, claimed that a new NFL franchise would generate $340 million in new income in the city and create 3,000 jobs. In a recent case, the Baltimore *Sun* reported in April of 1999 that a new study supported tearing down the existing 36-year-old Baltimore Arena and replacing it with a new $200 million facility. This investment, the study claims, will raise city taxes by $3.8 million and state taxes by $6.3 million. In addition, the facility could generate up to $100 million in new earnings for the citizens of the city of Baltimore.

Contrast these recent figures with information from the 1994 edition of the *County and City Data Book*. In 1990, the last year for which city and state tax collections are reported, Maryland and Baltimore collected $3.4 billion and $528 million in taxes, respectively. For the city, the tax gain from the replacement arena is, if the figures are correct, only about 0.7 percent of 1990 tax collections.

For the state, the new tax collections are less than two-tenths of a percent of 1990 tax collections. Earnings in Maryland were $68 billion and personal income in Baltimore was $13.9 billion. Projected earnings from the arena are about 0.15 percent of state earnings for 1990 and about 0.72 percent of Baltimore's total personal income. Although the absolute numbers seem large and impressive, they are small compared with the existing tax revenues and local economy, even if one grants that the proponents' estimates are correct.

The Flaws in Advocacy Studies

There are strong reasons to doubt the accuracy of the estimated benefits claimed by economic impact studies. These impact studies rely upon input-output models of the local or regional economies into which the team and its new stadium will be placed and estimate the economic impact prospectively. These studies ask the question: what will happen if a new franchise and stadium enter this community? The results of these studies invariably reflect the desires of those who commission them, and advocates of stadiums and franchises typically produce impact studies that find large economic impacts, translated as benefits, from building a stadium or enticing a team to enter the city.

The Mythical Multiplier The methodology used by impact studies has been criticized on a variety of grounds. All impact studies use multipliers to estimate the effect of each dollar spent directly on sports on the wider local economy. Critics argue that at best the multipliers used in prospective impact studies overstate the contribution that professional sports make to an area's economy because they fail to differentiate between net and gross spending and the effects of taxes. In computing the benefits of the investment in a stadium, the appropriate focus is on net benefits, that is, on benefits that would not have occurred in the absence of the stadium. Impact studies rarely consider this issue. One could think of this concern as the substitution effect. Specifically, because of sport- and stadium-related activities, other spending declines as people substitute spending on one for spending on the other. If the stadium simply displaces dollar-for-dollar spending that would have occurred otherwise, then there are no net benefits generated. To consider the spending on stadium- and sport-related activities as all benefits is, therefore, to widely overstate the value of the investment. A key issue for getting the right sense of the value of the stadium investment is, consequently, how much of stadium-related spending substitutes for otherwise intended spending and how much is net gain in spending.

An important question related to the size of these substitution effects, and on the appropriate size of sports spending multipliers, is the size of the relevant geographic area. A stadium or arena will have more added effects on a very narrowly defined community than on a largely encompassing community. The reason for this is that the more narrowly the host community is defined, the more of the spending at the stadium and the nearby restaurants, bars, and hotels will come from outside the community. However, that spending will come largely at the expense of the home communities of the fans that travel into the stadium from outlying areas. The substitution effect for the broadly defined area is quite large, but for the narrowly defined stadium community it is much smaller. What this points out is that stadiums and sports teams may be a tool for redistributing income in which the people from suburbs subsidize businesses in the city.

Efficiency Is Irrelevant   Impact studies typically do not address alternative uses of

public funds. Indeed, politicians often seem to think that the means of financing the stadium generates free resources that have no alternative uses whatsoever. For example, when the state of Maryland discussed plans to lure the Cleveland Browns to Baltimore, they made clear that part of the funding for the construction of a new stadium would come from the state lottery. In state senate hearings on the issue, it was pointed out that lottery funds were essentially constant in recent years and that they were already dedicated, at least in part, to paying off the bonds issued to finance Oriole Park at Camden Yards. If lottery funds did not grow, then to add the financing of the football stadium would require that the state dip into general tax revenues either to pay interest on the baseball stadium related bonds or to spend on the other public services supported out of lottery revenues. Alternatively, the state could choose to stop supporting other public services at all. The senators dismissed this concern out of hand. As the example makes clear, the revenues have opportunity costs.

But the issue is more than simply that there are alternative uses of the taxes used to pay for the stadium. The fundamental issue is that a stadium is a public investment in real capital. As such, the rules for sensible public investment apply to stadium finance as much as they apply to public provision of highways, schools, and airports. Specifically, the key is comparing the return on the investment in the stadium with the return on the same dollar investment in any alternative public use, including tax reduction. Efficient use of public resources requires that any given funds go into the uses that provide the highest return. This, of course, makes estimation of the return on the stadium and other investments very important. But measurement of these returns is complicated by the fact that there are substantial services of the stadium and sports franchises that do not pass through the marketplace.

Let Them Eat Civic Pride   Stadium and team advocates, for example, raise the issue of civic pride and the image of cities. According to this logic, only cities with professional sports teams are truly world class. The gain in civic pride is, of course, very difficult to measure. The benefits that accrue to individuals who never or rarely attend games at the stadium but who derive enjoyment from following the team in the newspaper or via the radio and television broadcasts are also difficult to measure. Such benefits are the result of an externality, a good or service provided by one individual or group that provides benefits to other individuals or groups and for which the latter provide no compensation to the former. The existence of these external benefits could justify some public participation in the provision of stadiums and sports franchises.

The Sordid Truth About Economic Impact

In stark contrast to the results claimed by most prospective economic impact studies commissioned by teams or stadium advocates, the consensus in the academic literature has been that the overall sports environment has no measurable effect on the level of real income in metropolitan areas. Our own research suggests that professional sports may be a drain on local economies rather than an engine of economic growth.

Many Sports, Many Cities   The difference between the impact studies commissioned by teams or cities and the academic literature is more than simply prospective versus retrospective methodology. Academic studies consider a large number of metropolitan areas with major league professional sports over a long period of time and examine other factors

that are likely to predict aggregate economic activity as well as a broadly conceived view of the sports environment. In other words, these studies look specifically for the net effect of the sports environment on the economic vitality of metropolitan areas.

Our research examines all 37 U.S. cities that had one or more professional football, basketball, or baseball franchises at some point during the 1969–1996 period. This represents the universe of cities with such professional sports franchises during this period. The sample contains a wide variety of franchise moves and new stadium and arena construction. Twenty-three percent of these metropolitan areas attracted a basketball franchise, 10 percent attracted a football franchise, and 7 percent attracted a baseball franchise; 2.5 percent built a new baseball stadium, 10 percent built a football stadium, 10 percent built a new combined football and baseball stadium, and 21 percent built a new basketball arena.

Quantifying the Sports Environment   Because it is not clear whether pro-stadium studies claim that the stadium will raise the level or the growth rate of income, we focus on identifying factors that affected either the level or growth of income per person. Although attracting a new football team or building a new basketball arena might have had some effect on these variables, other factors certainly played an important role. Our approach is to quantify the sports environment, including the presence of franchises, franchise entry and departure, stadium construction and renovation, the location of new stadiums and arenas, and the "novelty" effect of a new stadium or arena for professional football, basketball, and baseball. We then estimate econometric models of the determination of the level or growth rate of income in metropolitan areas and include the variables reflecting the sports environment.

We take two different approaches to estimating the models. First, taking advantage of the time-series cross-sectional nature of our data, we are able to control for city-specific factors that affect income or income growth, including trend growth, the decline of rust-belt cities and booms in sun-belt cities, and the effect of the business cycle. The use of city-specific effects, and these other variables, means that we are able to make sure that the estimated effects of the sports environment variables are not contaminated with other historical or location-specific influences on the economic vitality of the cities.

Second, we use an event study approach to analyze the effect of professional sports on local economies. This method uses the sports environment variables as a means of explaining why a particular city differs from the average city. This technique is widely used to examine the effects of changes in laws or regulations on the market value of firms in the finance and regulation literature. This approach can also be used to examine the impact of professional sports on local economies. In this approach, one regresses the level of income in each city on the average level of income across all the cities and a set of dummy variables reflecting changes in the sports environment. If the sports environment variables are statistically significant, the difference between that city and the average of all cities is not purely random but is a function of its different sports environment. The main drawback to this approach is that city-specific variables cannot be used. That is why we place more reliance on the results of the first approach described above. But the event study is a viable alternative to the other econometric models we estimate, and the results of the event study approach serve as a check on the robustness of our other results.

Results. Our results indicate:

• The professional sports environment in the 37 metropolitan areas in our sample had no measurable impact on the *growth rate* of real per capita income in those areas.

• The professional sports environment has a statistically significant impact on the *level* of real per capita income in our sample of metropolitan areas, and the overall impact is *negative*.

The presence of professional sports teams, on average, reduces the level of real per capita income in metropolitan areas. This result differs from much of the existing literature, which generally has found no impact at all. However, we used a broader and longer panel of data and a richer set of variables reflecting the sports environment than previous studies.

Because we developed a wide variety of measures of the sports environment in metropolitan areas, many of the individual elements have a positive impact that is offset by another element that carries a negative impact. For example, the arrival of a new basketball franchise in a metropolitan area increases real per capita income by about $67. But building a new arena for that basketball team reduces real per capita income by almost $73 in each of the 10 years following the construction of the arena, leading to a net loss of about $6 per person. Similarly, in cities that have baseball franchises, the net effect of an existing baseball team playing in a 37,000-seat baseball-only stadium (the average capacity of the baseball stadiums in our sample) is a $10 reduction of real per capita income.

The results from the event study regressions are similar: sports environment variables are correlated with negative deviation from the average level of per capita income. However, the size of the estimated negative effect of the sports environment on the level of real per capita income generated by the event study regressions is considerably larger than the size of the estimated impact from the other reduced-form econometric models. The impact of an existing baseball franchise playing in a stadium of average size is a reduction in real per capita income of over $850 per year below the average level of income across the cities in our sample, based on the event study estimates. We tend to put more trust in the smaller estimated impact based on the reduced-form econometric models of income determination than in the larger impact implied by the event study regressions because the exclusion of city-specific trends and other factors from the event study regressions may force the average income variable to carry too much of the explanatory weight in these regressions.

How Sports Subsidies Reduce Income

If, as prospective team owners, developers, and politicians would have us believe, professional sports can be an important engine of economic growth, how can our estimates be correct? How can the professional sports environment reduce the level of real per capita income in a metropolitan area? A recently published volume edited by Roger Noll and Andrew Zimbalist (*Sports, Jobs, and Taxes*) contains a number of essays that examine in detail the relationship between professional sports and local economies. The essays in this volume suggest a number of possible answers to these questions, which fall into several broad categories.

Substitution in Public Spending   Public funds are often used to subsidize professional sports teams and the stadiums or arenas they play in. These public funds have alternative uses, such as maintaining local infrastructure; increasing the quality or provision of public health, safety, or education; and attracting new businesses to the area. The deterioration of local public capital or services could diminish the ability of the local economy to produce

other non-sports-related goods and services, which in turn would reduce local income.

Substitution in Private Spending Households face budget constraints; they must meet their unlimited wants with a limited amount of income. The arrival of a professional sports team in a city provides households with a new entertainment option. Households that choose to attend games will spend less on other things, perhaps going out to dinner, bowling, or the movies. If the impact of each dollar spent on these forgone alternatives has a larger effect on the local economy than the impact of each dollar spent on professional sporting events, the local economy will contract and income will be lower. Why would the impact of each dollar spent going to a professional basketball game be smaller than the impact of each dollar spent on bowling? This could easily occur if the revenue generated by the basketball team and arena, which in turn becomes the income made by the players and team owners, escapes the flow of transactions that make up the local economy to a greater extent than the income made by the owners and employees of the bowling alley or movie theater.

Compensating Differentials in Income Perhaps professional sports do not directly reduce the level of real per capita income in a metropolitan area. Instead, our results reflect a "compensating differential" related to the presence of professional sports in some cities. Residents of cities with professional sports teams derive non-pecuniary benefits from the teams' presence and, because of those non-pecuniary benefits, are willing to accept lower income in return for living in these cities, other things being equal. This rationale implies that a recent college graduate might be willing to take a lower-paying job in a city with a professional sports franchise instead of a slightly higher-paying job in a city that has no professional sports franchises. The determining factor in the choice is whether the value of those non-pecuniary benefits is high enough. In other words, we may observe lower per capita income in cities with a professional baseball franchise because residents of those cities are willing to accept lower wages or salaries to have local access to a baseball franchise.

Negative Effects on Productivity   Productivity, broadly defined as the amount of output that a worker with a given amount of capital, experience, and education can produce, is an important determinant of income and explains much of the observed difference in per capita income across countries. The factors that affect the productivity of workers are notoriously difficult to pin down precisely, but small differences in productivity can lead to large differences in per capita income when those differences persist over time. Workers in cities with professional sports teams may spend more work time discussing the outcome of last night's game, organizing an office pool, or other similar activities than workers in cities without professional sports teams. These differences could, over a period of many years, lead to differences in income per capita.

Conclusions

The policy implications of our results are no different from those of the previous studies that found no relationship between the professional sports environment and local economies. Still, they bear repeating. The evidence suggests that attracting a professional sports franchise to a city and building that franchise a new stadium or arena will have no effect on the growth rate of real per capita income and may reduce the level of real per capita income in that city. Yet government decision-makers and politicians continue to try to attract professional sports franchises to

cities, or use public funds to construct elaborate new facilities in order to keep existing franchises from moving. According to public finance theory, the decision-makers who attempt to attract a new franchise or build a new stadium or arena must value the total consumption benefits, including all non-pecuniary benefits, more than the total costs, including the opportunity costs. The total consumption benefits cannot be directly measured because of the non-pecuniary component of those benefits; in order for these policies to make sense, the total value of the consumption benefits associated with these policies must be larger than was previously imagined. However, regardless of the size of the non-pecuniary benefits, one thing is clear from the evidence on professional sports franchises: owners are reaping substantial benefits in the value of their teams because they are so skilled at the stadium gambit.

References

Robert A. Baade. "Professional Sports and Catalysts for Metropolitan Economic Development." *Journal of Urban Affairs* 18 (1996): 1.

Robert A. Baade and Richard F. Dye. "The Impact of Stadiums and Professional Sports on Metropolitan Area Development." *Growth and Change* 12 (1990): 1.

Dennis Coates and Brad R. Humphreys. "The Growth Effects of Sport Franchises, Stadia and Arenas." *Journal of Policy Analysis and Management* 18 (1999): 601.

John L. Crompton. "Analysis of Sports Facilities and Events: Eleven Sources of Misapplication." *Journal of Sports Management* 9 (1995): 14.

Roger G. Noll and Andrew Zimbalist. *Sports, Jobs, and Taxes: The Economic Impact of Professional Sports Teams and Stadiums.* Washington, D.C.: The Brookings Institution, 1997.

James P. Quirk and Rodney D. Fort. *Pay Dirt: The Business of Professional Team Sports.* Princeton: Princeton University Press, 1992.

Mark S. Rosentraub, David Swindell, Michael Przybylski, and Dan Mullins. "Sports and Downtown Development Strategy: If You Build It, Will Jobs Come?" *Journal of Urban Affairs* 16 (1994): 221.

CHAPTER 40

The Changing Nature of America's Sports Facilities

Chad Seifried *and* Dave Shonk

Howard (1999) found over 120 new or significantly renovated sport facilities emerged in the United States for around $16 billion between 1990 and 1999. Other reports generated similar conclusions about this decade's spending. For instance, Bernstein (1998) suggested professional sport facility construction totaled nearly seven billion dollars during the 1990s. For Major League Baseball (MLB) and the National Football League (NFL) the 1990s specifically produced $4.4 billion ($5.7 inflation adjusted) in new facility spending. The future demonstrates this construction trend will continue in MLB and the NFL (2000–2012) for approximately $13 billion. Despite adjusting for inflation, extreme and massive costs noticeably increased versus the previous decade's spending on new sport facilities by $8.5 billion. Interestingly, this recent construction period (1990–present) reveals more than half of MLB and NFL organizations will compete in new facilities built since 1990.

The current era of professional sport facility construction owes its substantial cost increase to a strict focus on accommodating all the needs of the owners, players, investors, and

media or its various stakeholder groups (Seifried, 2005). Eisinger (2000) and others also posit entertaining spectators also dramatically altered the shape and function of today's, and therefore size and cost of sport facilities (Bess, 1999; Ritzer & Stillman, 2001; Seifried, 2005). Ron Turner, a Sr. Vice President and Director of Kansas City's Sport Architecture firm, Ellerbe Becket, described this allowed the professional sport facility to evolve into a "miniature city," which unsurprisingly consumes tremendous amounts of energy (Gunts, 1992 p. 87). Other works overwhelmingly support this conclusion (Bess, 1999; Weiner, 2000). Bess (1999) distinctively demonstrates this "miniature city" and energy cost description through his discovery that architectural designs increased current sport facility volumes nearly 500 percent from previous sport building projects. Consequently, the average MLB and NFL facility built since 1990 averages an astounding 27.87 acres.

The colossal retractable roof facilities completed during the 1990s and throughout this decade also demonstrate the dramatic rising costs vividly as they average $416,266,667

Originally published as "American Professional Sports Facilities: Considerations for the Future," *Working Paper Series*, Paper No. 07–24, June 2007, by the International Association of Sports Economists, Limoges, France. Reprinted with permission of the publisher.

($485,230,367 inflation adjusted) per build from 1990 to 2006, while their outdoor counterparts average another $298,292,857 ($356,667,779 inflation adjusted) of damage. Sharma (1999) additionally reveals retractable roof facilities inflict at least another $300,000 more in maintenance costs annually than un-roofed facilities to further the burden. Fasci-natingly, the retractable roof exists as a massive and costly structure primarily due to its engi-neering and sheer weight (Leventhal, 2000; Seifried, 2005). For instance, Miller Park's (Milwaukee) pivoting roof panels occupy ap-proximately eleven acres and weigh roughly twenty-four million pounds (Seifried, 2005). Safeco Field (Seattle) possesses a sliding re-tractable roof approximately nine acres in size. Additionally, this structure weighs twenty-two million pounds so it can protect itself against six to seven feet of snow and winds approach-ing seventy miles per hour (Seifried, 2005). Finally, Sherman (1998) describes Chase Field (Phoenix) as so immense it can hold eight America West Arenas, Phoenix's 19,023-seat basketball venue, inside.

Bess (1999 p. iii) believes these outra-geous costs stem from the unwillingness and inability of community officials to devise ap-propriate limitations on sport team owners. This inability or unwillingness to limit spend-ing likely surfaces from a fear teams will leave them for a new location because of the com-petition for major league status. Essentially, this fear produces a tremendous amount of leverage for the professional sport organiza-tion during facility discussions because a move can strip a city of its precious image (Euch-ner, 1993; Gunts, 1992). The owners, as a financially driven group, seek facilities, which increase revenues to offset rising player salaries and improve the overall worth of their team (Euchner, 1993; Gunts, 1992; Howard & Crompton, 1995; Ritzer & Stillman, 2001; Rockerbie, 2004; Smith, 2000; Sullivan,

2001). Consequently, adding structures, which significantly enhance the spectator's experi-ence and thus the size of the facility, appears necessary to assuage ownership requests and increasing attendee comfort and entertainment demands. Interestingly, despite the additional features new stadiums embrace, these civic monuments produce few if any tangible benefits for their communities (Baade & Dye, 1988; Bess, 1999; Blickstein, 1995; Euch-ner, 1993; Noll & Zimbalist, 1997; Seifried, 2005).

Some examples like AT & T Park and its 5,200 square foot medical clinic and Turner Field's day care center serve as exceptions but on the average these types of community ori-ented activities fail to find a home in the pro-fessional sport facility (Epstein, 1998b; Smith, 2000). Weiner (2000) and others recommend sport facilities attempt hosting community-oriented businesses and services to increase the tangible worth of their likely large public in-vestment (Baade & Dye, 1988; Bess, 1999; Eu-chner, 1993). Clearly, this exists as a sound ob-jective because it appears difficult to justify hundreds of millions of the public's dollars when teams and other professional events uti-lize sport facilities so few days of the year.

Again, professional sport facilities today function as entertainment zones and generally do not support community activities because that is not their primary purpose (Baade & Dye, 1988; Bess, 1999; Smith, 2000, 2003; Weiner, 2000). This is important to under-stand. Typically, professional sport facilities focus their services and benefits towards im-proving the financial condition of the profes-sional organization and its stakeholders (i.e. owners, sponsors, media). Euchner (1993, p. 182) enthusiastically promotes American cities need to do a better job of developing policies that "enhance stability in fundamen-tal services and activities such as energy, trans-portation, housing, health care, and education." This work proposes the professional sport facility could serve to help accomplish this need. Furthermore, this inquiry seeks to suggest three areas future professional sport facility designers should consider so they can accommodate this call from the scholarly field identified above and still create an attractive bottom line for sport organizations. The three areas include reducing the size, considering the environment, and embracing interaction and telecommunication technology.

Research Design and Method

This research was part of a larger study dealing with the evolution of the professional sport facility in the United States. It utilized historical methods to study this phenomenon. Historical research is the attempt to systematically establish conclusions, trends, and facts about past environments based on evidence collected and interpreted from valid or authentic sources (Ary, Jacobs, & Razavieh, 1996; Johnson & Christensen, 2000). Using historical sources, from this study's perspective, provides an excellent opportunity toward a more complete understanding of past culture but also how the future may be altered. Essentially, studying the past helps us understand the future.

Historical study requires the researcher to pursue primary (e.g. newspapers, pictures, interviews, architectural plans) and secondary (e.g. journal articles, scholarly books) sources and examine these materials through completing a historical criticism. The historical criticism completed for this work aimed to certify the validity and reliability of the primary and secondary source evidence so accurate conclusions or predictions could be prepared. Internally, the researchers evaluated the information used for this manuscript by asking whether or not each source provided accurate or trustworthy information (Wineberg, 1991; Ary et al., 1996). Externally, this research inquiry; "ask if the documentation includes valid techniques, and if the source in question has been falsified in any way" (Ary et al., 1996; Berg, 1998 p. 350). This check was especially helpful when analyzing biographical information on sport facilities like ballpark dimensions or construction costs. Thompson (1967) suggests completing a historical criticism appears important for developing or acknowledging a theme within a larger event. In this case, the theme concerns expectations about the future of facility construction.

Finally, the process of examining trends of sport facility construction required the researchers to perform triangulation. Triangulation benefits this study because valuable and important causal inferences can be appropriately established (Brewer & Hunter, 1989). Denzin (1978) supports this point as he argues for combining numerical data and written information because it supplements or enhances individual strengths and reduces weaknesses of arguments or predictions. Overall, triangulation appears logical and necessary for this paper because findings from this technique improve the overall validity of its position.

Reduce the Size

Professional sport facilities today often include structures like restaurants, halls of fame, hotels, and entertainment zones like playgrounds, arcades, and pools to create the "miniature city" identified above (Jenkins, 1998; Leventhal, 2000; Sherman, 1998; Smith, 2000, 2003). Sheard (2001) argues the current era of professional sport facilities uniquely provide these structures to keep spectators at the venue for longer periods of time during and in between events so they can provoke as much spending as possible. Interestingly, sport facilities did not always solely focus on removing money from their patrons. For example, historical records show the space within the sport facility accommodated areas for other activities like rifle shooting and indoor track (Serby, 1930). Additionally, early modern era (1903–1952) facilities acted as dormitories or community housing areas, laboratories, horse/ cattle stables, and automobile repair, wood-working, or machine shops (*American Architect*, 1920; Serby, 1930). Weiner (2000) recommends we can better address the needs of the professional sport facility's surrounding community and therefore justify its cost better by using the stadium's innards like they did in the past. The "innards of a stadium" are those areas underneath the seating arrangements and within the actual site of the building.

The University of Pennsylvania's Franklin Field II demonstrates many of these areas. For instance, editions of the *American Architect* (1923) and *Architectural Forum* (1923) both describe multiple rooms existing inside Franklin Field II. This facility expectedly accommodated team rooms, storage areas, showers, training rooms, ticket counters, a physician's office, and administrative space. However, two squash courts with a seating gallery, five regular squash courts, one rifle range, a dirt surface large enough to practice indoor track events like the pole vault or jumping (i.e. long jump, broad jump, triple jump), and university housing also appeared within the structure. Overall, most early modern sport facilities exploited their available space under stands and within concourses or hallways to maximize the use of the facility (Serby, 1930). Appropriately, this directly kept the size and cost of the venue from spiraling out of control.

It appears surrounding the professional sport facility with vast amounts of automobile parking also does little to help the community because it does not prompt individuals and groups to stay, participate, and interact with local neighborhood's commercial ventures, which surround the perimeter of the sport facility (Euchner, 1993). According to Seifried (2005), this was a major criticism of the Late Modern era (1953–1991) of sport facility development. The current "Post Modern" era of professional sport facilities often create their own community and encourage onsite spending by building the "miniature city" and its associated structures described above. However, spending at this "miniature city" typically only benefits the sport organization and not necessarily the locals who provided funds for its construction. Therefore, Bess (1999) and Seifried (2005) suggest future ballparks should look to encourage spending around the periphery of the sport facility through community-based activities (e.g., housing, health care, or education) offered or supported using the innards of the ballpark so ultimately the size of the venue will not continue to expand and construction costs will remain low.

Bess (1999) and Parrish (1998) both recommend avoiding a suburban location and choosing an urban setting for professional sport facilities because site constraints imposed by the urban environment force sporting venues to be smaller. A smaller physical footprint should persist as a desirable objective because it serves to reduce the cost of the overall project for those private investors and the public (Bess, 1999). Specifically, Bess (1999) assumes sport facilities emerging one-third less in size create half as much construction spending, even in an urban location. Recent examples and discussions from New York, Dallas, and San Francisco demonstrate this idea could be important to sport organizations because many cities expect their teams to contribute more financially to facility funding if not all for their construction.

Bess (1999) recommends fighting our compulsion to abolish all obstructed seating positions could help realize this goal for the contributing public and sport organizations. Obstructed viewpoints created from expansion efforts of the early modern era of sport facility design provoked recent stadium developers to position upper decks farther away from the field and introduce vertical circulation systems outside the constraints of the structure to make sport facilities larger (Bess, 1999; *Progressive Architecture*, 1971; Rader, 2002; Richmond, 1993; Ritter, 1992; Seifried, 2005). Ideally, we could limit the size of the professional sport facility by placing vertical circulation and parking structures inside, underneath or above the confines of the building's location rather than expanding out.

Improved engineering techniques and innovative building materials clearly allow us the opportunity to accomplish this feat. For example, the Great American Ballpark in Cincinnati currently possesses a large parking garage underneath the facility. Even as far back as 1931, Serby suggested an athletic organization could design parking in these locations for large stadiums requiring ten acres or more of parking accommodations. A side consequence of this action might produce smaller concourses with fewer amenities (e.g. concession options and merchandise stands) but with improving seating options (i.e. smart seats — described below) people can order these items delivered to their seat without suffering a loss of quality in the product, service, or spectator experience.

Consider the Environment

In order to help pay off their staggering costs, Parrish (1998) and others recommend professional sport facilities also attempt to utilize ecologically friendly or renewable sources of energy such as wind, sun, water, and geo-thermal activities (Blickstein, 1995; Sheard, 2001; Temko, 1993). For example, the kinetic energy produced by the wind could operate turbines capable of producing tremendous amounts of renewable electricity. The power output necessary to work the turbines typically requires a wind speed range many offshore or high altitudes places produce (Archer & Jacobson, 2005). Perhaps cities like Denver, Chicago, and San Francisco could take advantage of their location to capture this source of energy. Likewise, a tide, wave, or current's hydroelectric power generates endless supplies of energy which facilities could harness to alleviate operating costs. Several major league cities like Pittsburgh, Jacksonville, and Cincinnati, to name a few, host sport facilities near or next to water bodies which act as available sources of energy. Solar power also appears as a viable methods to offset construction and annual expenditures. For instance, the energy collected by cells on solar panels can generate electricity and heat buildings or food areas through heat pumps and ovens. Clearly, these structures work best in places with plenty of direct sunlight. Thus, places like Arizona, Southern California, and Texas appear as prime places to capture solar power. Interestingly, Sheard (2001) also claims solar heating can help benefit the environment because it produces seventy percent less carbon dioxide emissions. Clearly, those facilities harnessing these types of power would do a lot to increase attitudes concerning the environment because the energy produced would relieve costly burdens current structures often impose on the public and sport organizations.

Wind fans and thermal chimneys also serve to reduce sport facility size and costs by decreasing our dependence on massive air conditioning units. Sherman (1998, p. 218) adds Chase Field in Phoenix, AZ, surfaced as a 21.9 acre facility partially due to its, "six massive chillers which would cool the stadium on those 110-degree days." Wind fans and thermal chimneys, like the one at the Royal Selangor Turf Club in Kuala Lumpur, Malaysia and others in the Pacific side of the world demonstrate the success of using natural ventilation. Thermal chimneys perform this activity by allowing convective currents created through hot air's desire to rise out of a building (Lomas, Eppel, Cook, & Mardaljevic, 1997). The thermal chimney is produced by providing a warm area with an exterior outlet at the top of the facility. Ultimately, this ventilates the structure and allows the airflow to deliver a nice breeze throughout the venue. This type of structure is particularly excellent for tropical or excessively hot or humid climates to reduce heat and move air inside the facility. Future facilities in the southern United States could benefit greatly from incorporating thermal chimneys.

Temko (1993) predicted improvements with high strength steel and other new materials along with accompanying innovative construction techniques would produce truly incredible structures in the future. Many of the skyrocketing costs of professional sport facilities concerns the selection of building materials with their exceptional design. This work suggests future professional sport facility designers should utilize durable low-maintenance materials like pre-cast concrete, glass, plastic, fiberglass, and Teflon as they cost less yet still remain aesthetically pleasing and strong enough to keep costs manageable and designs fresh (Blickstein, 1995). Temko (1993) encourages the use of natural light and tall windows where possible for the illumination of the facility. This appears appropriate for professional sport facilities because internal and exterior lighting often consume a large amount of energy used by the venue. Energy saving lamps and light reflector technology can help reduce power consumption while remaining bright and lasting longer than conventional lamps.

This study offers combining tall windows, with a self-cleaning glass feature, will also overtime help reduce costs to the facility. Obviously, the use of natural light cuts down on the amount of electricity used to light up the structure but the self-cleaning glass serves as an added bonus because it harnesses solar power through the use of a metal oxide coating on one side of window to remove debris (Romeas, Guillar, & Pichat 1999). When raindrops fall they form sheets of water on the window and wash away loose particles. On sunny days, the ultraviolet energy from the sun activates the oxide coating to accelerate the decomposition of organic matter attempting to collect on the window's surface. Overall, this combination reduces illumination costs and the need for manpower armed with perhaps toxic chemicals to clean the facility under potentially dangerous conditions (e.g. working in elevated lifts/baskets or rapelling from the side of a building).

Improving the comfort level for all participants at a professional sport facility is important and clearly providing the appropriate levels of humidity, temperature, wind, and illumination, as identified above, appears necessary to accomplish this objective (Parrish, 1998). Puhalla, Krans, & Goatley's (2002) work suggests the growing senior population in the United States is one major group in the future who should be carefully considered before sport facility design. Specifically, Crompton (1999) discovered roughly one-eighth of the U.S. population included people sixty-five and older in 1990. However, based on current demographic trends proposed by the U.S. Census Bureau (2004), this figure is expected to increase to approximately one-fifth (20.7 percent) of the total American population (419,854,000) by 2050. This work believes the senior group's needs should emerge as a main consideration because of the vast amount of leisure time and disposable income they enjoy.

For example, in 1948 almost 50 percent of those sixty-five and older continued to participate in regular employment but by the finish of the 1990s, this number declined to 15 percent (Crompton, 1999). Appropriately, Blickstein (1995) predicts future generations of professional sport facilities will develop based on market forces because the sport industry may need to convince people to attend the facility rather than watch at home. Clearly, focusing on comfort with the appropriate aesthetic look for seniors is a potentially profitable investment for future professional sport facilities because the growing senior market will likely look for places to go and events to spend their well-earned retirement.

Embrace Interaction and Telecommunications

The professional sport facility generates, processes, and disseminates information for those in direct and remote or virtual attendance (Seifried, 2005 p. 291). Mitchell (1995) supports two types of presence, physical and virtual. The growth of computer technology survives as the most significant development of the late 20th century because people exponentially depend on computer technology to provide them with cultural, economic, educational, and social forms of interaction (Adams, 1997). Necessarily, future professional sport facilities will need to continue their evolution into high tech buildings and television studios because of the way spectators desire to view and interact with professional sport (Boyle & Haynes, 2000; Seifried, 2005; Sheard, 2001; Smith & Patterson, 1998).

Interaction with the sporting event is important to recognize because Sweet (2001) and others predict sport spectators will continue to desire more interaction with pro-

fessional sport in the future (Seifried, 2005; Sheard, 2001; Smith & Patterson, 1998). Sack (1997) suggests interaction regularly produces meanings through the shared social relationships and behaviors. Sheard (2001) expects the spectator of the future to participate more with the facility itself rather than exist as a passive member of the audience. Oriard (2001) supports this as he argues football spectators understand they need to become active participants in order to make the event a great spectacle. Appropriately, Chema (1996) and others believe individuals interacting more with the facility spend more money when they believe they can effectively impact the event because it provides them with some powerful experience (Smith & Patterson, 1998). Thus, future sport facilities should include opportunities for direct and remote interaction because experiencing interaction or contact is valuable socially and economically (Chema, 1996; Smith & Patterson, 1998).

Gershman (1993) and Golenbock (2000) demonstrate the benefits of direct interaction with their descriptions of how former St. Louis Browns (MLB) owner Bill Veeck (1951–1953) provided Sportsman's Park spectators several chances to interact with his American League team. Specifically, spectators attending St. Louis Browns games interacted with Manager Zack Taylor's on-the-field decisions by holding up signs with the words "hit" or "bunt." This marketing strategy served to produce record attendance and profits for the St. Louis Browns during this time period. Similarly, in the late 1980s and early 1990s, Pokey Allen, head football coach of Portland State University, embraced a similar fan involvement strategy to increase attendance and profits for his institution (Canzano, 2005). During these football seasons, Allen allowed fans with "run" or "pass" cards and "go" or "punt" signs to determine what strategy he used during the game. Allen also provided his fans another opportunity to interact with the sporting event through submitting plays to him they drew up for the game. During one football season, Allen would pick one play out for each home game and execute it during the contest. Expectantly, this campaign was wildly popular with the fans and helped produce significantly improved attendance at home football games.

Smart Seat technology now appears in a variety of facilities across the country to promote direct interaction experiences between spectators and event to produce a better experience (King, 2001). Currently, facilities like Tropicana Field (Tampa, FL) and San Diego Stadium installed "Choice Seats," as they are also called, in a small section of their venue. These special seats, "incorporate a touch screen computer monitor linked to an inhouse television network so spectators can view immediate replays of game action, read game information or statistics, and order food or beverage service" (Seifried, 2005 p. 264). Smart Seats like these also allow other entertainment opportunities like the watching of television programs, playing video games, and the ordering of concessions or merchandise to enhance the overall experience (Alm, 1998; Bernstein, 1999; Blickstein, 1995; Davis, 1998; John & Sheard, 2000). Williams (2001) believes professional football and baseball will also soon enjoy the ability to control camera angles for their viewing pleasure through personal video recording (PVR) in their smart seats. Blickstein (1995) and others show us many current smart seats also possess the ability to generate warmth for customers on cold days and cool spectators during hot weather (John & Sheard, 2000).

Clearly, this technology appears impressive when comparing them to the old wooden or metal seats provided in the previous eras of sport facility development and this work proposes these types of seats will eventually find a home throughout all major professional sport facilities. Additionally, we should not be surprised if smart seat and home Internet technology is eventually used to covertly allow fans to call plays for their team like the handheld signs, described above, did in the past to enhance the spectator experience. Essentially, this work supports the idea spectators will get the opportunity to impact the core product (i.e. the sporting event). Sport organizations with poor or dwindling interest could recognize this as an opportunity to generate improved fan support through this direct and remote interactive experience. Additionally, this type of fan involvement could also produce better job security for head coaches, as they might not always be solely accountable for their team's performance.

Euchner (1993) suggests, in the future, professional sport facility planners should also consider those in virtual/remote attendance as much as those physically at the facility. Consequently, the next modern professional sport facilities should also embrace telecommunication and computer needs within its design because it no longer represents a space to be filled and emptied strictly for those attending athletic events. Adams (1997) implies the Internet and television allows multidirectional instantaneous interactions, which would provide individuals the ability to occupy a place different from the one they literally rest. This concept is also known as extensibility. Mitchell's (1995) work implies we should view computer and television networks as a living place because a variety of individuals possess the ability to travel to this location instantly through the voluminous amount of sensory information they provide.

Future professional sport facilities will need to work toward this goal of extensibility to increase the popularity and spending upon the sports they host. Consequently, the number of television camera locations will likely multiply throughout the facility much like they did over the past fifty years. Sheard (2001) acknowledges older facilities of the Late Modern era (1953–1991) rarely contained more than four television locations. However, the current professional sport facilities support adequate room for twenty or more television camera locations (Sheard, 2001). In the future, we should expect this figure to increase because television producers often utilize multiple shots (i.e., close-ups, long shots, and over the field views) to generate more interest in the event for both direct and remote spectators (Chandler, 1988; Sheard, 2001). Bess (1999) assumes most professional baseball contests will likely take place at night so the sport facility should identify the most important concerns with night game productions and implement conditions best broadcasting these contests. Producing the event in this manner makes it a dramatic event and therefore easier to captivate the audience and change their interaction with the event from a passive viewer to an active participant.

Conclusion

The professional sport facility can be identified as a primary place because it is an artificial structure which influences, affects, and controls a variety of people and activities. Primary places possess rules on exclusion and inclusion to differentiate one group of people from another (Sack, 1997). Sack's (1986, 1997) work indicates the territorial partitioning of individuals within a professional sport facility naturally accompanies the increasing maturation or evolution of the sport itself. The enclosure efforts sport entrepreneurs brought to professional sport facilities will not likely subsist because people generally seek to control an appropriate amount of space to meet their psychological and physical needs. Therefore, the large areas occupied by luxury boxes will not likely fall in the future because again most individuals tend to acquire enough space to improve their privacy or opportunities for choice (Sundstrom, Town, Brown, Forman, & McGee, 1982).

The future could likely produce more luxury boxes or turn a greater percentage of current facility seats into this structure, which will not aid in decreasing facility operating and construction costs or increase community benefits. However, we are capable of reducing the size and costs of future professional sport facilities in a variety of ways to benefit the community, sport organization, and league (e.g. NFL Stadium Fund) both financially and socially as called for by the aforementioned scholars. First, we can make attempts to eliminate the "miniature city" most contemporary facility support today. We can better utilize the innards of the stadium to support community-oriented activities while still accommodating the necessary structures to fiscally run a professional sport facility. Again, Bale (1988) suggests future developers of professional sport facilities will receive a tremendous amount of pressure to make certain their structures host more events other than sporting activities. Selecting an urban location serves to limit the area a professional sport facility can consume. Considering the physical and biological environment also helps us achieve a reduction in size and improve the debt through the using of renewable sources of energy (e.g. sun, water, wind) and the introduction of structures like wind fans and thermal chimneys. Recently, the San Francisco Giants announced their plans to install 590 solar panels at AT&T Park to provide energy to the local grid as an example of contributing back to the community (McIntire-Strasburg, 2007). Careful selection of construction materials and design of the facility also serve to keep costs low while maintaining an aesthetically pleasing location. Finally, embracing interaction and telecommunication technology will help improve the experience and impact of the professional sport facility by providing more choices and options for people to participate directly or remotely to an event.

References

Adams, P.C. "Introduction: Cyberspace and Geographical Space." *Geographic Review*, vol. 87, no. 2 (1997): 139–145.

Alm, R. "Technology Puts Sports Fans in Front Row." *Dallas Morning News* (July 21, 1998): 2F.

Archer, C.L., and M.Z. Jacobson. "Evaluation of Global Wind Power." *Journal of Geophysical Research: Atmospheres* (2005): retrieved June 11, 2006, from www.agu.org/pubs/crossref/2005.../2204JD 005462.shtml.

Ary, D., L.C. Jacobs and A. Razavieh. *Introduction to Research in Education*, 5th ed. Philadelphia, PA: Harcourt Brace, 1996.

Baade, R., and R. Dye. "Sports Stadiums and Area Development: A Critical Review." *Economic Development Quarterly*, vol. 2, no. 3 (1988): 265–275.

Bale, J. "The Changing Face of Football: Stadiums and Communities." *Soccer and Society*, vol. 1, no. 1 (1988): 91–101.

Berg, B.L. *Qualitative Research Methods for the Social Sciences*. Boston: Allyn and Bacon, 1998.

Bernstein, A. "Video Monitors Cater to Fans." *Sports Business Journal*, vol. 2, no, 35 (1999): 35.

Bernstein, M.F. "Sports Stadiums Boondoggle: Building Hopes in the City." *The Public Interest*, vol. 22, no. 45 (1998).

Bess, P. *City Baseball Magic: Plain Talk and Uncommon Sense about Cities and Baseball Parks*. Minneapolis, MN: Minneapolis Review of Baseball, 1999.

Blickstein, S. *Bowls of Glory Field of Dreams: Great Stadiums and Ballparks of North America*. Encino, CA: Cherbo, 1995.

Boyle, R., and R. Haynes. *Power Play: Sport, the Media and Popular Culture*. New York: Pearson, 2000.

Brewer, J., and A. Hunter. *Multimethod Research: A Synthesis of Styles*. Newbury Park, CA: Sage, 1989.

Canzano, J. "Biggest Question for PSU Is Why Should We Care?" *The Oregonian* (September 14, 2005): retrieved June 12, 2006, from www.oregon live.com/sports/Oregonian/john_canzano/index.ssf ?base/sports/112669557856010.xml&coll=7.

Chandler, J.M. *Television and National Sport*. Urbana, IL: University of Illinois Press, 1988.

Chema, T. "When Professional Sports Justify the Subsidy." *Journal of Urban Affairs*, vol. 18, no. 1 (1996): 19–22.

Crompton, J.L. *Financing and Acquiring Park and Recreation Sources*. Champaign, IL: Human Kinetics.

Davis, M. "Old Ball Game Has High-Tech Look." *Kansas City Star* (August 22, 1988): B1.

Denzin, N.K. *The Research Act: A Theoretical Introduction to Sociological Methods*. New York: McGraw-Hill, 1978.

Eisinger, P. "The Politics of Bread and Circuses: Building a City for the Visitor Class. *Urban Affairs Review*, vol. 1 (2000): 316–333.

Epstein, E. "Clinic Rents Space at Giants' Park; Medical Care to Be Offered to Fans, Players, Residents." *San Francisco Chronicle* (November 20, 1998): A21.

Euchner, C.C. *Playing the Field: Why Sports Teams Move and Cities Fight to Keep Them*. Baltimore, MD: Johns Hopkins Press.

Gershman, M. *Diamonds: The Evolution of the Ballpark*. New York: Houghton Mifflin, 1993.

Golenbock, P. *The Spirit of St. Louis: A History of the St. Louis Cardinals and Browns*. New York: Harper-Collins, 2000.

Gunts, E. "Grandstand." *Architecture*, vol. 81 (1992): 64–71.

Howard, D. "The Changing Fanscape for Big League Sports: Implications for Sport Managers." *Journal of Sport Management*, vol. 13 (1999): 78–91.

Howard, D.R., and J.L. Crompton. *Financing Sport*. Morgantown, WV: Fitness Information Technology, 1995.

Jenkins, B. "Arizona's Park Nicely Combines Old, New." *San Francisco Chronicle* (April 4, 1998): E1.

John, G., and R. Sheard. *Stadia*, 3rd ed. Boston: Architectural, 2000.

Johnson, B., and L. Christensen. *Educational Research Quantitative and Qualitative Approaches*. Boston: Allyn and Bacon, 2000.

King, B. "NFL Gets Comfy with Choice Seat." *Sports Business Journal*, vol. 3, no. 46 (2001): 5.

Leventhal, J. *Take Me Out to the Ballpark: An Illustrated Tour of Baseball Parks Past and Present*. New York: Black Dog and Leventhal, 2000.

Leventhal, J. *Take Me Out to the Ballpark: An Illustrated Tour of Baseball Parks Past and Present*. New York: Black Dog and Leventhal, 2000.

Lomas, K.J., H. Eppel, M. Cook and J. Mardaljevic. "Ventilation and Thermal Performance of Design Options for Stadium Australia." International Building Performance Simulation Association (1997): retrieved June 11, 2006, from www.ibpsa.org /%5Cproceedings%5CBS1997%5CBS97_P160. pdf.

McIntire-Strasburg, J. "San Francisco Giants to Install Solar Panels." *Treehugger* (March 22, 2007): retrieved May 17, 2007, from www.treehugger.com/ files/2007/03/solar_baseball.php.

Mitchell, W.J. *City of Bits: Space, Place, and the In-fobahn.* Cambridge, MA: MIT Press, 1995.

Noll, R.G., and A. Zimbalist. "Sports, Jobs, and Taxes: The Economic Impact of Sports Teams and Stadiums." Washington, D.C.: Brookings Institution.

Oriard, M. *King Football: Sport and Spectacle in the Golden Age of Radio and Newsreels, Movies and Magazines, the Weekly and the Daily Press.* Chapel Hill: University of North Carolina Press, 2001.

Parrish, J. "Environmentally Sustainable Development of Sport Venues." In P. Thompson, J.J. Tolloczko, and J.N. Clarke, eds., *Stadia, Arenas and Grandstands,* New York: Routledge (1998): 337–343.

Puhalla, J., J. Krans, and M. Goatley. *Sport Fields: A Manual for Construction and Maintenance.* Hoboken, NJ: John Wiley and Sons, 2002.

Richmond, P. *Ballpark: Camden Yards and the Building of an American Dream.* New York: Simon & Schuster, 1993.

Ritter, L.S. *Lost Ballparks: A Celebration of Baseball's Legendary Fields.* New York: Viking Studio, 1992.

Ritzer, G., and T. Stillman. "The Postmodern Ballpark as a Leisure Setting: Enchantment and Simulated de-McDonaldization." *Leisure Sciences,* vol. 23 (2001): 99–113.

Rockerbie, D.W. *The Economics of Professional Sport* (2004): retrieved on January 13, 2005, from http://people.uleth.ca/~rockerbie/SportsText.pdf.

Romeas, V., C. Guillar and P. Pichat. "Testing the Efficacy and the Potential Effect on Indoor Air Quality of a Transparent Self-Cleaning TiO2-Coated Glass through the Degradation of a Fluoranthane Layer." Industrial & Engineering Chemistry Research, vol. 38, no. 10 (1999): 3878–3885.

Sack, R.D. *Homo Geographicus.* Baltimore, MD: Johns Hopkins University Press, 1997.

Seifried, C.S. *An Analysis of the American Outdoor Sport Facility: Developing an Ideal-Type on the Evolution of Professional Baseball and Football Structures.* Doctoral dissertation, Ohio State University (2005): retrieved May 1, 2007, from www.ohiolink.edu/etd/send-pdf.cgi?acc%5Fnum=osu116446330.

Serby, M.W. *The Stadium: A Treatise on the Design of Stadiums and Their Equipment.* New York: American Institute of Steel Construction, 1930.

Sheard, R. *Sports Architecture.* New York: Spon, 2001.

Sherman, L. *Big League, Big Time: The Birth of the Arizona Diamondbacks, the Billion-Dollar Business of Sports, and the Power of the Media in America.* New York: Pocket, 1998.

Smith, A., and R. Patterson. "Epilogue: The Future." In A. Smith and R. Patterson, eds., *Television: An International History,* New York: Oxford University Press (1998): 264–267.

Smith, C. *Storied Stadium: Baseball's History Through Its Ballparks.* New York: Carroll and Graf, 2003.

Smith, R. *The Ballpark Book: A Journey Through the Fields of Baseball Magic.* St. Louis, MO: Sporting News, 2000.

Sullivan, N.J. *The Diamond in the Bronx: Yankee Stadium and the Politics of New York.* New York: Oxford University Press, 2001.

Sundstrom, E., J. Town, D. Brown, A. Forman, and C. McGee. "Physical Encloser, Type of Job, and Privacy in the Office." *Environment and Behavior,* vol. 14 (1982): 543–559.

Sweet, D. "The Future Holds Technology at the Touch of a Button." *Sports Business Journal,* vol. 4, no. 17 (2001).

Temko, A. *No Way to Build a Ballpark and Other Irrelevant Essays on Architecture.* San Francisco, CA: Chronicle, 1993.

Thompson, D. "The Writing of Contemporary History." *Journal of Contemporary History,* vol. 2 (1967): 25–34.

U.S. Census Bureau. "Projected Population of the United States by Age and Sex: 2000 to 2050<in> (2004): retrieved May 15, 2007, from www.census.gov/ipc/www/usinterimproj/natprojtab02a.pdf.

Weiner, J. *Stadium Games: Fifty Years of Big League Greed and Bush League Boondoggles.* Minneapolis: University of Minnesota Press, 2000.

Williams, P. "Being Part of the Design Key for Concessionaires." *Sports Business Journal,* vol. 4, no. 15 (2001): 24.

Wineberg, S.S. "Historical Problem Solving: A Study of the Cognitive Processes Used in the Evaluation of Documentary and Pictorial Evidence." *Journal of Educational Psychology,* vol. 27 (1991): 73–87.

CHAPTER 41

Sports Facilities, Public Benefits, and the Future

Jordan Rappaport *and* Chad Wilkerson

Over the last few decades the number of U.S. metropolitan areas large enough to host a franchise from one of the four major professional sports leagues has soared. Even as the National Football League, Major League Baseball, the National Basketball Association, and the National Hockey League have expanded to include more franchises, demand by metro areas continues to exceed supply. As a result, metro areas have been forced to compete with each other to retain and attract franchises.

Large public expenditures on the construction of new sports facilities have been the main form of this competition. Sports stadiums and arenas are extremely expensive. A new football or baseball stadium costs approximately $325 million; a new basketball or hockey arena costs approximately $200 million. The public's share of these costs has averaged $200 million and $100 million, respectively. During the 1990s more than $6 billion in public funds was spent on construction of sports stadiums and arenas. Almost $4 billion has already been allocated toward new facilities scheduled to open by the end of 2004.

The large public spending on sports facilities has been controversial. Usually these costly projects are justified by claims that hosting a sports franchise spurs local economic development by creating numerous new jobs and boosting local tax revenue. However, independent economic studies suggest that taxpayers may not be getting such a good deal. In seeking to quantify the job creation and tax revenue benefits produced by a sports franchise, these studies overwhelmingly find that the benefits are much smaller than the outlay of public funds.

Does this mean that public funding of sports franchises is not justified? Perhaps not. An important element missing in the debate is the impact of a sports franchise on a metro area's quality of life. While difficult to measure, the contribution of a sports franchise to quality of life may exceed more traditional job creation and tax revenue benefits. If so, when quality-of-life benefits are included in the calculation, public spending may not appear to be such a bad investment for some metro areas.

The first section of this chapter reviews the current rush by metro areas to build sports

Originally published as "What Are the Benefits of Hosting a Major League Sports Franchise?" *Economic Review*, Vol. 27, No. 1, First Quarter 2001, by the Federal Reserve Bank, Kansas City, MO.

facilities and lays out the arguments both in favor of and against using public funds to do so. The second section shows why the job creation and tax revenue benefits from hosting a major league franchise fall far short of typical public outlays on constructing a new sports facility. The third section argues that the large quality-of-life benefits associated with hosting a major league team may justify the public outlays.

The Debate on Public Financing for Sports Stadiums

More than half the U.S. population lives in one of the 38 metro areas that host one or more teams from the four major professional sports leagues. And millions more live in rapidly growing metro areas with populations large enough to make them a potentially attractive place to locate a team. With demand for hosting major league teams exceeding supply, both current and potential host metro areas have been forced to compete to retain and attract franchises. Doing so almost always requires allocating large public expenditures to the construction of sports stadiums and arenas.

This section documents the scope and magnitude of public spending on professional sports franchises. It then summarizes the claims made to justify such spending as well as the critique of these claims by independent economists.

The Scope and Magnitude of Public Financing for Sports Stadiums

The National Football League (NFL), Major League Baseball (MLB), the National Basketball Association (NBA), and the National Hockey League (NHL) are the four most widely followed professional sports leagues in the United States. Of the 121 teams

in these four leagues, 111 play in 92 stadiums and arenas in 38 U.S. metro areas. The remaining ten teams play in eight stadiums in six different Canadian metro areas.

Since 1994, more than $8 billion has been spent constructing new stadiums to host major league teams. Another $1 billion has been spent on major renovations of existing stadiums. While a few of the stadiums were financed privately, most received large contributions from local and state governments. Public spending on these new and renovated stadiums has totaled $5.4 billion. An additional $3.7 billion in public funds has already been allocated toward the construction of stadiums and arenas scheduled to open by the end of 2004. As a result of all this spending, by 2004 more than two-thirds of the 111 major league teams in the United States will be playing in venues that either opened or were heavily renovated in the previous ten years.

Sports stadiums and arenas are expensive. For the 17 football and baseball stadiums built since 1994, the average public contribution has been $188 million, or 66 percent of the total cost. For the 19 basketball and hockey arenas built during the same period, the average public share has been $84 million, or 45 percent of the total. The average public contribution toward stadiums and arenas currently under construction is even higher: $230 million for baseball and football stadiums (63 percent of the total), and $114 million for basketball and hockey arenas (51 percent of the total).

To finance their contributions toward stadium and arena projects, local and state governments issue bonds. Such bonds are usually paid off through various sorts of taxes enacted especially for this purpose. Sales taxes directed at tourists (for example, on hotel rooms, rental cars, and convention space) have been an especially popular method used to repay stadium bonds. Also common are general sales taxes that can apply across multiple counties or only in the county or municipality where the stadium is located. Other means of repaying stadium bonds in recent years have included gate taxes (surcharges on tickets to events at the sports facilities), state lottery proceeds, taxes on businesses in specially designated districts, and local and state government general funds.

Justifying Public Spending on Sports Facilities

Supporters of using public expenditures to finance the construction of sports facilities argue that hosting a major league franchise helps spur economic development. Impact studies commissioned by stadium proponents attempt to quantify how hosting a team affects a variety of local economic indicators such as output, personal income, jobs, and tax revenue. Stadium advocates suggest that increases in these indicators justify the large public outlays on sports facilities.

A 1996 study argued that the NFL Seahawks in their former stadium increased total Seattle annual output by $69 million, increased total Seattle annual personal income by $41 million, created 1,264 Seattle jobs, and raised $3.3 million in state and local taxes per year. Impact studies also often label the expenditures and jobs associated with the construction phase of stadium projects as economic benefits. For instance, a 1996 study supporting the public financing of separate new sports stadiums for Cincinnati's NFL Bengals and MLB Reds suggests that the construction of these two stadiums would generate $1.1 billion in economic activity for the Cincinnati metro area and create 18,461 temporary jobs.

These impact studies that justify stadium projects can be subject to a number of criticisms. Many of the studies look at only the positive effects of hosting a major league franchise. Taking account of negative effects such as offsetting job losses, however, would produce much lower estimates of the net impact on local economic development. Moreover, the impact studies almost always fail to measure benefits in a form that can be compared with public outlays. While increases in output, increases in personal income, and job creation all measure increases in underlying economic activity, how should a metro area value these increases?

In response to the shortcomings of such impact studies, independent economists have attempted to measure the effect of professional sports teams on metro areas in a number of ways. One method is to compare growth rates of metro areas with and without professional teams, after controlling for other variables. For example, in a study of the growth of per capita personal income in 48 metro areas from 1958 to 1987, Baade (1994) found no significant difference between metro areas with major league teams and those without. In a study of 46 metro areas from 1990 to 1994, Walden actually found a negative relationship between economic activity and the presence of a sports team.

A second way of measuring the impact of teams is to examine the subsequent growth of cities that acquire new teams. Baade and Sanderson did this for ten metro areas that obtained new franchises between 1958 and 1993 and found no significant increases in employment or output. Results from Coates and Humphreys showed that per capita income fell when metro areas added teams.

Still another approach to measuring the impact of professional sports teams is to analyze the specific economic activity generated by specific teams in specific locations. For example, Hamilton and Kahn measured the annual returns to Maryland residents from Baltimore's NFL Ravens at approximately $1 million, compared to a $14 million annual public cost for their new stadium. Similarly, Baade (1997) measured the annual returns to Washington state residents from Seattle's MLB Mariners at between $3.8 and $5.1 million, compared to a $28 million annual public cost for their new stadium.

Regardless of method, none of the academic studies has so far been able to find significant economic development benefits sufficient to justify the large public outlays. As Siegfried and Zimbalist concluded in a recent survey of the economics of sports facilities,

> Few fields of empirical economic research offer virtual unanimity of findings. Yet, independent work on the economic impact of stadiums and arenas has uniformly found that there is no statistically significant positive correlation between sports facility construction and economic development.

Similarly, Noll and Zimbalist introduced a collection of 14 essays on the economics of sports stadiums by stating, "The overriding conclusion of this discussion is that the economic case for publicly financed stadiums cannot credibly rest on the benefits to local business, as measured by jobs, income, and investment."

So which view is correct? Do sports teams promote economic development as claimed by the impact studies? Or are such economic development benefits illusory as suggested by the independent economists? The next section examines whether the economic development benefits from hosting a major league franchise justify typical public outlays on sports stadiums and arenas.

Measuring Job Creation and Tax Revenue Benefits

To measure the benefits associated with hosting a professional sports team, both stadium proponents and their critics focus on the increased economic activity and additional tax revenue that may be generated by a team's presence. The most common measure of economic activity is the creation of new jobs. Correctly measuring the benefit from job creation requires both accurately accounting for the net number of new jobs associated with a team's presence along with valuing the benefit of these jobs to the host metro area. Increased tax revenue resulting from the presence of the professional sports team arises from sales taxes and income taxes. Estimates of the combined benefits from net job creation and increased tax revenue fall considerably short of typical public outlays on new sports stadiums and arenas.

Measuring Job Creation Benefits

Net job creation is a relatively good measure of the possible increase in economic activity associated with hosting a professional sports team. Estimated net job creation can be explicitly valued in terms of its benefit to a metro area's existing residents. Such an approach provides an estimate of benefits that can be directly compared with the public outlay costs while avoiding double counting that may arise from other methods. A possible limitation of this approach is that an increase in economic activity may benefit a metro area's existing residents even without any net job creation — for instance, if hosting a team causes everyone's wages to increase. However, the findings in numerous independent studies suggest that using net job creation to measure economic activity does not miss any large benefits.

Estimating net job creation. To estimate the number of jobs created from hosting a professional sports team, it is necessary to distinguish between gross and net job creation. Gross job creation is the number of jobs that can be observably linked to the presence of a sports team. Such observable jobs are created mainly within the stadium itself and at nearby businesses catering to people who attend sports events. But the presence of a professional sports team also creates job losses, because individuals who spend money to attend sports events have less to spend at businesses elsewhere in the host metro area. Less spending results in job losses. And benefits generally arise only from a net increase in jobs.[1]

Gross jobs created at a sports stadium include the players and other team employees; stadium management, maintenance, and support staff; and the various vendors selling goods at stadium events. Gross jobs created at nearby stadium businesses arise from the before-game and after-game spending of people attending sports events. Depending on the specific design and location of a sports stadium, such spending may support a number of local businesses, such as parking lots, restaurants, nightclubs, and souvenir shops. Some additional tourism-related jobs that can be linked to the presence of a sports team may also be created further away from stadiums. These arise from the spending of people who visit a host metro area to attend a sports event — for instance, at hotels and restaurants located throughout the metro area.[2]

Both stadium and nearby-stadium job creation may be offset by job losses throughout a host metro area. Such job losses must be subtracted from the above job gains to obtain an estimate of net job creation. In particular, economic research shows that people's total spending on entertainment is not affected by the presence of a professional sports team. For example, the more people spend on attending sports events, the less they may spend on movies and restaurants (Baade and Sanderson). Similarly, the more people spend at restaurants and nightclubs located near a stadium, the less they may spend at restaurants and nightclubs located elsewhere. Because the job losses from lower spending are spread across a large number of businesses and a wide geographic area, they usually cannot be observably linked to the presence of a sports team.

In addition to observable gross jobs, hosting a professional sports team also creates unobservable "local multiplier" jobs. These jobs arise from changes in local spending due to gross job creation and the offsetting job losses. For example, local spending by team players supports jobs across a range of local service industries, including at restaurants, nightclubs, and retail stores. Hence the total number of jobs created in a host metro area is some multiple of the observable number of jobs created. Similarly, the reduced local spending of people who lose jobs causes additional, again unobservable, job losses. Hence the total number of jobs lost is some multiple of the "initial" (also unobservable) number of jobs lost.[3]

Because local multiplier jobs cannot be easily linked to a sports team's presence, the size of the local multiplier is controversial. Estimates of total job creation in the stadium impact studies use local multipliers as high as 2.5. In other words, these studies assume that 2.5 total jobs are created for each initial observable job created from hosting a sports team. In contrast, the independent economic studies suggest that the appropriate local multiplier to apply to the gross jobs created from hosting a sports team is probably no more than 1.25 (Hamilton and Kahn; Siegfried and Zimbalist). The lower local multipliers used by the independent studies appear more reasonable because a large portion of local spending goes to purchase goods and services produced outside the host metro area. In addition, many professional sports players reside outside the metro area in which they play, either during the off-season or following retirement.

Taking explicit account of job losses and using estimates of the local multiplier from independent studies suggest that the net number of jobs created from hosting a professional sports team is quite low. It is almost certainly less than 1,000 and likely to be much closer to zero. For example, the methodology and numbers reported in Hamilton and Kahn suggest that Baltimore's hosting of the Orioles baseball team has created just 770 jobs in the Baltimore metro area. Statistical analysis reported in Baade and Sanderson found evidence of positive net job creation in only three of ten metro areas examined; their highest estimate of the number of net jobs created from hosting a sports team was 356 (associated with the Kansas City Royals). Surveying the economics literature, Siegfried and Zimbalist concluded that hosting a sports team might actually be associated with net job destruction rather than net job creation.[4]

Valuing the benefits from net job creation. To measure the benefit from increased economic activity, it is not enough just to estimate the net number of jobs created. It is also necessary to value explicitly the benefit of these jobs to the metro area.

It is important to realize that a metro area's existing residents may not benefit at all from net job creation. Consider the case of metro area residents who already have high paying jobs which they enjoy. How do they benefit from more jobs in a metro area? On the positive side, property prices are likely to rise and local governments may be able to raise revenues from a larger tax base, in turn allowing for lower tax rates. On the negative side, a rise in property prices could make housing less affordable, and traffic and other sorts of congestion may increase. For some existing residents, the net result may be that they are hurt rather than helped by net job creation.[5]

Whether and how much a metro area benefits from net job creation is an empirical question that a number of economists have attempted to answer. In particular, statistical techniques have been used to look at the correlations across metro areas among population, employment, wages, and house values. For a given increase in population and employment, benefits accrue through associated rises in wages or house values. For people who do not own their homes, net benefits are likely to be negligible as any rise in wages is offset by the higher cost of housing. But for residents who already own a home, there is no offset and so benefits may be positive.

Using such techniques, economists have estimated metro area benefits to range from $0 to $1,500 per net job created (Rosen; Roback; Gyourko and Tracy; and Hamilton and Kahn).[6] At one extreme, if the benefit per net job created is indeed zero, metro areas will not benefit at all from any possible net job creation from hosting a professional sports team. At the other extreme, even if the benefit per net job created is at its upper bound estimate of $1,500, the total benefit to a metro area from any net jobs created will be far smaller than the total of the associated salaries.

Valuing the net job creation benefit from a team requires combining the above estimates of the number of net jobs created with the value of these jobs to the host metro area. Using the lower and upper bound estimates, respectively, values the net job creation benefit at $0 and $1.5 million per year. Using the midpoints from each of these ranges as a baseline values the net job creation benefit at $375,000 per year (500 jobs times $750 per job).

Measuring Tax Revenue Benefits

The second main source of benefits on which both stadium advocates and independent economists focus is the increased tax revenues that may arise from hosting a team. Fans' spending before, during, and after games is likely to be subject to local and state sales taxes. And the income accruing to any net increase in jobs is often subject to local and state income taxes.

Estimating imported sales tax revenue. The main way in which increased sales tax revenue benefits a host metro area is if it is paid by non-local residents. Non-local sports fans visiting to attend games pay sales taxes on all local purchases before, during, and after games. Such spending "imports" tax revenue, which in the absence of a professional sports team would have accrued to governments outside the host metro area. Imported sales tax revenue benefits the host metro area by reducing the amount of taxes that need to be raised from local residents.[7]

Estimating the imported sales tax revenues associated with hosting a team is straightforward. To do so, first the number of non-local fans who visit to attend sports games must be estimated. This estimate is then multiplied by the fans' estimated average spending before, during, and after games. Finally, this latter result must be multiplied by the relevant local sales tax rate. The difficult part, of course, is estimating the number of visitors and how much they spend on average. Among the four major professional sports leagues, specifics such as ticket prices, average attendance, and the number of home games per season vary enough to require separate estimates. And regardless of league, it is necessary to distinguish non-local sports fans who visit for the purpose of attending a game from non-local visitors who happen to attend a game.

The estimated imported sales tax benefit from hosting a team from each of the four major sports leagues are examined. The listed percentages of non-local visiting fans are toward the high end of estimates from a number of impact and economic studies.[8] For calculating the imported sales tax revenue benefit attributable to hosting a sports team, what matters is not the number of non-local residents who attend games but rather the number of

non-local residents whose visits are explicitly motivated by the presence of a team. The distinction is crucial. Non-local residents who attend games may be visiting the host metro area for non-game-related reasons such as business or family. If so, their spending at games most likely represents a shifting away from spending on other forms of local entertainment and hence the associated imported tax revenues should not be attributed to the presence of the sports team.[9]

Average spending by visiting sports fans is estimated to range from $63 for MLB games to $99 for NBA games. The concession portion of average spending is based on the purchase of a representative bundle of food, merchandise, and parking at the average 2000 season price in the respective league (FoxSports.com). The out-of-stadium portion of average spending is based on a survey of fans attending Baltimore Orioles games in 1992, converted to 2000 dollars (Hamilton and Kahn).

The imported tax revenue from a given amount of visitors' spending obviously depends on the applicable rate of sales tax. Assuming an extremely high local sales sports team imports from $696,000 per year for an NHL team to $1,537,000 per year for an MLB team. At a more typical local sales tax rate of 2 percent, imported sales tax revenues for the four types of teams range from just $278,400 per year for an NHL team to $614,800 per year for an MLB team.[10]

Estimating income tax revenue. Many of the localities in which professional sports teams play levy local income taxes. If so, the income tax revenue on salaries due to any net job creation is imported in the sense that in the absence of a professional sports team, it would be paid to other localities. Such imported income tax revenue does not necessarily benefit the host metro area since at least in part it goes to cover any additional costs in providing municipal services to accommodate the growth in employment and population.[11]

Nevertheless, because player salaries are extremely high, the associated income taxes are likely to far exceed the marginal cost of any municipal services used by players. This is especially so since many players reside outside the host metro area for a significant portion of the year. Moreover, because they tend to be young, few players have children in local public schools. Income taxes on the relatively high salaries of a team's general manager and head coach are also likely to exceed the marginal cost of the additional municipal services these individuals use.

The estimated imported income tax benefit from hosting a team from each of the four major sports leagues were studied. Applying a 2 percent income tax rate to the estimated team payrolls suggests that increased local income taxes range from $868,000 per year for NHL teams to $1.4 million per year for NFL teams. The assumed 2 percent local income tax rate is toward the high end of the rate at which local governments tax income. Indeed, many professional teams play in metro areas whose local governments do not levy income taxes. On the other hand, many state governments tax income at higher than a 2 percent rate. Using the highest combined state and local income tax rate from the metro areas that host teams (10.6 percent for New York City) establishes an upper bound on the imported annual income tax benefit ranging from $4.6 million for an NHL team to $7.5 million for an NFL team.

Comparing Job Creation and Tax Revenue Benefits to Public Outlays

How do benefits of estimated job creation and tax revenue compare with typical public outlays on sports facilities? Adding together the annual estimated benefit values of the net job creation, imported sales taxes, and increased income taxes yields baseline estimates of the value of hosting a franchise ranging from $1.9 million per year for an NHL team to $2.9 million per year for an NFL team.

A last necessary step toward the goal of comparing benefits and costs is to convert benefits quantified on an annual basis into benefits quantified on a net present value basis. The question is, how much should a metro area be willing to spend for each dollar of *annual* benefits associated with hosting a franchise? Calculating the answer is straightforward. Assuming that metro areas can borrow (by issuing municipal bonds) at a 6 percent interest rate and that the proceeds are used to purchase an annual stream of benefits starting one year in the future and lasting for 30 years (a reasonable estimate for the life of a sports stadium), it follows that each $1 of annual benefits is worth $13.76 to the metro area.[12]

On a net present value basis, the estimated value of the combined jobs and tax benefits from a franchise range from $26.7 million for an NHL team to $40.3 million for an NFL team. Such values fall far short of typical public outlays on sports facilities. The average public outlay on new baseball and football stadiums completed between 1994 and 2000 was $188 million. Thus, for most sports stadium projects, costs exceeded the above estimated benefits by well over $100 million. The average public outlay on new basketball and hockey arenas completed over the same period was $84 million. Thus, for most sports arena projects, costs exceeded the above estimated benefits by well over $50 million. The amount by which public costs exceed estimated jobs and tax benefits is even higher for the sports stadiums and arenas currently under construction.

If anything, the baseline values estimated above likely overstate rather than understate the benefits they measure. As discussed, there is much doubt that hosting a professional sports team creates any jobs. Moreover, many host metro areas tax spending at a rate lower than the assumed 5 percent baseline. And, many do not tax income at all. As a result, it is reasonable to believe that the net present value of the jobs and tax benefits may be no more than $5 million from hosting an NBA or NHL team and no more than $10 million from hosting an NFL or MLB team. Even using the upper-bound estimates from the analysis above suggests that the public outlays on current sports facility projects far exceed any associated jobs and tax benefits.

The bottom line, then, is that the benefit to a host metro area from increased economic activity as measured by net job creation and increased tax revenues appears to fall far short of the public outlays typically needed to retain and attract professional sports teams. Nevertheless, metro areas continue to approve ever-larger public outlays on new sports facility construction. If such public outlays represent good investments, there must be some other large benefit from hosting a team that the above analysis is not measuring. The next section explores whether a professional sports team's contribution to a host area's quality of life may be exactly such a benefit.

Quality-of-Life Benefits from Hosting a Major League Franchise

The presence of a major league sports franchise can help make a metro area an attractive place to live. Nearly all analyses of the benefits from hosting professional sports teams recognize this contribution to a metro area's quality of life. But because quality-of-life benefits are difficult to quantify, stadium proponents and critics usually pay them little attention beyond such acknowledgment.

The term "quality of life" used in this ar-

ticle is meant to capture the satisfaction, or happiness, residents derive from shared metro area attributes. Examples of shared attributes include pleasant weather, scenic vistas, and natural recreational opportunities. Of course, residents' happiness also depends on their individual circumstances, such as having a good job and living in a nice house.

This section discusses how the presence of a major league franchise contributes to the quality of life of a host metro area's residents. Three possible ways of valuing this benefit are presented. Together they suggest that hosting a major league franchise contributes substantially to quality of life and perhaps justifies public outlays on sports stadiums and arenas.

How Hosting a Professional Sports Team Contributes to Quality of Life

Professional sports teams contribute to a metro area's quality of life primarily by increasing the happiness of sports fans. The most visible source of fan happiness comes from attending home games. However, only part of this happiness actually counts as a quality-of-life benefit attributable to hosting a team. This is because fans must pay to attend games. In the absence of a professional sports team, fans could instead use what they paid for game admissions on other sources of happiness, such as watching a movie or traveling to a different metro area to attend a game.

Formally, the quality-of-life benefit to a particular fan who attends a sports game is the amount above the admission price they would have been willing to spend to attend the game. For instance, if someone is willing to spend $30 to attend a game that only costs $20, they receive a $10 quality-of-life benefit. Adding up the individual quality-of-life benefits of all residents who attend games yields the total metro area's quality-of-life benefit from game attendance.[13]

A second source of happiness for fans

comes from rooting for a team more generally, independent of actually attending games in person. Fans watch games on television, listen to them on the radio, and read about them in local newspapers. Games serve as an occasion for parties and barbecues. Teams' performance is the subject of long discussions among friends. And second-guessing team decisions is the subject of nearly continuous banter on local talk radio.

It is also possible that hosting a franchise increases the happiness of all metro area residents, regardless of their being sports fans. Home games and rooting for a sports team provide for shared community experiences. And hosting a sports team may increase civic pride — for instance, by contributing to a sense that one lives in a "world class" city.

On the other hand, hosting a team may also decrease the happiness of some metro area residents. Home games impose traffic and congestion in the vicinity of sports facilities. And television viewers face interruption of their favorite syndicated shows by local game broadcasts. Such possible negative contributions must be subtracted from positive contributions in valuing the net contribution to quality of life from hosting a team.

Valuing Quality-of-Life Benefits

Valuing the happiness metro area residents derive from the presence of a major league team is extremely difficult. A person's happiness from attending a game or from watching one on television is not observable. Nevertheless, there are several possible approaches to valuing quality-of-life benefits. A first approach is to ask a sample of metro area residents how much they would be willing to pay to retain or attract a team. A second approach uses variations in metro area wages and house prices to implicitly value quality-of-life attributes that may be similar in magnitude to hosting a major league franchise. A third

approach looks at the actions of metro areas that have lost sports franchises and so may have the best information on the quality-of-life benefits from hosting a team.

Surveying residents. The most direct approach to valuing the quality-of-life benefits from hosting a team is to ask local residents how much they would be willing to pay to keep their team from moving.

In the only major study of this kind, Pittsburgh metro area residents were asked during the winter of 2000, "What is the most you would be willing to pay out of your own household budget each year in higher city taxes to keep the Penguins in Pittsburgh?" (Johnson, Groothuis, and Whitehead). The responses implicitly valued the quality-of-life benefits from hosting the NHL Penguins at somewhere between $0.83 to $2.30 per Pittsburgh metro area resident per year. Given metro Pittsburgh's population of 2.4 million and converting to a net present value basis using a 6 percent interest rate, as described in the previous section, the value of hosting the Penguins for 30 years is estimated to fall somewhere in the range of $26.9 million to $74.7 million.

Note that the lower-bound estimate of the quality-of-life value of hosting the Penguins is nearly the same as the baseline estimate of the job creation and tax benefit value of doing so. The upper-bound estimate of the quality-of-life value of hosting the Penguins begins to approach the $84 million average public contribution to NBA/NHL sports arenas completed between 1994 and 2000.

Moreover, there are several reasons to believe that the quality-of-life benefits to Pittsburgh from hosting the Penguins may be low relative to such benefits associated with other major league teams. First, the quality-of-life benefits from hosting an NHL team are probably the lowest of the four leagues considered in this article. For instance, only 15 of the 24

NHL teams currently have local network television contracts. And when NHL games are broadcast, their ratings tend to be less than half those for MLB games (*SportsBusiness Journal*). Second, Pittsburgh also hosts the NFL Steelers and the MLB Pirates. So even if it were to lose the Penguins, Pittsburgh would still host two major league teams. Economic theory argues that the additional benefit of something decreases the more you have of it. Third, at the time the survey was conducted, the Penguins organization was in Chapter 11 bankruptcy proceedings. Whatever problems caused the Penguins' financial difficulties may also have lowered the team's contribution to Pittsburgh's quality of life. Fourth, as will be argued below, it may be that only by losing a team do metro area residents come to accurately value the team's contribution to quality of life.[14]

Comparing to quality-of-life valuations of other attributes. The second approach to valuing the quality-of-life contribution from hosting a team considers the valuations of other attributes that also contribute to quality of life. For instance, the quality-of-life net present value associated with one extra day per year of pleasant weather for 30 years turns out to be similar in magnitude to many of the recent public outlays on stadium projects. So if the contribution to quality of life from hosting a major league team is at least as great as the contribution from one extra day per year of pleasant weather, then the public outlays on sports stadiums and arenas may be justified.

The quality-of-life benefits of certain attributes that naturally differ across metro areas, such as the weather, can be measured by variations in wages and house prices. All else equal, metro areas with attributes that positively contribute to residents' happiness attract population inflows. This puts downward pressure on local wages and upward pressure on local house prices as people who move in try to find jobs and housing. The lower wages and higher house prices serve as negative "compensation" for the high quality of life. Conversely, metro areas that offer low levels of happiness lose population, putting upward pressure on local wages and downward pressure on local house prices as firms try to retain workers and the people who move out vacate housing. The higher wages and lower house prices serve as positive "compensation" for the low quality of life.[15]

Using data on a large number of individuals and households living in more than 100 different metro areas, statistical techniques can measure the variations in wages and house prices that are due to each of several metro area attributes. The quality-of-life value of a given metro area attribute can then be calculated as the sum of the lower wages individuals are willing to accept and the higher house prices they are willing to pay to live in an area with such an attribute.[16]

The quantitative benefits from quality of life are found to be quite large. For instance, the estimates suggest that the annual value to a metro area of one extra sunny day per year is between $7 to $12 per person. So a metro area with two million people should be willing to pay between $14 million and $24 million per year for the extra annual sunny day (or roughly between $193 million and $330 million up front for an average extra sunny day over each of the subsequent 30 years). Quantitatively similar valuations are estimated for the quality-of-life benefits of one less rainy day per year and one inch less snow per year.

Unfortunately, this second approach cannot be used directly to value the quality of life from hosting a major league team. The reason is that nearly all teams choose to locate in metro areas with high levels of population and employment. This makes it impossible to distinguish between the variations in wages and house prices that are due to the presence of a sports team and those that are due to the high population and employment.

Nevertheless, the high valuations of the quality-of-life benefits that flow from geographic attributes such as pleasant weather serve as a useful benchmark for the quality-of-life benefits from hosting a major league team. In particular, large public outlays to attract and retain a major league team may make sense if the team's contribution to the area's quality of life is similar in magnitude to that of one extra sunny day per year (or one less rainy day per year or one inch less snow per year). Fan willingness to endure extreme weather to attend games at outdoor stadiums suggests that the positive contribution to happiness from hosting a professional sports team may exceed such a threshold.

The experience of metro areas that lost teams. A third approach to valuing quality-of-life benefits points to the actions of metro areas that hosted a major league team that then moved elsewhere. These metro areas should be among those with the best information on the quality-of-life benefits from hosting a team since they can compare happiness both with and without a team. Subsequent to losing a team, many of these metro areas were willing to significantly increase the size of their public outlays on constructing new sports facilities. This willingness suggests that residents revised upward their estimates of a major league team's contribution to their happiness. The resulting success of such metro areas in attracting replacement teams indicates that quality-of-life benefits may indeed justify the large public outlays.

Since 1980, only 12 U.S. metro areas have lost major league teams.[17] Six of these lost National Football League teams: Oakland (1983), Baltimore (1984), St. Louis (1988), Los Angeles (two teams in 1995), Cleveland (1997), and Houston (1997). Four metro areas lost National Hockey League teams: Atlanta (1980), Denver (1982), Minneapolis/St. Paul (1993),

and Hartford (1997). And two metro areas lost National Basketball Association teams: Kansas City (1984) and San Diego (1984).

Losing a football team seems clearly to have caused metro area residents to revise upward their estimates of the associated quality-of-life benefits.[18] Of the metro areas that lost NFL teams, all but Los Angeles subsequently allocated considerably more public financing to attract a new NFL team than it would have cost to keep their old team. For example, St. Louis' NFL Cardinals departed in 1987 after the city refused to allocate $120 million toward the construction of a new football stadium (Quirk and Fort). Less than three years later, St. Louis voters approved $280 million in public funds for a new football stadium — even before they had a team to play in it.[19] And two years following the departure of the NFL Browns, Cleveland allocated $214 million toward construction of a football stadium for a newly awarded expansion team. The owner of the former Cleveland Browns commented, "The only regret I have, to be honest with you, is that if they gave me half of what they're doing now, I'd still be in Cleveland" (Meyer). Similarly, Oakland, Baltimore, and Houston each increased by at least one-third the amount of public funds they were willing to spend on building new football stadiums.[20]

The experience of metro areas that lost NHL and NBA teams has been more mixed. Minneapolis-St. Paul would probably have needed to spend only about $17 million to prevent the 1993 departure of its NHL team (Bremner). But in 1999 it decided to allocate $130 million to attract a new NHL team. At the same time, Atlanta and Denver managed to endure the loss of their NHL teams for 19 and 13 years, respectively. They were eventually able to attract replacement NHL teams at what is probably a lower public cost than what would have been required to prevent the original losses. Hartford has been more aggressive in attempting to attract an NFL team rather than a replacement for its departed NHL team. And neither Kansas City nor San Diego has made an extensive effort to replace their NBA teams.[21]

Taking Account of Quality-of-Life Benefits

The previous section's discussion of the job creation and tax revenue benefits from hosting a major league franchise suggested that such benefits fall far short of typical public outlays on the construction of new sports facilities. Can quality-of-life benefits make up the difference?

Based on results of a survey asking Pittsburgh metro area residents how much they would be willing to be taxed to keep the NHL Penguins, the answer may be yes. However, caution warns against generalizing the results from a single survey.

Alternatively, results of economic studies of compensating differentials provide a benchmark in assessing quality-of-life benefits. For instance, if the contribution to metro area residents' happiness from hosting a major league sports franchise is similar in magnitude to that from an additional day of pleasant weather per year, the net present value quality-of-life benefit may indeed approach the magnitude of recent public outlays on sports facility construction.

Finally, the aggressive bids by metro areas to replace teams that have departed further supports the view that the overall value to a metro area from hosting a professional sports team may exceed the associated large public expenditures. Of course, this will not always be the case as is illustrated by the metro areas that have not made extensive efforts to re-attract lost teams. But for those metro areas that have bid aggressively, this would almost certainly have to be due to a large contribution to residents' quality of life.

Summary and Conclusions

U.S. metro areas have had to compete with each other to retain and attract major league sports franchises. The resulting large public outlays to finance the construction of sports facilities have been quite controversial. Proponents of using public funds to finance stadium construction argue that the benefits from increased economic activity and increased tax revenue collection exceed the public outlays. But independent economic studies universally find such benefits to be much smaller than claimed.

So does it makes sense for metro areas to use public funds to attract and retain major league sports franchises? The answer is definitely not if benefits are limited to increases in economic activity and tax revenue collection. A strong case can be made, however, that the quality-of-life benefits from hosting a major league team can sometimes justify the large public outlays associated with doing so.[22]

Quality-of-life benefits are rarely explicitly included in the debate on using public funds to attract and retain a major league sports franchise. Acknowledging that the main benefit from hosting a team comes from improved metro-area quality of life should help to value this contribution. Doing so does not require impact studies. Residents and elected officials who understand that the benefits of a sports team are the same sort that flow from parks, zoos, museums, and theater can decide on their own how much hosting a major league team is worth.

Notes

1. Benefits may also arise when high-paying jobs replace low-paying ones.
2. Impact studies usually attribute to the presence of a professional sports team gross job creation due to all local spending by non-local residents who attend a sports game. But some of this spending is likely to

have occurred anyway, as many of the non-local residents who attend a game may be visiting the metro area for other reasons (e.g., to visit family or for business).

3. Equivalently, local multiplier jobs can be thought of as implying that total net job creation will be some multiple of observable jobs created less unobserved jobs lost.

4. Many impact studies also claim large benefits from the actual construction jobs associated with building stadiums. But such jobs are unlikely to produce large metro area benefits. Except in the depths of a recession, any very large construction project must either hire workers from elsewhere who temporarily relocate into a metro area or else hire local workers away from other local construction projects.

5. The ambiguity of whether a metro area benefits from net job creation sharply contrasts with the common perception that local net job creation is a benefit in and of itself. The perception is easy to understand given that net job creation usually reflects beneficial underlying metro area fundamentals.

6. To the extent that such statistical techniques fail to control for underlying fundamentals that cause simultaneous increases in jobs, wages, and property values, they will overestimate the benefits associated with increases in employment.

7. A second way that increased sales tax revenue benefits a host metro area is if it is due to local residents' spending a greater proportion of their entertainment dollars within the host metro area rather than elsewhere.

8. Of course, depending on particular circumstances, visits by non–MSA fans may vary tremendously.

9. However, any revenue due to such visitors' spending at games being taxed at higher than average rates does count as a benefit attributable to hosting a sports team.

10. On the other hand, 5 percent is not an uncommon state sales tax rate. But for states, imported tax revenue accrues only from visits by out-of-state sports fans, which is likely to be a smaller percentage than for non-metro sports fans.

11. To the extent that any increased income tax revenue from net job creation does exceed the marginal cost of providing any associated increased municipal services, the resulting benefit is largely what underlies the explanation of how net job creation benefits a metro area's existing residents. To include it again as an imported income tax benefit would be to double count.

12. Using a 5 percent interest rate instead implies that each dollar of annual benefits is worth $15.37. Using a 7 percent interest rate implies that each dollar of annual benefits is worth $12.41.

13. This aggregate quality-of-life benefit is known as "consumer surplus." Estimates of consumer surplus from major league game attendance range from

$2 million to $54 million per team per year (Alexander et al., Irani).

14. On the other hand, many economists argue that people overestimate their willingness to pay for things when answering surveys (Diamond and Hausman).

15. Population inflows drawn to high quality of life may also result in large-scale job creation. The straightforward intuition is that firms desire to locate where they can affordably hire good workers.

16. More specifically, individuals' wages are regressed on individual-specific characteristics and metro area characteristics. Negative coefficients on the metro area characteristics measure positive contributions to quality of life. House prices are regressed on house-specific characteristics and metro area characteristics. Positive coefficients on the metro area characteristics measure positive contributions to quality of life.

17. In addition, two relatively small Canadian metro areas, Quebec and Winnipeg, lost NHL teams in the mid–1990s.

18. It could also be that the metro areas revised upward their estimates of the job creation and tax revenue benefits. But this seems unlikely given economists' unanimous inability to find evidence of any large such benefits.

19. Additional incentives were later added to lure the NFL Rams in 1995.

20. Los Angeles, as well, committed to a $100 million public outlay in a bid to win an NFL expansion team that was awarded in 1999. Given the large quantity and variety of alternative entertainment venues in the Los Angeles metro area (e.g., four major league teams, two top college athletic programs, four major amusement/theme parks, beaches, nearby mountains), it is not surprising that the quality-of-life benefits from hosting an additional team may be lower to Los Angeles than they are to other metro areas.

21. One reason that Kansas City and San Diego may not have done so is that both cities already host both an MLB and an NFL team. As was argued above with regard to the NHL Pittsburgh Penguins, the additional quality-of-life benefit from a third team may be much smaller than the benefit from a first or second team. In addition, both of the departing NBA teams had losing records in the several seasons prior to leaving, which also may have lowered their contributions to quality of life.

22. A conceptually different question is whether metro areas would be better off if all public contributions to the building of sports stadiums were prohibited.

References

Alexander, Donald L., William Kern, and Jon Neill. 2000. "Valuing the Consumption Benefits from

Professional Sports Franchises," *Journal of Urban Economics*, September.

Baade, Robert A. 1997. "Mariner Economic Analysis," prepared for Citizens for Leaders with Ethics and Accountability Now, March.

_____. 1994. "Stadiums, Professional Sports, and Economic Development: Assessing the Reality," Heartland Institute Policy Study, No. 62.

Baade, Robert A., and Allen R. Sanderson. 1997. "The Employment Effect of Teams and Sports Facilities," in Roger G. Noll and Andrew Zimbalist, eds., *Sports, Jobs, and Taxes: The Economic Impact of Sports Teams and Stadiums*. Washington: Brookings Institution Press.

Blomquist, Glenn C., Mark C. Berger, and John P. Hoehn. 1988. "New Estimates of Quality of Life in Urban Areas," *American Economic Review*, March.

Bremner, B. 1990. "Ice Folly in Minneapolis," *Business Week*, February 26.

CSL International. 2000a. "Green Bay Packers Impact Analysis," prepared for the Green Bay Packers.

_____. 2000b. "Houston Rockets Impact Analysis," prepared for Central Houston, Inc.

Center for Economic Education, University of Cincinnati. 1996. "The Effects of the Construction, Operation, and Financing of New Sports Stadia on Cincinnati Economic Growth," prepared for the Hamilton County Administrator, January.

Coates, Dennis, and Brad R. Humphreys. 2000. "The Stadium Gambit and Local Economic Development," *Regulation*, no. 2.

Conway, Dick, and Associates. 1996. "Seattle Seahawks Economic Impact," prepared for HOK Sport and King County, March.

Diamond, Peter A., and Jerry A. Hausman. 1994. "Contingent Valuation: Is Some Number Better Than No Number?" *Journal of Economic Perspectives*, Fall.

Gyourko, Joseph, and Joseph Tracy. 1991. "The Structure of Local Public Finance and the Quality of Life," *Journal of Political Economy*, August.

Hamilton, Bruce W., and Peter Kahn. 1997. "Baltimore's Camden Yards Ballparks," in Roger G. Noll and Andrew Zimbalist, eds., *Sports, Jobs, and Taxes: The Economic Impact of Sports Teams and Stadiums*. Washington: Brookings Institution Press.

Irani, Daraius. 1997. "Public Subsidies to Stadiums: Do the Costs Outweigh the Benefits?" *Public Finance Review*, March.

Johnson, Bruce K., Peter A. Groothuis, and John C. Whitehead. 2001. "The Value of Public Goods Generated By a Major League Sports Team: The CVM Approach," *Journal of Sports Economics*, February.

Johnson, C.H., Consulting, Inc. 1999. "Economic Impact Analysis of the Proposed Ballpark for the Boston Red Sox," prepared for Greater Boston Convention and Visitors Bureau and Greater Boston Chamber of Commerce, June.

KPMG. 1998. "Economic and Fiscal Impact Analysis for a Proposed New Stadium to Host the New England Patriots in Hartford, Connecticut," prepared for State of Connecticut, November.

Meyer, Ed. 1997. "Cleveland Sells NFL on Its Abilities," *Akron Beacon Journal*, January 22.

Mid-America Regional Council. 2001. Update to "Economic Impact of the Kansas City Chiefs and Kansas City Royals on the State of Missouri," prepared for Jackson County Executive, January.

National Sports Law Institute of Marquette University Law School. 2000. *Sports Facility Reports*, vol. 1, no. 2.

Noll, Roger G., and Andrew Zimbalist, eds. 1997. *Sports, Jobs, and Taxes: The Economic Impact of Sports Teams and Stadiums*. Washington: Brookings Institution Press. Office of Business and Economic Research, Maryland Department of Business and Economic Development. 1999. "Impact of the Baltimore Ravens Pro Football Team on the Maryland Economy: 1999 Update," October.

Pollack, Elliott D., and Company. 1998. "Economic and Fiscal Impact of BankOne Ballpark and the Arizona Diamondbacks," prepared for Downtown Phoenix Partnership, September.

Quirk, James, and Rodney Fort. 1992. *Pay Dirt: The Business of Professional Team Sports*. Princeton: Princeton University Press.

Rappaport, Jordan. 2000. "Why Are Population Flows So Persistent?" Federal Reserve Bank of Kansas City, working paper no. 99–13, August.

_____, and Jeffrey Sachs. Forthcoming. "The U.S. as a Coastal Nation," Federal Reserve Bank of Kansas City, working paper.

Roback, Jennifer. 1982. "Wages, Rents, and the Quality of Life," *Journal of Political Economy*, December.

Rosen, Sherwin. 1979. "Wage-Based Indexes of Urban Quality of Life," in Miezkowski and Straszheim, eds., *Current Issues in Urban Economics*. Baltimore: Johns Hopkins University Press.

Siegfried, John, and Andrew Zimbalist. 2000. "The Economics of Sports Facilities and Their Communities," *Journal of Economic Perspectives*, Summer.

Street and Smith's SportsBusiness Journal. 2000. "Special Report: Broadcast Media," April 17–23.

Texas Perspectives, Inc. 1999. "The Role of the Spurs in the San Antonio Economy," prepared for City of San Antonio.

Walden, Michael. 1997. "Don't Play Ball," *Carolina Journal*, October/November.

CHAPTER 42

Major Issues Shaping America's Sports Industry

John Sweeney

Sports leagues and fans bow in reverence to tradition and history, but the fact is that much in the world of sports has radically changed. The Manchester United football (soccer) team can claim not only the expected 7.5 million fans in the United Kingdom, but 14 million fans in Thailand as well.

In creating a university's sports communication program, I have had to wrestle with the many changes in sports and its role in culture and the economy. I see the future of the sports industry being shaped by the following 10 controversial issues. The way that these controversies are managed will make a major impact on the prosperity of the games we so enjoy.

The Turbulent Brand

Sports leagues and events have learned that unifying as a singular brand in the marketplace can increase wealth. A singular brand such as the National Football League (NFL) can put media rights out to bid from major networks, attract lucrative sponsorships, and

sell licensed fashions and merchandise. Everything moves in lockstep — under a tight political organization and unified identity — to reach out for national and, increasingly, international revenues. Sports organizations have learned to cooperate and organize, just as McDonald's learned that there is a lot of money to be made by organizing hamburgers and fries together. Unlike with McDonald's, however, the "hamburgers" and "fries" in sports are rivals who'd like to humiliate and defeat each other.

Prosperity will be won by those who can brand themselves not only with a recognizable logo, but also with a genuine attitude of cooperation. The NFL currently does it best and the results are obvious. The League leads in television ratings and gets $3 billion a year in media rights, another $3 billion in licensing, average attendance of nearly 70,000 a game, and leading sponsors like Motorola paying over $20 million a year to associate with the League.

The simple question is, Who will do it better in the years ahead? Who will avoid the feuds, lockouts, strikes, and business soap op-

Originally published in *The Futurist*. Used with permission from the World Future Society, 7910 Woodmont Avenue, Suite 450, Bethesda, Maryland 20814 USA. Telephone: 301-656-8274; www.wfs.org.

eras that keep fans and revenues away? It may be another league or perhaps newly formed groups, such as the National Thoroughbred Racing Association — the brand name for more than 70 racetracks. Another successful brand story could be for an entire sport, like Strike Ten Entertainment for bowling. The future belongs not just to those who understand branding, but to those able to achieve the enormous political discipline necessary to make it work.

The Shattered Media

Once upon a time in the 1960s, the United States had three television networks that reached an entire nation with programming. Today, the vast power and influence of the three broadcast networks has been diluted by hundreds of cable networks, satellite channels, pay-per-view choices and video-on-demand options. More jockeying for attention would come from new technologies for increasingly specialized audiences, such as VCRs, DVDs, cell phones, home computers, Internet sites, and videogame consoles. Even more threatening to broadcasters' dominance are inventions like Tivo that challenge the entire advertising revenue model of broadcast media.

Naturally, the shattering of media also extends to magazines, newspapers, radio, and other media. In the United States, magazine racks made space for 5,000 new titles between 1998 and 2006 and now offer more than 18,000 choices.

The new world of sports will be one where a passionate group of fans can band together commercially far below the audience requirements of broadcast television networks. Few people would consider skateboarding a major commercial sport, yet renowned skateboarder Tony Hawk has transformed his championship image into a $10 million annual business.

The Women's Revolution

The bad old days for women's sports were indeed pretty bad. One study of network television's coverage of women's sports between August 1972 and September 1973 showed that NBC devoted just one hour to women's sports out of 366 hours of athletic coverage, while CBS was only slightly more generous with 10 out of 260 hours. Participation was little better: Fewer than 300,000 women were participating in high-school sports at that time, compared with 3.5 million men.

The numbers have changed dramatically. Today, more than 2.5 million women participate in high school sports. Women purchase more than half of health-club memberships, and leagues such as the Ladies Professional Golf Association and the Women's Tennis Association are successful organizations with a national television schedule. Women's events in the 1996 Olympic Games sold more tickets than did men's events, and the 1999 Women's World Cup sold out the Rose Bowl for the final game and was a ratings smash on television.

However, the women's revolution has not fit the model of men's sports in terms of marketing. The Women's National Basketball Association (WNBA) has stalled in television ratings and declined in attendance. Women's United Soccer Association (WUSA) — the startup league that evolved from the World Cup — suspended operations in 2003. *Sports Illustrated* and Condé Nast started — and ultimately shelved — women's sports publications.

Internet-based ventures such as Nike Goddess may prove successful for women's sports, especially if they focus on fitness rather than competition. Nike's dual-platform approach offers a "personal stylist" (online catalog) for buying Nike gear as well as a "personal trainer" (videos) for working out with a virtual coach.

While the revolution in participation is clear, there is as yet no clear appetite for women's sports as commercial media products that in any way parallels that of men's sports. This is not a criticism. The commercial expression of women in sports is only beginning. It will be through experimentation in the years ahead that the real place of women in athletics will be decided and it will be enormous.

Heretic Games

Baseball dominates the historical memory of the United States in a powerful way that is mirrored by football in Europe. However, the fastest-growing sports are snowboarding and mountain biking, and the leading sports in terms of new media coverage are bull riding and bass fishing.

Not only are sports dramatically different but the entire culture surrounding them can seem more like a rock song than an inspirational anthem. In many sports, uniforms are now more individualistic and the attitudes of leading performers are far from the reverent, wholesome persona of the Olympian.

In terms of established sports, many sacred traditions have become a historical footnotes. Imagine basketball without a shot clock and three-point line or baseball without interleague play and the designated hitter. Each of these was an innovation in its day that seemed heretical to old-time fans.

The big sports won't be put out of business, but niche sports may join the major leagues, as NASCAR did in the 1990s, or an offbeat activity may find a launching pad on a small network and explode across the mainstream. How about taking 10 characters playing poker and call it a sport?

The Haves and Have-Nots of Sports

In sports, as in so much of national life, wealth is becoming increasingly concentrated. The payrolls for teams in Major League Baseball recently ranged from $180 million at the top to just $31 million at the bottom. The top six conferences in college football made ten times the income as the second six. A top NASCAR team requires a budget of more than $20 million a year to be competitive. Those without deep pockets need not dream.

The Olympic Games were conceived as a festival celebrating athletic endeavor, but the poor performance of the United States in the 1988 Winter Olympics led to the creation of the Podium Program, which supported athletes with the best chance to win medals. The United States won just six medals in 1988 and an impressive 25 in the 2006 Torino Games, second only to Germany. While this is a nice result, the Olympic spirit was not founded on the domination of the wealthiest countries based on their ability to subsidize athletes.

The concentration effect also goes to those who can benefit from the rare impact player. Golfer Tiger Woods has been known to bring more than a million households to a Sunday television broadcast. This audience only tunes in when he is in contention. Similarly, basketball superstar LeBron James's arrival to the Cleveland Cavaliers created a 50 percent increase in sponsorship and attendance and more than 200 percent increase in television ratings. Little wonder James was paid $80 million by the Cavaliers to extend his contract.

The Lost Mission

The endless summer days that youth once spent on the neighborhood sports field have been replaced by countless hours sitting before a computer screen playing a game about a sport rather than a sport itself. And this virtual sport is far more exciting than the real thing. The afternoon soft drink has been replaced by the 64-ounce Super Gulp and the daily physical education class has been dropped in favor of academics.

The loss of real sport in young people's lives has contributed to an obesity epidemic; among adults, it is a matter of unfortunate choices, but among kids aged 6 to 11, the epidemic is a matter of neglect. The result of a "customer is king" lifestyle is a tripling of obesity with monster burgers and mega-size ice cream shops finding buyers while health clubs are stalled and participation in sports is declining.

Those kids who do pursue today's sports increasingly find it a place of competitive elite leagues. Serious players now need to specialize in a single sport, causing an epidemic of repetitive stress injuries. Elite competitors in figure skating, for instance, are increasingly subjected to hip injuries due to the stress of longer practices for difficult jumps and complicated footwork. Not surprisingly, nearly 70 percent of children drop out of sports by age 14, leaving themselves without a support system for physical fitness.

Ski resorts are working to restrict the pollution from snow-making equipment and minimize the impact on rivers and streams. They are also trying to walk the thin line between extravagant resort construction and the original spirit of the wilderness that remains the essence of the sport.

Reefs and mountains face growing threats from climate change, as well as from the increased number of divers and climbers. Both reefs and summits have been made far more accessible for the average tourist through breakthroughs in scuba gear and the rise of mountain guide companies. The results have been harsh for many fragile destinations.

The Caribbean country of Bonaire declared all its surrounding water up to a depth of 200 feet to be a protected national park. Nepal put strict environmental rules on Everest expeditions as a move to save the mountain from remaining "the world's tallest garbage dump."

Policies that promote environmental sensitivity — whether "catch and release" for marlin fishing or a camera replacing a gun for safari — will be a fundamental priority for sports tourism, regardless of the beliefs of individual customers.

The Environmental Tightrope

Sports take place on many of the most extraordinary landscapes and seascapes on our planet. For this reason, environmentalism will play an increasingly important role in the management of golf courses, ski resorts, and coral reefs.

The leading golf course architects are working to design courses with minimal needs for chemicals and greater protection of wildlife diversity. This isn't a matter just of good will, but of survival as well, since many communities now passionately oppose all development.

The Engineered Athlete

The revolution in technology has complicated the purity of athletic pursuit in a variety of ways. Some uses of the new technologies will continue to scandalize traditionalists. The ability of "designer" drugs to escape detection with current testing will put the temptation of doping in front of every player in certain sports. It will also force organizations to confront uncomfortable questions about random testing and punishment.

Technology's uses, though, are not always negative. The development of amazing new surgeries have extended careers and given top athletes the ability to recover from injuries that once destroyed players' futures in a flash. The breakthrough application of arthroscopic surgery to sport injuries earned Robert Jackson, M.D., accolades as one of "40 for the ages" in a *Sports Illustrated* commemorative issue.

Technology will remain controversial because it affects performance, but innovation will continue to accelerate. From metal composite golf clubs that challenge the classic designs of old courses to powerful graphite rackets that eliminate long rallies in tennis, innovation will continue to force every sport to define the nature of competition — and even its very soul.

The Global Destiny

Satellites can bring the world together virtually in an instant. Thanks to satellite transmission of its games, the National Basketball Association can claim audiences in nearly every country of the world. Moreover, more than half of its Web hits are from users outside the United States.

A global event such as the Volvo Ocean Race, in which boats travel the world over eight months, can claim a cumulative television audience of more than 800 million viewers, plus 15,000 published articles reaching 686 million readers.

In 2006, England's tradition bound, 119-year-old Wimbledon tennis championship hired a two-year old firm in San Francisco for its first global Internet broadcast. The innovative X-Games have become a major event for action sports and, like the Olympics, have been held all over the world, from Los Angeles to Dubai, Seoul, Bangkok, and Kuala Lumpur.

New events such as the World Baseball Classic and golf's President's Cup show the capacity to invent sports as a global enterprise, connected by communication in a way virtually unimaginable in 1960. As we enter the world of global sports, new questions emerge: Can America's NASCAR challenge Europe's Formula One in auto racing? Will Major League Soccer in the United States survive when European professional soccer is just a click or remote button away?

The Moral Connection

It is a cliché in sports marketing to use the language of entertainment to discuss the sports business. While it is true that both spectator and participatory sports are leisure pursuits, there is a reason why sports are integrated into universities and varsity metal bands are not. The difference is the fundamental belief that sports both reveal and enhance character.

There is a moral connection that ties an 8-year-old child to the glory and traditions of a sport in a way that is more than the tie to a comic book character. It is why the best leagues are continuously reaching out to the community to promote involvement and participation. Yes, part of the success of the PGA Tour is due to Tiger Woods's popularity, but significantly more is due to the $1 billion that PGA tour events have raised for charity throughout the organization's history. Now it is commonplace for celebrity athletes to support charities or establish their own. For example, skateboarder Tony Hawk has a foundation for youth recreation programs, and Olympic champion speed skater Joey Cheek donated his entire gold medal bonus ($40,000) to the Right to Play organization devoted to using sport and play in the development of children. Cheek earmarked his money to go to the refugee children of Darfur.

The almost spiritual belief in the redemptive power of sports to bring out the best in human beings is one that is constantly challenged in a time of millionaire prodigies and drug scandals. While no major sport will go out of business, it is instructive to see the declines in television and attendance that follow a league when it shows a cynical reality behind its athletes. Major League Baseball lost an estimated 20 percent of its audience due to the 1994 strike and slowly drew them back.

The undoing of this great belief in the greater meaning of sport does not mean the industry will disappear with the next mismanaged scandal. But teams and leagues that disregard this special connection with the culture and communities that support them will see that support erode. This will translate into cutting off funds for taxpayer-supported stadiums, boycotting increasingly expensive skyboxes, and searching for alternative viewing from among literally hundreds of choices.

Sports are not just entertainment. If the industry makes the mistake of acting like it is, the future will see more organizations subtly troubled and caught in decline.

CHAPTER 43

The Future of the Sports Industry in America

Irving Rein, Philip Kotler, *and* Ben Shields

There is probably no better place to examine the media landscape in the next decades than the sports arena, especially the first big players in this highly lucrative, multi-billion dollar worldwide industry. We are now seeing a massive readjustment in what has historically been a synergistic relationship between the sports leagues and teams and the media. In this transformation, new alliances will be formed, media giants will be sorely pressed to operate, and viewers — i.e., fans or customers — will have unprecedented access to information on numerous and yet-to-be-determined distribution channels.

In the United States, today's sports-media model was pioneered on television by ABC's *Wide World of Sports,* NBC's coverage of the Olympics, and CBS's Sunday afternoon football. This relationship was clear: The sports properties sold their rights to the media, who then sold the sports content to advertisers, who gained audiences and potential customers for their products. The model was primarily built on network television and was largely responsible for turning professional and college sports into a multibillion-dollar busi-

ness. Over time, this model began to change as cable television networks entered the sports rights fee arena and, because of cable subscriptions revenues, began competing with network television and what was once a scarcity-driven market.

The best example of a current winner is ESPN (Entertainment and Sports Programming Network), the synergistic sports-media brand that communicates with its fans through every distribution channel imaginable. From its flagship television network, the company has spawned other networks (ESPN2, ESP-NEWS, ESPN Classic, ESPN Deportes), syndicated radio stations (ESPN Radio), a magazine *(ESPN the Magazine),* an interactive Web site with streaming video, audio, insider information, and fantasy games (ESPN.com), a mobile phone content provider (Mobile ESPN), and sports-themed restaurants (The ESPN Zone). Throughout most of the cable network's history, if a sport wasn't covered by ESPN, it didn't exist.

In the next stage, sports leagues and teams, because of technological innovations, are beginning to communicate differently with

Originally published in *The Futurist.* Used with permission from the World Future Society, 7910 Woodmont Avenue, Suite 450, Bethesda, Maryland 20814 USA. Telephone: 301-656-8274; www.wfs.org.

fans. For the first time, the content providers are developing pipelines directly aimed at their fans. A leader in this transformation is Manchester United, the billion-dollar English football (soccer) club, which has adapted and expanded ESPN's blueprint to its own one-city team. It has a television channel (MU TV), radio station (MU Radio), magazine *(United)*, mobile phone service (MU Mobile), team-themed restaurants (the Red Cafe), and interactive Web site (Manutd.com) with streaming video, audio, insider information, and a fantasy game. Outdoing ESPN, it even has its own financial services, including car insurance, credit cards, and mortgages; a ManU lottery; and a host of other attractions. As an English football club outside of London, Manchester United has transformed itself into a global lifestyle brand through innovative partnerships and new media communication strategies.

The signals of this future trend are everywhere. Sports properties are becoming their own media companies, interacting directly with their consumers without the filter of traditional media. For example, the most valuable television property in sports is America's National Football League (NFL). For most networks, the NFL is sought after not only for its high ratings but also for the promotional lead-ins to the rest of the network's schedule and as a competitive asset in the television content wars.

Despite their league's television rights monopoly, the NFL has been building its own television channel, the NFL Network, which competed against ESPN with its own NFL draft show and broadcast eight regular season games in the 2006 season. Rather than selling its Thursday and Saturday night television package to other networks, the NFL is investing in its own media brand, using the network as a backup plan for the time when or if television networks won't pay the rights fees. The

NFL Network has also bought the rights to several college bowl games, covers the league's teams all year round from the draft to training camps, and builds the legends of the league with its popular NFL Films content. For the traditional sports media, the NFL Network — along with the National Basketball Association's NBATV, the Baseball Network, and other team only channels — is redefining sports television and transforming the once-reliable sports rights infrastructure.

The Internet is another area in sports media where rules are being rewritten and the marketplace is rapidly changing. Major League Baseball (MLB), for example, through its Advanced Media division, has built a substantial Internet infrastructure for streaming live video of baseball games throughout the season. For a one-time subscription fee, fans can watch almost every baseball game of the season on their computer.

The streaming video business has been a substantial revenue generator for the league, and it is defining the ways that leagues and teams broadcast sports on the Internet and make a profit in the process. When the National Collegiate Athletic Association decided to stream the Final Four college basketball tournament, it turned to MLB because it had the capacity and skill to do so. MLB has become one of the benchmarks for integrating new technology into its communication strategies to meet the changing expectations of fans, and MLB's current success only means that other sports properties will begin emulating and reconfiguring their formula.

A final indicator of the changing sports-media relationship is the increasing amount of fan-driven content on the Internet. A good example is Deadspin.com, a sports news Web site that is operated out of the New York City apartment of the site's founder. Deadspin covers sports news like any other newspaper and magazine, provides forums for fans to discuss the latest sports controversies, and is sometimes the first media outlet to break a story. Deadspin's influence has become so important that even members of the traditional media often get their material from the site. That fans have also become the distributors of information demonstrates how the traditional media's role as filter is diminishing, and both sports properties and the fans themselves are increasingly filling the channels.

The radical realignment of sports is the canary in the coal mine for the future of media. It's only a matter of time before the professional sports model becomes the standard in college and high-school sports. The Big Ten Conference, for example, has plans to begin a satellite channel to provide content to its fans. Other entertainments such as film, fashion, and music are also developing their own content and media pipelines to reach targeted fan bases.

It's fair to say that the media landscape over the coming decades will look considerably different than it does now. Moreover, the storytellers and strategists who formerly worked in these media channels will increasingly find employment with the content providers and nontraditional information distributors. If the traditional media pipelines are going to survive, they will have to seek new alliances and look to connect to the content providers in innovative ways. Already we see increased bartering, cost-sharing, and integrated multi-platform distribution strategies. The only certainty about the sports marketplace is that it is adapting, and for the stakeholders, this means constant monitoring of change and a commitment to innovation.

Appendices

Containing A. Glossary; B. Acronyms and Abbreviations; C. Periodical Bibliography; D. Bibliography; E. Foundation Resources; F. Federal Reserve Bank Resources; G. Federal Government Resources; H. Regional Resource Directory; I. National Resource Directory; J. International Resource Dictionary

A. Glossary*

Basic employment: Associated with business activities that provide services primarily outside the area via the sale of goods and services, but whose revenue is directed to the local area in the form of wages and payments to local suppliers.

Business attraction or recruitment: Marketing or other activities designed to persuade businesses to choose a community as a location for expansion.

Business Retention and Expansion (R&E): Supporting and assisting local businesses with an expansion or helping them to overcome an obstacle that prevents them from remaining competitive, usually done through company visits and/or surveys.

Capital costs: The costs a business pays for major physical improvements, such as buildings, equipment, or machinery.

Commission: A group of citizens organized under statute to perform certain tasks or duties in the public interest. An economic development commission is a good example of citizens who have been appointed to the task of developing strategies to improve the local economic base.

Community profile: Information about a community including taxes, transportation networks, health and recreation facilities, labor rates and skill levels, market proximity, available sites and industrial parks, nearest major cities, companies already doing business in the community, utilities, government organizations, and educational facilities, that is usually presented in or with a brochure to an attraction project.

Development Authority: An independent agency of local government that possesses certain powers beyond those of city government. A public housing authority is a good example because it has the ability to issue special bonds for public housing.

Economic base: The major business activities that create and bring wealth into a community (e.g. manufacturing services, tourism, etc.)

Eminent domain: The authority of a government to take, or to authorize the taking of, private property for public use, almost always with adequate compensation to the owner.

Entrepreneurship: Starting a business, taking a product or service from idea stage to market.

Guaranteed loan: A loan that is guaranteed partly or fully by a specific governmental agency for the benefit of protecting a lender against possible losses.

Industrial park: A tract of land that is divided and developed according to a plan for the location or expansion of industries, with the basic infrastructure installed before the sites are sold.

Infrastructure: The physical structure that supports and sustains communities and economic

*Source: Center for Economic and Community Development, School of Extended Education, Ball State University, 2000 West University Avenue, Carmichael Hall 109, Muncie, Indiana 47306.

223

development (e.g. roads, waste treatment systems, utility systems, railroads, telecommunications).

Insured loan: A loan insured by a governmental agency or a private mortgage insurance company.

Interest subsidy: A grant designed to lower the interest costs of borrowing. The subsidy either goes directly to the borrower or is paid on his or her behalf.

Land-use planning: Planning for proper use of land, taking into account such factors as transportation and location of business, industry, and housing.

Leveraging: A means of multiplying the availability of funds for economic development or community development programs by using one pot of money as a match or lever to access a larger amount of money.

Option to buy: An arrangement to permit one to buy or sell something within a specified period of time, usually according to a written agreement.

Ordinance: A rule or law established by the local governing body to control actions of citizens and the effects of their activities on others.

Public works: Facilities constructed for public use and enjoyment with public funds, such as ramps, highways, sewers, in contrast to maintenance activities, such as street cleaning and painting school buildings.

Quasi-public agency: Usually a non-profit corporation with a privately appointed board of directors whose purpose is to assist governmental agencies and the private sector to improve the general living standards of citizens. The majority of funds for such activities come from public agencies.

Revolving loan fund: Pool of local and/or state monies loaned to businesses at low interest rates for expansion and retention; the interest generated from the loans goes back into the pool to create additional funds to be loaned in the future.

Small business incubator: A facility that offers low rent and inexpensive shared business services to start up businesses for a designated period of time. Usually associated with an indigenous growth strategy pursued by a community.

Tax abatement: A reduction in property taxes for a specific property over a certain period of time.

Tax incentives: Tax reductions, abatements and programs designed to persuade companies to locate in a state or community.

Technical assistance: Providing information, data, and know-how in establishing, implementing and evaluating economic development initiatives and activities.

Value added: Adding market value (monetary) to raw materials or a product by processing, handling, labeling, packaging, transporting, etc.

Workforce development: Public and private education and training programs designed to increase skills, abilities and knowledge of members of the workforce.

B. Acronyms and Abbreviations*

AASHTO—American Association of State Highway & Transportation Officials
ACOE—Army Corps of Engineers
ADA—Americans with Disabilities Act
ADT—Average Daily Traffic (or Average Daily Trips)
AEP—American Electric Power
AFT—American Farmland Trust
AICP—American Institute of Certified Planners
AO—Airport Overlay
AP—Agricultural/Rural Preserve
APA—American Planning Association
APFO—Adequate Public Facilities Ordinance
APTA—American Public Transit Association
APTS—Advanced Public Transportation System
APWA—American Public Works Association
AR—Agricultural/Residential
ARB—Architectural Review Board
ASCE—American Society of Civil Engineers
ATM—Advanced Traffic Management System
AVR—Average Vehicle Ridership
B—Business zone
BID—Business Improvement District
BLM—Bureau of Land Management (U.S.)
BMP—Best Management Practice
BOA—Board of Appeals or Board of Adjustment

*Source: Department of Planning, Bedford County, 122 East Main Street, Suite G-03, Bedford, Virginia 24523, modified slightly by the editor.

BOCA— Building Officials and Code Administrators, International

BOS— Board of Supervisors

BP— Building Permit

BZA— Board of Zoning Appeals

C— Commercial zone

CofA— Conditions of Approval

CAA— Clean Air Act

CAD— Computer Aided Design

CBD— Central Business District

CBF— Chesapeake Bay Foundation

CBLAD— Chesapeake Bay Local Assistance Department

CBPA— Chesapeake Bay Preservation Act

CDBG— Community Development Block Grant

CDC— Community Development Corporation

CFS— Cubic Feet per Second

CHAS— Comprehensive Housing Affordability Strategy

CIP— Capital Improvements Program

CMAQ— Congestion Mitigation and Air Quality Program

CMP— Corrugated Metal Pipe

CMSA— Consolidated Metropolitan Statistical Area

CO— Certificate of Occupancy

CO— Corridor Overlay

COCS— Cost of Community Services

COG— Council of Governments

CUP— Conditional Use Permit

DEIS— Draft Environment Impact Statement

DOE— Department of Energy

DOT— Department of Transportation

DU— Dwelling Unit

ECO— Emergency Communications Overlay

EDA— Economic Development Authority

EDA— Economic Development Administration

EIR— Environmental Impact Report

EIS— Environmental Impact Statement

EPA— Environmental Protection Agency

ESC— Erosion and Sediment Control

ESCO— Erosion and Sediment Control Ordinance

ETC— Employee Transportation Coordinator

EZ— Enterprise Zone

FAA— Federal Aviation Administration

FAR— Floor Area Ratio

FCAA— Federal Clean Air Act

FCC— Federal Communications Commission

FEMA— Federal Emergency Management Agency

FEIS— Final Environmental Impact Statement

FERC— Federal Energy Regulatory Commission

FHA— Federal Housing Administration

FHWA— Federal Highway Administration

FIA— Fiscal Impact Analysis

FIRE— Finance, Insurance and Real Estate

FO— Floodplain Overlay

FOIA— Freedom of Information Act

FSA— Farm Services Agency

GDP— General Development Plan

GFA— Gross Floor Area

GIS— Geographic Information Systems

GM— Growth Management

GPS— Global Positioning System

HMP— Hazard Mitigation Plan

HO— Historic Overlay

HOD— Highway Overlay District

HOV— High Occupancy Vehicle

HTF— Housing Trust Fund

HUD— U.S. Department of Housing and Urban Development

I— Industrial Zone

ICMA— International City/County Managers Association

IDA— Industrial Development Authority

IDO— Interim Development Ordinance

IHS— Interstate Highway System

ISTEA— Intermodal Surface Transportation Efficiency Act

ITE— Institute of Transportation Engineers

LDP— Land Disturbing Permit

LEDO— Local Economic Development Organization

LOMA— Letter of Map Amendment

LOMR— Letter of Map Revision

LOS— Level of Service

LRTP— Long Range Transportation Plan

LUGS— Land Use Guidance System

LUI— Land Use Intensity

M— Manufacturing Zone

MGD— Million Gallons per Day

MPD— Master Planned Development

MPO— Metropolitan Planning Organization

MSA— Metropolitan Statistical Area

MTP— Metropolitan Transportation Plan

MTS— Metropolitan Transportation System

MXD— Mixed Use Development

NAHB— National Association of Home Builders

NARC— National Association of Regional Councils

NAHRO— National Association of Housing & Redevelopment Officials

NAICS— North American Industrial Classification System

NC— Neighborhood Commercial

NEPA— National Environmental Policy Act
NFIP— National Flood Insurance Program
NHPA— National Historic Preservation Act
NHS— National Highway System
NIMBY— Not In My Back Yard
NPDES— National Pollution Discharge Elimination System
NRCS— Natural Resources Conservation Service
NTHP— National Trust for Historic Preservation
NWI— National Wetlands Inventory
PC— Planning Commission
PCD— Planned Commercial Development
PDC— Planning District Commission
PDR— Purchase of Development Rights
PID— Planned Industrial Development
PO— Park Overlay
POSWCD— Peaks of Otter Soil and Water Conservation District
PPB— Parts per Billion
PPM— Parts per Million
PRD— Planned Residential Development
PSA— Public Service Authority
PUD— Planned Unit Development
QOL— Quality of Life
R— Residential Zone
REDO— Regional Economic Development Organization
RFP— Request for Proposals
RFQ— Request for Qualifications
ROW— Right of Way
RPA— Regional Planning Agency
RPC— Regional Plan Commission
RTPA— Regional Transportation Planning Agency
SAD— Special Assessment District
SAV— Submerged Aquatic Vegetation
SEPA— State Environmental Protection (or Policy) Act
SEQA— State Environmental Quality Act
SFD— Single Family Dwelling
SIC— Standard Industrial Classification (Code)
SML— Smith Mountain Lake
SMP— Shoreline Management Plan
SMSA— Standard Metropolitan Statistical Area
SOB— Sexually Oriented Business
SOV— Single Occupancy Vehicle
STIP— Statewide Transportation Improvement Plan
STP— Surface Transportation Program
SUP— Special Use Permit
SWCD— Soil and Water Conservation District
SWM— Stormwater Management
SWMO— Stormwater Management Ordinance
SWMP— Stormwater Management Plan

TAP— Technical Assistance Program
TAZ— Traffic Analysis Zone
TDM— Transportation Demand Management
TDR— Transfer of Development Rights
TEA-21— Transportation Equity Act for the 21st Century
TIF— Tax Increment Financing
TIP— Transportation Improvement Program
TIS— Traffic Impact Statement
TIS— Technical Information Service
TMDL— Total Maximum Daily Load
TOD— Transportation Oriented Development
TOD— Transit Oriented Design
TRC— Technical Review Committee
TSM— Transportation System Management
TSP— Transportation System Plan
TTC— Transportation Technical Committee
UGB— Urban Growth Boundary
ULI— Urban Land Institute
UMTA— Urban Mass Transit Administration
URPI— Urban and Regional Planning
USDA— U.S. Department of Agriculture
USDI— U.S. Department of the Interior
USDOC— U.S. Department of Commerce
USFS— U.S. Forest Service
USFWS— U.S. Fish and Wildlife Service
USGS— U.S. Geological Survey
USPLS— U.S. Public Land Survey
WCF— Wireless Communication Facility
WCO— Wireless Communication Overlay
WHP— Well-head Protection Overlay
WIA— Workforce Investment Act
WQMP— Water Quality Monitoring Project
WQMP— Water Quality Management Plan
ZBA— Zoning Board of Adjustment (or Appeals)
ZLL— Zero Lot Line
ZO— Zoning Ordinance

C. Periodicals Bibliography

This listing includes major periodicals in the United States that focus on contemporary issues in communities, as well as functional disciplines in the areas of building, economic development, the environment, land and water, planning, public works, real estate, and major sports issues.

American City & County
Penton Media, Inc.
http://www.americancityandcounty.com/

APWA Reporter
American Public Works Association
http://www.apwa.net/

Building Design & Construction
Reed Construction Data
http://www.WDCnetwork.com/

Economic Development Quarterly
SAGE Publications
http://edq.sagepub.com/

Governing
Congressional Quarterly Inc.
http://www.governing.com/

Journal of the American Planning Association
American Planning Association
http://www.planning.org/

Land and Water
Land and Water, Inc.
http://www.landandwater.com/

National Real Estate Investor
Penton Media, Inc.
http://www.nreionline.com/

The Next American City
The Next American City Inc.
http://www.americancity.org/

Planning
American Planning Association
http://www.planning.org/

Planning and Environmental Law Journal
American Planning Association
http://www.planning.org/

Public Management
International City/County Management Association
http://www.icma.org/

Public Works
Hanley Wood Business Media
http://www.pwmag.com/

Regulation
The Caito Institute
http://www.regulationmagazine.com/

The Sport Journal
U.S. Sports Academy
http://www.thesportjournal.org/

Sports Business News
Sports Business News, Inc.
http://www.sportsbusinessnews.com/

Urban Land
Urban Land Institute
http://www.uli.org/

D. Books and Articles Bibliography

This listing includes major published works in the United States that focus on significant sports issues, sports facilities such as stadiums and arenas, economic development as it relates to sports teams, the public financing of sports facilities, as well as their development and maintenance, and related issues.

Archer, C.L., and M.Z. Jacobson. "Evaluation of Global Wind Power." *Journal of Geophysical Research: Atmospheres* (2005): retrieved June 11, 2006, from www.agu.org/pubs/crossref/2005.../2204JD005462.shtml.

Adams, P.C. "Introduction: Cyberspace and Geographical Space." *Geographic Review*, vol. 87, no. 2 (1997): 139–145.

Alm, R. "Technology Puts Sports Fans in Front Row." *Dallas Morning News* (July 21, 1998): 2F.

Ary, D., L.C. Jacobs and A. Razavieh. *Introduction to Research in Education*, 5th ed. Philadelphia, PA: Harcourt Brace, 1996.

Baade, R., and R. Dye. "Sports Stadiums and Area Development: A Critical Review." *Economic Development Quarterly*, vol. 2, no. 3 (1988): 265–275.

Bale, J. "The Changing Face of Football: Stadiums and Communities." *Soccer and Society*, vol. 1, no. 1 (1988): 91–101.

Berg, B.L. *Qualitative Research Methods for the Social Sciences*. Boston: Allyn and Bacon, 1998.

Bernstein, A. "Video Monitors Cater to Fans." *Sports Business Journal*, vol. 2, no. 35 (1999): 35.

Bernstein, M.F. "Sports Stadiums Boondoggle: Building Hopes in the City." *The Public Interest*, vol. 22, no. 45 (1998).

Bess, P. *City Baseball Magic: Plain Talk and Uncommon Sense about Cities and Baseball Parks*. Minneapolis, MN: Minneapolis Review of Baseball, 1999.

Blickstein, S. *Bowls of Glory Field of Dreams: Great Stadiums and Ballparks of North America*. Encino, CA: Cherbo, 1995.

Boyle, R., and R. Haynes. *Power Play: Sport, the Media and Popular Culture*. New York: Pearson, 2000.

Brewer, J., and A. Hunter. *Multimethod Research: A Synthesis of Styles*. Newbury Park, CA: Sage, 1989.

Canzano, J. "Biggest Question for PSU is Why Should We Care?" *The Oregonian* (September 14, 2005): retrieved June 12, 2006, from www.oregonlive.com/sports/Oregonian/john_canzano/index.ssf?base/sports/112669557856010.xml&coll=7.

Chandler, J.M. *Television and National Sport*. Urbana, IL: University of Illinois Press, 1988.

Chema, T. "When Professional Sports Justify the Subsidy." *Journal of Urban Affairs*, vol. 18, no. 1 (1996): 19–22.

"Construction Work Starts on Huge Seattle Stadium." *The American Architect*, vol. 117 (1920): 806–807.

Crompton, J.L. *Financing and Acquiring Park and Recreation Sources*. Champaign, IL: Human Kinetics.

Davis, M. "Old Ball Game has High-Tech Look." *Kansas City Star* (August 22, 1988): B1.

Denzin, N.K. *The Research Act: A Theoretical Introduction to Sociological Methods*. New York: McGraw-Hill, 1978.

Eisinger, P. "The Politics of Bread and Circuses: Building a City for the Visitor Class. *Urban Affairs Review*, vol. 1 (2000): 316–333.

Epstein, E. "Clinic Rents Space at Giants' Park; Medical Care to be Offered to Fans, Players, Residents." *San Francisco Chronicle* (November 20, 1998): A21.

Euchner, C.C. *Playing the Field: Why Sports Teams Move and Cities Fight to Keep Them*. Baltimore, MD: Johns Hopkins Press.

"The Franklin Field Stadium, University of Pennsylvania." *The American Architect*, vol. 124 (1923): 366–373.

"The Franklin Field Stadium, University of Pennsylvania." *Architectural Forum*, vol. 39 (1923): 73–73.

Gershman, M. *Diamonds: The Evolution of the Ballpark*. New York: Houghton Mifflin, 1993.

Golenbock, P. *The Spirit of St. Louis: A History of the St. Louis Cardinals and Browns*. New York: HarperCollins, 2000.

Gunts, E. "Grandstand." *Architecture*, vol. 81 (1992): 64–71.

Howard, D. "The Changing Fanscape for Big League Sports: Implications for Sport Managers." *Journal of Sport Management*, vol. 13 (1999): 78–91.

Howard, D.R., and J.L. Crompton. *Financing Sport*. Morgantown, WV: Fitness Information Technology, 1995.

Jenkins, B. "Arizona's Park Nicely Combines Old, New." *San Francisco Chronicle* (April 4, 1998): E1.

John, G., and R. Sheard. *Stadia*, 3rd ed. Boston: Architectural, 2000.

Johnson, B., and L. Christensen. *Educational Research Quantitative and Qualitative Approaches*. Boston: Allyn and Bacon, 2000.

King, B. "NFL Gets Comfy with Choice Seat." *Sports Business Journal*, vol. 3, no. 46 (2001): 5.

Leventhal, J. *Take Me Out to the Ballpark: An Illustrated Tour of Baseball Parks Past and Present*. New York: Black Dog and Leventhal, 2000.

Lomas, K.J., H. Eppel, M. Cook and J. Mardaljevic. "Ventilation and Thermal Performance of Design Options for Stadium Australia." International Building Performance Simulation Association (1997): retrieved June 11, 2006, from www.ibpsa.org/%5Cproceedings%5CBS1997%5CBS97_P160.pdf.

McIntire-Strasburg, J. "San Francisco Giants to Install Solar Panels." *Treehugger* (March 22, 2007): retrieved May 17, 2007, from www.treehugger.com/files/2007/03/solar_baseball.php.

Mitchell, W.J. *City of Bits: Space, Place, and the Infobahn*. Cambridge, MA: MIT Press, 1995.

Noll, R.G., and A. Zimbalist. "Sports, Jobs, and Taxes: The Economic Impact of Sports Teams and Stadiums." Washington, D.C.: Brookings Institution.

Oriard, M. *King Football: Sport and Spectacle in the Golden Age of Radio and Newsreels, Movies and Magazines, the Weekly and the Daily Press*. Chapel Hill: University of North Carolina Press, 2001.

Parrish, J. "Environmentally Sustainable Development of Sport Venues." In P. Thompson, J.J. Tolloczko, and J.N. Clarke, eds., *Stadia, Arenas and Grandstands*, New York: Routledge (1998): 337–343.

Puhalla, J., J. Krans, and M. Goatley. *Sport Fields: A Manual for Construction and Maintenance*. Hoboken, NJ: John Wiley and Sons, 2002.

Richmond, P. *Ballpark: Camden Yards and the Building of an American Dream*. New York: Simon & Schuster, 1993.

Ritter, L.S. *Lost Ballparks: A Celebration of Baseball's Legendary Fields*. New York: Viking Studio, 1992.

Ritzer, G., and T. Stillman. "The Postmodern Ballpark as a Leisure Setting: Enchantment and Simulated de–McDonaldization." *Leisure Sciences*, vol. 23 (2001): 99–113.

Rockerbie, D.W. *The Economics of Professional Sport* (2004): retrieved on January 13, 2005, from http://people.uleth.ca/~rockerbie/SportsText.pdf.

Romeas, V., C. Guillar and P. Pichat. "Testing the Efficacy and the Potential Effect on Indoor Air Quality of a Transparent Self-Cleaning TiO2-Coated Glass through the Degradation of a Fluoranthane Layer." *Industrial & Engineering Chemistry Research*, vol. 38, no. 10 (1999): 3878–3885.

Sack, R.D. *Homo Geographicus*. Baltimore, MD: Johns Hopkins University Press, 1997.

_____. *Human Territoriality: Its Theory and History*. New York: Cambridge University Press, 1986.

Seifried, C.S. *An Analysis of the American Outdoor Sport Facility: Developing an Ideal-Type on the Evolution of Professional Baseball and Football Structures*. Doctoral dissertation, Ohio State University (2005): retrieved May 1, 2007, from www.ohiolink.edu/etd/send-pdf.cgi?acc%5Fnum=osu1116446330.

Serby, M.W. *The Stadium: A Treatise on the Design of Stadiums and their Equipment*. New York: American Institute of Steel Construction, 1930.

_____. "Stadium Planning and Design." *Architectural Record*, vol. 69, no. 2 (1931): 152–176.

Sharma, B.W. *An Economic Analysis of Stadium Construction in Professional Sports*. Unpublished bachelor's thesis, Pennsylvania State University, University Park (1999).

Sheard, R. *Sports Architecture*. New York: Spon, 2001.

Sherman, L. *Big League, Big Time: The Birth of the Arizona Diamondbacks, the Billion-Dollar Business of Sports, and the Power of the Media in America*. New York: Pocket, 1998.

Smith, A., and R. Patterson. "Epilogue: The Future." In A. Smith and R. Patterson, eds., *Television: An International History*, New York: Oxford University Press (1998): 264–267.

Smith, C. *Storied Stadium: Baseball's History through Its Ballparks*. New York: Carroll and Graf, 2003.

Smith, R. *The Ballpark Book: A Journey through the Fields of Baseball Magic*. St. Louis, MO: Sporting News, 2000.

"The Stadium: All-American Monument." *Progressive Architecture*, vol. 52 (1971): 78–87.

Sundstrom, E., J. Town, D. Brown, A. Forman, and C. McGee. "Physical Encloser, Type of Job, and Privacy in the Office." *Environment and Behavior*, vol. 14 (1982): 543–559.

Sullivan, N.J. *The Diamond in the Bronx: Yankee Stadium and the Politics of New York*. New York: Oxford University Press, 2001.

Sweet, D. "The Future Holds Technology at the Touch of a Button." *Sports Business Journal*, vol. 4, no. 17 (2001).

Temko, A. *No Way to Build a Ballpark and Other Irrelevant Essays on Architecture*. San Francisco, CA: Chronicle, 1993.

Thompson, D. "The Writing of Contemporary History." *Journal of Contemporary History*, vol. 2 (1967): 25–34.

U.S. Census Bureau. "Projected Population of the United States by Age and Sex: 2000 to 2050" (2004): retrieved May 15, 2007, from www.census.gov/ipc/www/usinterimproj/natprojtab02a.pdf.

Weiner, J. *Stadium Games: Fifty Years of Big League Greed and Bush League Boondoggles*. Minneapolis: University of Minnesota Press, 2000.

Williams, P. "Being Part of the Design Key for Concessionaires." *Sports Business Journal*, vol. 4, no. 15 (2001): 24.

Wineberg, S.S. "Historical Problem Solving: A Study of the Cognitive Processes Used in the Evaluation of Documentary and Pictorial Evidence." *Journal of Educational Psychology*, vol. 27 (1991): 73–87.

E. Foundation Resources[*]

The Annie E. Casey Foundation
http://www.aecf.org/

The Benton Foundation
http://www.benton.org/

Cargill Foundation
http://www.grantstation.com/

The Carnegie Corporation Foundation
http://www.carnegie.org/

The Council of Foundations Home Page
http://www.cof.org/

*Source: National Association of Development Organizations, 400 North Capitol Street, NW, Suite 390, Washington, DC 20001.

The Ewing Marion Kauffman Foundation
http://www.emkf.org/

The Fannie Mae Foundation
http://www.fanniemae.com/

The Ford Foundation
http://www.fordfound.org/

The Foundation Center
http://www.fdcenter.org/

The Foundation for the New South
http://www.fndmidsouth.org/

The Heinz Foundation
http://www.heinz.org/

The John D. & Catherine T. MacArthur Foundation
http://www.macfdn.org/

The Kentucky Foundation for Women
http://www.kfw.org/

Maine Development Foundation
http://www.mdf.org/

The Meadows Foundation
http://www.mfi.org/

National Association of Development Organizations Research Foundation
http://www.nado.org/

National Foundation for Women Business Owners
http://www.nfwbo.org

The Pew Charitable Trust
http://www.pewtrusts.org/

The Rockefeller Foundation
http://www.rockfound.org/

The Sloan Foundation
http://www.sloan.org/

Target Stores Community Giving Program
http://www.grantstation.com/

Teaching Tolerance: Mix It Up Grants Foundation
http://www.grantstation.com/

F. Federal Reserve Bank Resources*

Atlanta Federal Reserve Bank
District 6
Atlanta, GA
http://www.frbatlanta.org/

Boston Federal Reserve Bank
District 1
Boston, MA
http://www.bos.frb.org/

Chicago Federal Reserve Bank
District 7
Chicago, IL
http://www.chicagofed.org/

Cleveland Federal Reserve Bank
District 4
Cleveland, OH
http://www.clevelandfed.org/

Dallas Federal Reserve Bank
District 11
Dallas, TX
http://www.dallasfed.org/

Kansas City Federal Reserve Bank
District 10
Kansas City, MO
http://www.kansascityfed.org/

Minneapolis Federal Reserve Bank
District 9
Minneapolis, MN
http://www.minneapolisfed.org/

New York Federal Reserve Bank
District 2
New York City, NY
http://www.newyorkfed.org/

Philadelphia Federal Reserve Bank
District 3
Philadelphia, PA
http://www.philadelphiafed.org/

Richmond Federal Reserve Bank
District 5
Richmond, VA
http://www.richmondfed.org/

*Source: Board of Governors, The Federal Reserve System, 20th Street and Constitution Avenue, NW, Washington, DC 20551.

St. Louis Federal Reserve Bank
District 8
St. Louis, MO
http://www.stlouisfed.org/

San Francisco Federal Reserve Bank
District 12
San Francisco, CA
http://www.febsf.org/

Notes: Each district branch has a community development office with local, regional, and national resources related to timely and important economic development topics. Alaska and Hawaii are part of the San Francisco District.

G. Federal Government Resources

These national government websites focus on online technical resources available in the fields of brownfields remediation, demographic information, economic and community development, the environment, historic preservation, housing information, land revitalization, transportation information, urban development, and related issues.

Bureau of Economic Analysis
U.S. Department of Commerce
http://www.bea.gov/

Brownfields Support Center
U.S. Environmental Protection Agency
http://www.brownfieldstsc.org/

Census Bureau
U.S. Department of Commerce
http://www.census.gov/

Community Development Information
U.S. Department of Agriculture
http://www.ocdweb.sc.egov.usda.gov/

Economic Development Administration
U.S. Department of Commerce
http://www.eda.gov/

Environmental Protection Information
U.S. Environmental Protection Agency
http://www.epa.gov/

FedWorld Clearinghouse
U.S. Department of Commerce
http://www.fedworld.gov/

Government Documents
U.S. Government Printing Office
http://www.access.gpo.gov/

Historic Preservation
National Trust for Historic Preservation
http://www.nthp.org/

Housing Information
U.S. Department of Housing & Urban Development
http://www.hud.gov/

Land Revitalization Support Center
U.S. Environmental Protection Agency
http://www.brownfieldstsc.org/

Links to Federal Government Agencies
The White House
http://www.whitehouse.gov/

National Main Street Center
National Trust for Historic Preservation
http://www.nthp.org/

Rural and Community Development
U.S. Department of Agriculture
http://www.usda.gov/

Transportation Information
U.S. Department of Transportation
http://www.dot.gov/

Urban Development Information
U.S. Department of Housing & Urban Development
http://www.hud.gov/

H. Regional Resource Directory

City and County of San Francisco
http://www.sfgov.org/

City of Anaheim
http://www.anaheim.net/

City of Arlington
http://www.ci.arlington.tx.us/

City of Boise
http://www.cityofboise.org/

City of Boston
http://www.cityofboston.gov/

City of Chicago
http://www.cityofchicago.org/

City of Corpus Christi
http://www.cctexas.com/

City of Denver
http://www.denvergov.org/

City of Evansville
http://www.evansvillegov.org/

City of Fargo
http://www.ci.fargo.nd.us/

City of Frisco
http://www.ci.frisco.tx.us/

City of Glendale
http://www.glendaleaz.com/

City of Harrisburg
http://www.harrisburgpa.gov/

City of Houston
http://www.houstontex.gov/

City of Kansas City
http://www.kcmo.org/

City of Los Angeles
http://www.lacity.org/

City of Memphis
http://www.cityofmemphis.org/

City of Miami
http://www.ci.miami.fl.us/

City of Montgomery
http://www.montgomeryal.gov/

City of New York
http://www.nyc.gov/

City of Newark
http://www.ci.newark.nj.us/

City of Olympia
http://www.ci.olympia.wa.us/

City of Pasadena
http://www.ci.pasadena.ca.us/

City of Richmond
http://www.richmondgov.com/

City of Rock Hill
http://www.ci.rock-hill.sc.us/

City of St. Paul
http://www.stpaul.gov/

City of Salem
http://www.ci.salem.va.us/

City of Seattle
http://www.seattle.gov/

City of Sioux Falls
http://www.siouxfalls.gov/

City of Trenton
http://www.trentonnj.org/

Community of Landover
(See Prince George County)

District of Columbia
(See Washington, DC)

Prince George County
http://www.princegeorgecountymd.gov/

Town of East Rutherford
http://www.eastrutherfordnj.net/

Washington, D.C.
http://www.dc.gov/

I. National Resource Directory

This listing includes major national professional, membership, and research organizations serving public officials, as well as concerned professionals and citizens. Many of these organizations focus on various issues relating to cities and sports facilities, and major programs relating to this topic.

Alliance for National Renewal
http://www.ncl.org/anr/

American Economic Development Council
http://www.aedc.org/

American Planning Association
http://www.planning.org/

American Public Transportation Association
http://www.apta.com/

American Public Works Association
http://www.apwa.net/

American Real Estate and Urban Economics Association
http://www.areuea.org/

American Society for Public Administration
http://www.aspanet.org/

American Society of Civil Engineers
http://www.asce.org/

Association for Commuter Transportation
http://tmi.cob.fsu.edu/act/

Association of Metropolitan Planning Organizations
http://www.ampo.org/

Center for Compatible Economic Development
http://www.cced.org/

Committee for Economic Development
http://www.ced.org/

Community Association Institute
http://www.caionline.org/

Community Transportation Association of America
http://www.ctaa.org/

Congress of New Urbanism
http://www.cnu.org/

Council of State Governments
http://www.csg.org/

Council for Urban Economic Development
http://www.cued.org/

Creative Economy Council
http://www.creativeeconomy.org/

Downtown Development and Research Center
http://www.DowntownDevelopment.com/

Environmental Assessment Association
http://www.iami.org/eaa.cfm/

Institute of Transportation Engineers
http://www.ite.org/

Local Government Commission
http://www.lgc.org/

National Association of Counties
http://www.naco.org/

National Association of County Administrators
http://countyadministrators.org/

National Association of Development Organizations
http://www.nado.org/

National Association of Housing and Redevelopment Officials
http://www.nahro.org/

National Association of Regional Councils
http://www.narc.org/

National Association of State Development Agencies
http://www.nasda.com/

National Association of Town and Townships
http://www.natat.org/

National Association for Environmental Management
http://www.naem.org/

National Center for the Revitalization of Central Cities
http://www.uno.edu/-cupa/ncrcc/

National Civic League
http://www.ncl.org/

National Community Development Association
http://www.ncdaonline.org/

National Congress of Community Economic Development
http://www.ncced.org/

National Council for Urban Economic Development
http://www.cued.org/

National Development Council
http://nationaldevelopmentcouncil.org/

National League of Cities
http://www.nlc.org/

North American Association of Sports Economists
http://www.kennesaw.edu/naase/

Partners for Livable Communities
http://www.livable.com/

Partnership for Regional Livability
http://www.pfrl.org/

U.S. Conference of Mayors
http://www.usmayors.org/

Urban and Regional Information Systems Association
http://www.uli.org/

Urban Institute
http://www.urban.org/

Urban Land Institute
http://www.uli.org/

J. International Resource Directory

This listing includes major international professional, membership, and research organizations serving public officials, as well as concerned professionals and citizens. Many of these organizations focus on various issues relating to cities and sports facilities, and major programs relating to this topic.

Building Officials and Code Administrators International
http://www.bocai.org/

Cities Alliance
http://www.citiesalliance.org/

Community Development Society International
http://www.comm-dev.org/

International Association of Sports Economists
http://www.iasecon.net/

International City/County Management Association
http://www.icma.org/

International Conference of Building Officials
http://www.icbo.org/

International Council for Local Environmental Initiatives
http://www.iclei.org/

International Council of Shopping Centers
http://www.icsc.org/

International Downtown Association
http://www.ida-downtown.org/

International Economic Development Council
http://www.iedconline.org/

International Facility Management Association
http://www.ifma.org/

International Institute for Sustainable Development
http://www.iisd.org/

International Transportation Management Association
http://itma-houston.org/

International Union of Local Authorities
http://www.iula.org/

United Cities and Local Governments
http://www.cities-localgovernments.org/

About the Editor
and Contributors

Editor

Roger L. Kemp has been the chief executive officer of cities on the West and East coasts for more than two decades. He has served as municipal CEO in California, New Jersey, and Connecticut, and is a fellow of the Academy of Political Science in New York.

He has also been a visiting scholar, senior adjunct professor, and professorial lecturer at leading universities: he holds BS and MPA degrees from San Diego State University and MBA and PhD degrees from Golden Gate University, and is a graduate of the Program for Senior Executives in State and Local Government from the John F. Kennedy School of Government at Harvard University. He is listed in *Who's Who in America*.

Kemp has been an author, contributing author, or editor of nearly 50 books dealing with America's cities and their future and is a past president of several city management associations. He received an Outstanding Alumni of the Year Award for 2007 from the School of Public Affairs at San Diego State University.

Contributors

Affiliations are as of the times the materials contained in this volume were written.

American City & County, Penton Media, Inc., Overland Park, Kansas.

John Atlas, president, board of directors, National Housing Institute, Maplewood, New Jersey.

Robert A. Baade, professor of economics, Department of Economics and Business, Lake Forest College, Lake Forest, Illinois.

Gretchen Barta, associate editor, *Commercial Investment Real Estate*, CCIM Institute, National Association of Realtors, Chicago, Illinois.

Steve Bergsman, free-lance writer, Mesa, Arizona.

Howard Bloom, writer and founder, *Sports Business News*, Ottawa, Ontario, Canada.

Jim Brunner, staff reporter, *Seattle Times*, the Seattle Times Company, Seattle, Washington.

Gerald A. Carlino, senior economic advisor and economist, research department, Federal Reserve Bank, Philadelphia, Pennsylvania.

Parke M. Chapman, senior editor, *National Real Estate Investor*, Penton Media Inc., Skokie, Illinois.

Greg Clark, senior fellow, Urban Land Institute, Washington, D.C.

Dennis Coates, professor, Department of Economics, University of Maryland, Baltimore.

N. Edward Coulson, professor of economics, Department of Economics, Pennsylvania State University, University Park.

Alan Ehrenhalt, executive editor, *Governing*, Congressional Quarterly Inc., Washington, D.C.

Desiree French, free-lance writer, Washington, D.C.

Charles Gerena, economics writer, research department, Federal Reserve Bank, Richmond, Virginia.

Josh Goodman, staff writer, *Governing*, Congressional Quarterly Inc., Washington, D.C.

Marc Hequet, free-lance writer, St. Paul, Minnesota.

Brad R. Humphreys, associate professor, Department of Recreation, Sport and Tourism, University of Illinois, Urbana-Champaign, Champaign.

Madeline Janis-Aparicio, executive director, Los Angeles Alliance for a New Economy, Los Angeles, California.

Brian Judd, director of community planning and design, Planning Center, Costa Mesa, California.

Philip Kotler, distinguished professor, Kellogg School of Management, Northwestern University, Evanston, Illinois.

Rebecca Kuzins, free-lance writer, Pasadena, California.

Philip Langdon, free-lance writer, New Haven, Connecticut.

Charles Mahtesian, correspondent, *Governing*, Congressional Quarterly Inc., Washington, D.C.

Victor A. Matheson, assistant professor, Department of Economics, College of the Holy Cross, Worcester, Massachusetts.

David Nardone, associate, Geller Sport Inc., a Division of Geller DeVellis Inc., Boston, Massachusetts.

Betty Joyce Nash, economics writer, research department, Federal Reserve Bank, Richmond, Virginia.

Mimi Nikolova, student and staff assistant, Department of Economics and Business, Lake Forest College, Lake Forest, Illinois.

Jim Noles, partner, Environmental and Natural Resources Section, Balch & Bingham LLC, Birmingham, Alabama.

George A. Purefoy, city manager, Frisco, Texas.

Jordan Rappaport, economist, Federal Reserve Bank, Kansas City, Missouri.

Irving Rein, professor, Department of Communication Studies, Northwestern University, Evanston, Illinois.

Roberts Stadium Advisory Board, established by the mayor, Evansville, Illinois.

Chuck Ross, contributing editor, *Building Design and Construction*, Reed Business Information, Oak Brook, Illinois.

Chad Seifried, visiting assistant professor, Sports and Exercise Management Program, The Ohio State University, Columbus.

Ben Shields, doctoral candidate, Department of Communication Studies, Northwestern University, Evanston, Illinois.

Dave Shonk, assistant professor, Sports Administration Department, College of Education and Human Development, University of Louisville, Louisville, Kentucky.

Stadium Task Force, established by the governor and state legislature, St. Paul, Minnesota.

Jason Stevenson, journalist and free-lance writer, Washington, D.C.

John Sweeney, distinguished professor, School of Journalism, University of North Carolina, Chapel Hill.

Nancye Tuttle, free-lance writer, Lowell, Massachusetts.

Roxana Tynan, director, Community Benefits Project, Los Angeles Alliance for a New Economy, Los Angeles, California.

Janet Ward, associate publisher and editor, *American City & County*, Penton Media, Inc., Overland Park, Kansas.

David Wilkening, free-lance writer, Orlando, Florida.

Chad Wilkerson, associate economist, Federal Reserve Bank, Kansas City, Missouri.

Ronald A. Wirtz, editor, *Fedgazette*, Federal Reserve Bank, Minneapolis, Minnesota.

Stephanie Worrell, free-lance writer, Boise, Idaho.

Renée Young, contributing editor, *Building Design and Construction*, Reed Business Information, Oak Brook, Illinois.

Adam M. Zaretsky, economist, research division, Federal Reserve Bank, St. Louis, Missouri.

Index